A WORLD OF DISORDERLY NOTIONS

A
WORLD
of
DISORDERLY
NOTIONS

QUIXOTE AND THE LOGIC
OF EXCEPTIONALISM

Aaron R. Hanlon

UNIVERSITY OF VIRGINIA PRESS
Charlottesville and London

University of Virginia Press
© 2019 by the Rector and Visitors of the University of Virginia
All rights reserved
Printed in the United States of America on acid-free paper

First published 2019

1 3 5 7 9 8 6 4 2

Library of Congress Cataloging-in-Publication Data

Names: Hanlon, Aaron R. (Aaron Raymond), 1982– author.
Title: A world of disorderly notions : Quixote and the logic
of exceptionalism / Aaron R. Hanlon.
Description: Charlottesville : University of Virginia Press, 2019. |
Includes bibliographical references and index.
Identifiers: LCCN 2018044533 | ISBN 9780813942162 (cloth : alk. paper) |
ISBN 9780813942179 (ebook)
Subjects: LCSH: English fiction—18th century—History and criticism—Theory, etc. |
Characters and characteristics in literature | American fiction—19th century—History
and criticism—Theory, etc. | Exceptionalism in literature. | Cervantes Saavedra,
Miguel de, 1547–1616. Don Quixote. | English fiction—Spanish influences. |
American fiction—Spanish influences.
Classification: LCC PR858.C47 H36 2019 | DDC 823/.50927—dc23
LC record available at https://lccn.loc.gov/2018044533

Cover art: From vol. 1 of *Don Quixote*, Miguel de Cervantes (London: Cadell
& Davies, 1818). Proof with etched letters, print by Francis Engleheart,
after Robert Smirke. (Image © Trustees of the British Museum)

For Nhi,
crosser of boisterous oceans

A world of disorderly notions, picked out of his books, crowded into his imagination.

—Miguel de Cervantes, *Don Quixote*

CONTENTS

INTRODUCTION

Tilting at Concepts

Famished and irritable, his ears ringing and his helmet cracked from the latest assault, Don Quixote asks Sancho what there is to eat. Sancho dips warily into the saddlebag and pulls out an onion, a bit of cheese, and a few crusts of bread, then offers them to Quixote with apologies. "How mistaken you are!" Quixote erupts in response. "I would have you know, Sancho, that it is an honour for knights errant not to eat for a whole month . . . and you would know this well enough if you had read as many histories as I have."[1] Studies of *Don Quixote* (1605–15) tend to take moments like this as evidence of Quixote's madness. But Quixote is actually logical in a way that explains both the political capital of Quixote in the eighteenth-century Atlantic world and the vast proliferation of quixotic characters in eighteenth-century fiction.

Of course, trying to string a thread of logic through at least two hundred years of mad characters inspired by Miguel de Cervantes's *Don Quixote* is itself a quixotic enterprise. Jorge Luis Borges's Pierre Menard initially tried to transform himself into Cervantes to write *Don Quixote* anew but eventually thought better of it and proceeded to write the text as Pierre Menard.[2] I have tilted at more than a few windmills in writing this book. The literary and cultural influence of *Don Quixote* is so vast and intimidating that it takes a certain kind of madness to attempt a systematic study of quixotism. I look at the first plate of Gustave Doré's 1867 illustrated edition of *The History of Don Quixote* (fig. 1), in which Quixote sits, besieged on all sides by the fictional creatures of his books, and I feel a sense of kinship with the character who can no longer control all the spirits he has conjured. Quixote experiences what the Doré-illustrated *Don Quixote* describes as "a world of disorderly notions," an apt metaphor for the study of quixotism.

Figure 1. "A world of disorderly notions, picked out of his books, crowded into his imagination." (From Miguel de Cervantes, *The History of Don Quixote*, ed. J. W. Clark, illustrated by Gustave Doré [London: Cassell, Petter and Galpin, 1867])

When we follow the Quixote story beyond *Don Quixote,* it gets complicated in a way that few literary texts can match. Those who study the novel—particularly the eighteenth-century novel in English—will certainly have read about quixotism, which is instrumental in the work of Jonathan Swift, Henry Fielding, Charlotte Lennox, Tobias Smollett, Laurence Sterne, and many others. Beyond the eighteenth century, Austen's *Northanger Abbey* (1818), Dickens's *The Pickwick Papers* (1836), Graham Greene's *Monsignor Quixote* (1982), and Kathy Acker's *Don Quixote* (1986) all take quixotism as a guiding motif. Early American writers, too, embraced quixotism, which forms the basis of Hugh Henry Brackenridge's *Modern Chivalry* (1792–1815), Royall Tyler's *The Algerine Captive* (1797), and Tabitha Gilman Tenney's *Female Quixotism* (1801).

Because of this breadth of influence, quixotism hovers in the background of so much literary scholarship. We take its presence for granted but remain uneasy about inviting it to the table. Two of the best books on quixotism—Wendy Motooka's *The Age of Reasons* and Sarah Wood's *Quixotic Fictions of the USA*—confront the beast only to brush past it. For Motooka, quixotism is a conceit for describing the instability of eighteenth-century notions of universal reason, while for Wood, quixotism is a disembodied collection of allusions to Cervantes that never takes on a character of its own.[3] In these edifying books, nominally on quixotism, quixotism affords us invaluable insight about other things—eighteenth-century reason, early American democracy—while disclosing very little of itself. We have a mountain of scholarly writing on quixotism that amounts to a molehill's worth of agreement about what quixotism actually means.

When we call something "quixotic," whether as scholars describing one of many allusions to Miguel de Cervantes's iconic knight in eighteenth-century novels, or as pundits commenting on an unlikely presidential candidate's missteps, one is left to wonder fundamentally to which elements of *Don Quixote*'s massive influence we refer. Are we describing a propensity for travel, for bellicosity, for hijinks, for delusion, for comic irony, or for flawed reading or interpretive practices? Are we signaling a formal or stylistic relationship between the thing we describe and Cervantes's *Don Quixote* (the text), as opposed to an allusion to the behavior or worldview of Cervantes's Don Quixote (the character)? Are we necessarily speaking of a relationship between an original and a copy, or has the concept of the quixotic evolved beyond its immediate relationship to its Spanish progenitor?

In short, the quixotic has long since exceeded a critical mass of meaning, and today, as such, means very little of use, despite how frequently scholars apply it as a descriptor. Just as Don Quixote believes himself an exception to the laws of his modern Spain, *Don Quixote* has a vigilante's relationship to the laws of genre. Given both the inadequacy of generic treatment of things Quixote, and the prominence of Don Quixote in eighteenth-century British and American literatures and cultures, we should have a better understanding of what we mean when we pronounce a text or a character quixotic, particularly when interpreting the ranging influence of Cervantes on literatures in English.

As a consequence of this crisis of meaning, the abundant scholarship on rewrites and reconfigurations of *Don Quixote* in literatures in English has evolved primarily as a taxonomic enterprise. Just as a biologist might describe and organize the characteristics of a new organism to place it in relation to a known organism, literary scholars throughout the centuries since *Don Quixote* was published have been observing and flagging allusions to Cervantes's masterpiece. From Henry Fielding's 1752 review of Charlotte Lennox's *The Female Quixote* (1752) in the *Covent-Garden Journal* to contemporary studies like Wood's *Quixotic Fictions of the USA, 1792–1815* and J. A. G. Ardila's *The Cervantean Heritage: Reception and Influence of Cervantes in Britain,* the critical aim has been to catalogue "quixotic" texts as a genre, based on the rough standard of, as Wood concisely puts it, "*Don Quixote* as a generative literary source, a significant (though not necessarily a sole) literary model."[4] The numerous renditions of the Quixote story have understandably compelled us to try to wrangle and tag them like a herd of cattle.

Nevertheless, even when the quixotic mode appears not as a central topic of inquiry but as a chapter or aside in a study with a different focus, this Multiple Quixotes Problem—of too many differing representations standing in for one widely applied term—threatens to undermine not merely our understanding of the quixotic within such studies but also our larger arguments about the function of quixotism as a politically and didactically important motif, and an otherwise pervasive motif, in eighteenth-century studies. A definitive example of this appears in Cathy Davidson's justifiably influential *Revolution and the Word: The Rise of the Novel in America,* which nevertheless contains a chapter on "The Picaresque and the Margins of Political Discourse" in which none of the quixotic protagonists under discussion is a picaro.[5]

The Multiple Quixotes Problem thrives, then, not only on imprecision wrought by the quantity and variety of products of the Quixote's influence (including those that incorporate the ostensibly picaresque elements of *Don Quixote*) but also on the tendency to respond to multiple and conflicting representations of the Quixote by defaulting to the organizational principles of influence and allusion that Wood, among others, uses to describe texts and characters that plausibly but only generally relate to *Don Quixote* as a source-text. Rather than seeking to understand first the character of quixotism as it affects Don Quixote and his "offspring" in subsequent literary traditions, scholars have overlooked what precisely we mean by "quixotic" in an attempt to define quixotism as a genre, a collection of texts generally related to *Don Quixote*.

In this way, "quixotic" becomes a generic term (in more ways than one) and, as such, a great moving target that takes on new meaning with each new context or association we ascribe to it. This strategy made sense for eighteenth-century authors appropriating the quixotic mode and reconfiguring their quixotes for new national audiences and political purposes suitable to the contexts in which they wrote. For scholars aiming to clarify and illuminate, however, this approach can lead to confusion and contradiction in work that attempts to investigate not just which texts fall under the category of quixotic, but *how quixotism itself operates within a text or a wider culture.* That the quixotic mode in fiction is endlessly contingent and impossibly fragmented is the conclusion of so many of our studies of quixotism, a conclusion that is indeed "insufficiently exciting," as Thomas Scanlan wrote in 2008 in an otherwise favorable review of Wood's *Quixotic Fictions of the USA,* on grounds that "*Don Quixote* fails to provide ideological or some other sort of intellectual consistency to the text in which it appears."[6]

With this book I aim to challenge the impression that quixotism is without intellectual consistency, destined for eternity to confuse and mislead. I propose a character turn for the study of eighteenth-century quixotism that reveals intellectual consistency where none has been found. Because eighteenth-century readers were far more interested in the character of Don Quixote than in the formal elements of Cervantes's text, a character turn in the study of eighteenth-century quixotes is in part a character *return,* a way of reanimating in scholarship today those elements of Don Quixote that so compelled and inspired eighteenth-century readers and writers.[7]

Of course, by investigating the character of quixotism, focusing on characters themselves who think and behave as Don Quixote does, we can also confront the Multiple Quixotes Problem. By analyzing quixotism as a coherent character mode and studying the logic that drives and justifies quixotic behavior, we can gather multiple quixotes under a wieldier rubric that unites these figures and ultimately tells us more about what so many quixotic figures are doing in eighteenth-century literatures in English. To put it concisely, if *Don Quixote* cannot provide intellectual consistency to the texts that reenvision it, Don Quixote can.

This approach avoids putting the cart before the donkey, or compiling a genre of quixotic texts before looking systematically to that character whom Vladimir Nabokov so eloquently described as a "stroke of genius on the part of Cervantes, loom[ing] so wonderfully above the skyline of literature, a gaunt giant on a lean nag."[8] It makes little sense to construct a genre called quixotism or quixotic when figures like Don Quixote exist so prominently across genres (to say nothing of languages, nations, and periods). It makes more sense to develop a character canon of quixotism grounded in the features and raison d'être of Quixote, whom Nabokov identifies as the driving force of Cervantes's influence. This character focus is also germane in light of Roberto González Echevarría's incisive observation that it is certainly not *structural* unity that allows us to take parts 1 and 2 of *Don Quixote,* published ten years apart, as a singular work, but rather the "profound unity given the entire ensemble by the protagonist, who became the most famous literary character of the modern era."[9] Once we arrive at a more thorough and coherent understanding of the logic of quixotism as a behavioral mode in eighteenth-century literatures in English, we might return once again to the genre question armed with enough clarity of purpose to tilt at that windmill.

Focusing on the character of quixotism necessarily requires us to account for the ways quixotes are political. Indeed, the politics of this character type is essential to the unity this study lends to quixotic characters and narratives. A prominent literary term, "quixotic" is also a starkly political term, a part of our political lexicon, used regularly as such to describe policies and politicians. Avid readers of internet news and commentary—perhaps the most ubiquitous of contemporary written genres—will have come across more than a few headlines about the "quixotic" underdog candidate challenging the party favorite in the primary, the "quixotism" of the bold alternative energy plan, or the modern "Don Quixote" about to lose his legislative seat because he stubbornly resists the cultural changes happening around him. These are recurring examples of the usage, but an internet news search at any given time will reveal yet more specific instances of this usage. Each of these examples reflects a different characterization of what it means to act quixotically, and this multiplicity of meanings in political rhetoric mirrors the unwieldy multiplicity of meanings that plagues literary scholars interested in quixotism, whether as a topic unto itself or as it intervenes in countless period, genre, and author studies.

It might not matter whether politicians, pundits, and journalists are being historically and literarily precise when they invoke quixotism to describe such scenarios (I would not say the same for scholars), but there are ways in which the subject of this book—the politics of quixotism—does matter in the world of brick-and-mortar windmills (however "quixotically" formulated was that alternative energy plan for their construction). This is the case because Cervantes's Don Quixote—arguably the most renowned character in all of European fiction—follows a specific logic that makes him not unique, but self-replicating: Don Quixote and his logic are contagious. The Quixote's ability to step outside of the rules and customs that govern his surrounding society render the Quixote an exceptionalist figure, one whose sense of moral superiority makes him an attractive character model for writers looking to critique or support social, moral, and political exceptions.

This study posits a link between the logic of quixotism and the logic of exceptionalism. These shared logics draw together the literary and political elements of quixotism. While various discussions of what it means to construct exceptions have been influential in literary studies as well as in political theory, from Carl Schmitt's analysis of the exception in *Political Theology* (1922) (more recently reconsidered by Paul Kahn in his 2011 study by the same name)[10] to Giorgio Agamben's work on homo sacer, these discussions tend to quarantine the logic of exception to the spheres of juridical and state practices. In traditional terms, then, the exception is rendered by the state—or by sovereign authority or force—rather than assumed in the imagination or claimed by rhetorical or persuasive means. If we consider, as an example, the character of American exceptionalism today, we see that such a belief is not juridically *enforced* so much as rhetorically *insinuated*. It exists as an assumption in the minds of a populace regardless of counterevidence.

For quixotes, the rhetorical construction of exceptionality is the more germane of these two mechanisms (enforcement versus insinuation) for rendering exceptions, largely because the authority that quixotes assume by understanding themselves as exceptions is more often earned rhetorically than claimed by sovereign right. In Lennox's *The Female Quixote,* for example, when Arabella excoriates her lady's maid, Lucy, for failing to comprehend her romantic thoughts and actions, she is operating with sovereign authority; but in every other realm of Arabella's life, the influence of her exceptionalism is a matter of what and how she speaks to people more powerful than she is. As Sir Charles remarks of Arabella, "If she had been a Man, she would have made a great Figure in Parliament."[11] Arabella demonstrates her rhetorical prowess in passing off romantic fiction for ancient history in conversation with Mr. Selvin and Mr. Tinsel in Bath, the former believing Arabella to be "a Wit, and very learn'd in Antiquity" (281). This is to suggest that quixotic exceptionalism is not a matter of recognized sovereignty or power, and differs as such from the theories of exceptionalism offered by Schmitt or Agamben. Quixotic exceptionalism turns these theories of exceptionalism on their heads, because what matters for quixotes is not the power to pronounce the exception, but the belief in one's own exceptionality even in the face of powerful resistance to that idea.

We can say, then, that the exceptionalist mind-set that drives quixotes is neither a legal nor a forceful claim to exceptionality, not a form of sovereignty or juridical authority explained by the theoretical frameworks of Schmitt or Agamben. Quixotic exceptionalism is rather the *experience* of one's own exceptionality based in the belief in one's own exceptionality, of moving through the world convinced that all obstacles can and should be subordinated to the quixote's superior sense of purpose. Whereas the idealist expects to be challenged by the status quo and marks the distinction between the idealistic worldview and the routine from which it deviates, the exceptionalist quixote meets challenges with surprise and indignation, because for quixotes the guiding worldview and the assumed moral superiority of the quixote are inseparable. The quixote experiences exceptionality at every turn, even in and through resistance to quixotism, or challenges to whatever authority or exceptionality to which the quixote lays claim.

This book deals with the logic of exceptionalism in broader terms than what is conventional in the realm of political theory. My discussion of the exceptionalism of quixotes treats exceptionalist logic as something that quixotic people and characters use for themselves and on others as a consequence of their experiences of exceptionality, rather than only something states use on those subject to state authority. I argue further that the exceptionalist logic that quixotes deploy at the interpersonal level becomes a way of mediating in literature the exceptionalist practices of states and of those empowered within social and political hierarchies. What we call quixotic fiction has been a strategy for identifying and grappling with exceptionalist worldviews and practices, whether in geopolitics, legal systems, or class hierarchies, and allegorizing these in fiction. In these ways the connection between the logic of quixotism and the logic of exceptionalism is one of shared political and rhetorical practices. More than belligerence or knighthood, conservatism or radicalism, the experience of exceptionalism is what seventeenth- and eighteenth-century translators and authors consistently picked up in Don Quixote and reproduced in their quixotic characters.

PART I

The Character of Quixotism

1

Quixotic Exceptionalism

We tend to think of quixotes as mad or deluded, as idealists or dream-
ers, as figures at odds with reason, but this is not the whole story of
quixotism. Understanding the difference between the exceptionalism
of quixotes and marginalized madness, delusion, or idealism is essential for understanding how the logic of exceptionalism operates to the
advantage of quixotic figures. What would it mean, for example, to
approach the quixotes representing Cathy Davidson's "margins of political discourse" in the early US not as figures marginalized by their madness but as adept reasoners and manipulative rhetoricians, like Tabitha
Tenney's Dorcasina in *Female Quixotism?* In what ways is Henry Fielding's
Parson Adams a prescient observer of a wayward and corrupt English
society, not just a bumbling anachronism foolishly imitating a dated
moral code? To answer these kinds of questions we need to rethink the
role of quixotism in eighteenth-century fiction and to understand quixotes not merely as imitators of a mode, representatives of a genre, or
delusional overreaders, but as figures fundamentally guided by their
experience of exceptionalism. This demands in turn a more in-depth
foray into political theory to gain a precise sense of how exceptionalism
works. In the end we will find that existing theories of exceptionalism—
from Carl Schmitt to Giorgio Agamben to more recent theories of state
exceptionalism—do not sufficiently explain quixotism, and that quixotic exceptionalism is something new unto itself.

As we can observe in quixotic texts like *Gulliver's Travels* (1726) and
Launcelot Greaves (1760–62) (discussed at greater length in part 2 of this
study), quixotes proceed with an exceptionalist outlook. Gulliver can
only justify his sense of English superiority before the Brobdingnagian
king by understanding himself as an exception to the logic and customs of those around him, admitting that he lacks satisfactory answers

to the king's probing questions about English governance. Likewise, Launcelot can only make sense of how the law works for him but fails others—and justify stepping outside the law to correct its injustices—by proceeding with his own sense of justice above the law.

But "exceptionalism" remains another slippery term in need of clarification before we come to further examples of quixotic characters. Clarifying exceptionalism is a challenging task, in part because of the many different contexts in which scholars, journalists, and politicians invoke the term. Even in its most prominent context—the notion of "American exceptionalism"—we tend to have difficulty distinguishing between the logic of exceptionalism and the actual state of exceptionality. I will clarify how quixotic exceptionalism relates to and differs from other theories of exceptionalism and emphasize that what makes quixotic exceptionalism quixotic is its relation to fictionality.

The logic of exceptionalism operates most visibly in three major theories of sovereignty, all of which help explain the exceptionalism of quixotes even as they illustrate the need for a specific theory of quixotic exceptionalism. We have the exception of homo sacer, or "bare life," from Giorgio Agamben's landmark study *Homo Sacer: Sovereign Power and Bare Life* (1998); we have the definition of the sovereign as "he who decides on the exception," from Carl Schmitt's influential *Political Theology* (1922); and we have the broader concept of state exceptionalism, most prominently American exceptionalism, which scholars have traced back centuries before the founding of the US state.[1] The logic of exceptionalism underwrites each of these theories, yet they differ in important ways.

In Agamben's study of sovereignty and bare life, for example, the ancient Roman religious concept of homo sacer ("sacred man," who can be killed but not sacrificed) provides an example of exceptional status juridically enforced, leaving the figure of exception vulnerable: homo sacer could be killed without the killer being deemed a murderer.[2] One who breaks an oath or commits a violation worthy of being made to exist outside the protection of law is an exception to be sure, but a disempowered one. By contrast, in Schmitt's theory of sovereignty, the consequences for the exception may be favorable or unfavorable, but the focus is on what the power to decide on the exception means for sovereignty. In other words, whereas homo sacer is a figure acted upon and made vulnerable by state power, the sovereign for Schmitt is one who acts by and through state power to produce exceptions to the rule of law. To account for a political dynamic in which Schmitt's sovereign individual is instead the popular sovereign (as in the US democratic republic), Paul Kahn has updated this definition of the sovereign; yet even for Kahn the most important relationship is between the freedom and agency of individuals and the Schmittian concept of the juridically enforced exception.[3] What all of these forms of exceptionalism hold in common is a focus on the direct relationship between individual subjects or constituents and the sovereigns who hold power over them. Such relationships are characterized by what Joseph Nye calls "hard power," the ability to influence by coercion rather than persuasion.[4]

National exceptionalism—the idea that one's nation is exceptional to the extent that it should act and be treated according to a different set of rules from all others—is yet a different category of exceptionalism, because it concerns less the relationship between the sovereign and the people than between the sovereign state and the wider international community. As Kahn observes of American exceptionalism, the Schmittian exception from *Political Theology* "speaks directly to the relationship between constitutional law and political sovereignty," but American exceptionalism is made possible because "our belief that the Constitution is a product of popular sovereignty" makes us reluctant to vest sovereignty in extraconstitutional institutions like international law or international consortiums.[5] With national exceptionalism, a global hegemon like the US may have the "hard" power to decide on the exception to international law, but the belief in American exceptionalism among US citizens is not enforced by a sovereign's hard power. National exceptionalism certainly relies on "hard" power at the international level, but it functions at the domestic level as a belief with "soft" appeal. This explains why, as Donald Pease has shown, so much of the cultural battle over American exceptionalism has been fought on the battleground of American literary studies throughout the Cold War period: the "soft" rhetorical power of literature, how we read literature, and which literature our institutions encourage us to read have all played central roles in reinforcing the notion of American exceptionalism.[6]

While none of these political theories of exceptionalism map cleanly onto the exceptionalism of quixotes, together they tell us a great deal about the logic of quixotism. Quixotes are at times belligerent wielders of the lance ("hard" power), but their exceptionalist outlook is a "soft" product of persuasion, literary imagination, rhetorical deftness, and idealistic belief. In this sense the logic of quixotic exceptionalism resembles that of American exceptionalism more than that of vulnerable "bare life" or the "hard" power of a sovereign. On the other hand, quix-otes are individuals who decide on their own exceptionality, or who believe in their own exceptionality by virtue of the literary imagination. But in this way quixotes are not wholly sovereign. Rather, they are pos-itive exceptions in their own minds—visionaries who see a better way of living, redressers of grievance and injustice—but negative and some-times vulnerable exceptions in the eyes of onlookers whose examples of everyday experience are at odds with quixotic behavior. Quixotic exceptionalism out in the fictional world, like American exceptionalism out in the world, is liminal, and has as such the ability to confuse the belief in exceptionalism with the fact of exceptionality.

By analogy, earnest proponents of the idea that the US is an excep-tional nation frequently take "American exceptionalism" to mean "America's exceptionality," though these are not the same, and their conflation is a political as well as heuristic problem. A state of exception or exceptionality is a factual condition, whereas a belief in exception-ality is just that. The term "American exceptionalism," which, as I men-tioned, gained currency with scholars and political commentators in 1950–70 as a way of describing America's exceptionality, has given way to more critical readings of the idea of America's exceptionality.[7] Today, literary scholars, historians, and political theorists are more likely to use "American exceptionalism" to refer to the ideology of a historically untenable set of beliefs. This is not to suggest there is no relationship between belief in exceptionalism and the creation of exceptions. In some cases, as in Agamben's study of homo sacer, an exceptionalist ide-ology baked into a juridical system produces a state of exception or exceptionality: the fact of someone being treated as an exception is a consequence of an ideology that chooses its exceptions.

Importantly, then, quixotes are not necessarily exceptional figures, like Smollett's affluent and capable Launcelot Greaves, but they do nec-essarily believe they are exceptional figures. As it concerns quixotes, this is the crucial difference between belief in one's exceptionalism and the fact of exceptionality, the former being more important for quixotism than the latter. Quixotes show us that they need not be exceptional—in wealth, intellect, or ability—to believe they are exceptional, nor to con-vince others to treat them as exceptions, whether in earnest or in jest. Whereas Launcelot must be reckoned with because of his exceptional wealth and privileged access to the legal system he wields against his enemies, Gulliver needs only to believe he hails from the greatest nation

in the world to feel like a foreign dignitary among kings and princes, or
to derive from his ambivalent reception abroad the impression that he
is a wise cosmopolitan compared to the Brobdingnagian king. Octavio
Paz writes of Quixote, convinced that he "doesn't embody human history; he is the exception to it."[8]

As Agamben notes, an example and its exception are effectively
indistinguishable from one another, which is how they operate together
as a set:

> The exception is situated in a symmetrical position with respect to
> the example, with which it forms a system. . . . While the example
> is excluded from the set insofar as it belongs to it, the exception is
> included in the normal case precisely because it does not belong
> to it. . . . In every case (as is shown by the dispute between anom-
> alists and analogists among the ancient grammarians), exception
> and example are correlative concepts that are ultimately indistin-
> guishable and that come into play every time the very sense of the
> belonging and commonality of individuals is to be defined. In every
> logical system, just as in every social system, the relation between
> outside and inside, strangeness and intimacy, is this complicated.[9]

While it is important not to conflate an actual exception with a belief in
one, it is likewise important to understand that the logic of exceptionalism is meant to obscure or render irrelevant that distinction, at least
until the point at which it becomes politically expedient to acknowledge the distinction and produce an exception. Quixotism—as distinguished from simple madness, idealism, or marginality—contains just
such a paradox. The Brobdingnagian king may be wholly unconvinced
by Gulliver's defense of England, such that Gulliver appears to the king
like another example of the very inadequacies and petty querulousness
that characterize the English in Gulliver's account. But Gulliver sees
himself in no such way. Quixotism believes in its exceptional status
even as it appears outwardly like a marginal worldview in relation to the
steady stream of ordinary life, of recurring manifestations and examples
of social customs ideological norms. Don Quixote frequently appears
reasonable because he *is* reasonable. When he appears unreasonable,
it is because he reasons accurately and at times profoundly from the
exception rather than the example.

This paradox of quixotism is a consequence of the quixote's exceptionalist way of perceiving. We say conventionally that quixotes struggle

to see the difference between fiction and reality, so they suffer from a kind of ontological insensitivity. But quixotes are more complicated than that. An exceptionalist outlook—a belief in one's exceptionality, rooted in a given form of idealism—makes it yet more difficult to look out into the world and know, or even care about, the difference between the exception and the example. Just as we can imagine someone who believes the US is truly an exceptional country apprehending two charts, one on global infant mortality rates that shows the US in a lower position than other wealthy nations next to another, on global GDP, that shows the US in a leading position, and dismissing the former for its failure to reinforce the notion of American exceptionalism, we can picture Launcelot Greaves working himself into a bout of frustration and confusion when the legal system that works so well for him (exception) fails to work the same for the less fortunate (example). Such moments can appear as instances of myopia, psychological disavowal, or refusal of counterevidence, but more precisely they are decisions to operate from evidence of the exception rather than evidence of the example. Such decisions perpetually reinforce the exceptionalist outlook, as they find, circularly, the evidence they expect from their guiding worldview while ignoring the rest. That the idea of a "quixotic America" is not uncommon in policy and international relations circles suggests further the long-standing similarities between quixotic and American exceptionalists.[10]

Because quixotes operate based on a worldview fostered by the literary imagination, the exceptionalism of quixotes reconfigures the root paradox of exceptionalism—the relationship between exception and example—as a paradox of fictionality. What is "real" to the quixote is the quixote's example and reality's exception. In this way, when we speak so often of *Don Quixote*'s role as a historical marker of the novel or of fictionality, at issue is not only the generic and structural relationships between *Don Quixote* and the eighteenth-century British novel it so widely influenced but also the very logic of fictionality.

As Catherine Gallagher has shown, readers and critics have taken narrative implausibility as a way of loosely defining fictionality, based on the idea that "fiction somehow suspends, deflects, or otherwise disables normal referential truth claims about the world of ordinary experience."[11] Fictional "suspension" is the framework with which critics have read Quixote from the beginning: as one whose madness leads him to assume a referential relationship between implausible, fantastical fictions and the real world. Yet what Gallagher identifies as the eighteenth-century novelistic convention of writing plausible stories that nevertheless rely on generic character names to suspend direct referentiality to the world of "real" people—Fielding's *Tom Jones*, for example—is a convention eighteenth-century readers could have considered a form of lying before they developed the framework of fictionality.[12] For Gallagher, then, the eighteenth-century novel provided simultaneously "a conceptual category of fiction" and "believable stories that did not solicit belief," a combination that tied the rise of fictionality directly to the mid-eighteenth-century novel and gave rise to fictionality as a paradox. "Fictionality," writes Gallagher, "only became visible when it became credible, because it only needed conceptualizing as the difference between fictions and lies became less obvious, as the operators of fictionality became multiple and incredibility lost its uniqueness."[13] The paradox of fictionality, then, is also a paradox of examples and exceptions. Once it became more difficult to distinguish between fictions and lies, there arose a need to account for fiction as an exception to the lie, neither a solicitation of belief in its truth value, nor a manifestation of the truth.

We can follow this aspect of the logic of exceptionalism—the relationship between exception and example—from Agamben's theory of exceptionalism through quixotism and fictionality. Quixotes conceive of themselves as exceptional, so define their relationship to their surroundings paradoxically as one of the quixote's entirely justifiable existence and a surrounding world of unfathomable exceptions to the just order of things. This condition of quixotism hinges on the quixote's concept of fictionality, which is not that the surrounding world is like chivalric romance (or a quixote's given hobbyhorse), but that the surrounding world is full of baffling exceptions to what ought to look more like the world of chivalric romance. This is the effect of quixotic exceptionalism: for the quixote, the exception is the example, and the example is the exception.

Accordingly, quixotic exceptionalism offered eighteenth-century readers a rigorous test of fictionality. Because quixotes reason from the exception rather than the example while at the same time soliciting belief in their quixotism—and because, as Wendy Motooka has argued, they "embody individual madness, while reproducing the conditions of universal rationality"—quixotes put immense pressure on the question of how a narrative wields or undermines its own plausibility.[14] And because the quixote is for surrounding characters a manifestation of implausible fiction, the quixotic narrative forces readers to reckon with representations of implausible romance in an otherwise plausible story. The many eighteenth-century novels featuring quixotes employ realist conventions of the period while portraying the quixote as romantically at odds with those conventions. When quixotic exceptionalism leads either to a narrative that privileges the quixote's visionary or heroic qualities, or a narrative that pillories quixotic exceptionalism, readers are forced to practice what Gallagher calls "cognitive provisionality," "a competence in investing contingent and temporary credit" in the quixotic narrative's political and representational claims.[15] Quixotic exceptionalism forces us to evaluate a narrative's stance toward its own fictionality and, in the process, to evaluate the narrative's stance toward exceptionalist politics. We witness this kind of test most starkly in the conclusion of Lennox's *The Female Quixote,* in which a Samuel Johnson figure—"the Doctor"—convinces Arabella to abandon her quixotism on the grounds that the romances Arabella reads are fictional, absurd (which is to say, implausible), and therefore dangerously criminal in their capacity to mislead people about what is real and what is not (368).[16]

For this reason quixotism is a highly desirable medium for expressions or critiques of exceptionalist politics. The exceptionalism of quixotes becomes the engine of their character inexhaustibility, the tendency of authors and readers to meet exceptionalist politics—and ensuing injustices—in the physical world with a continual reproduction of quixotic characters. Right away, then, we can draw associations between quixotic exceptionalism and the national exceptionalisms of imperial Spain in the seventeenth century, the Atlantic British Empire in the eighteenth century, and the emergent US Empire in the eighteenth and nineteenth centuries, all periods that generated quixotic narratives to address matters social and political. But to refine these associations we need to understand more precisely the historical circumstances that made possible the proliferation of exceptionalist quixotes in Spanish, British, and early US literatures, as well as the desire for characters who invoke and put pressure on fictionality. As Sarah Kareem notes, the eighteenth century witnessed "numerous historical circumstances that valorized uncertainty as a rational response to the modern world," including "debates over the nature (or existence) of divine intervention, over the epistemological value of strange facts, and exposure to different peoples and cultures through travel and imperialism." Quixotic exceptionalism—the imagination-driven belief that one should act and be treated differently from everyone else as one progresses along a more righteous path—made sense as a response to ongoing confusion of the example and the exception in theology, epistemology, economics, and global and domestic politics. Further, in light of quixotic exceptionalism's ties to fictionality, what Kareem calls the power of eighteenth-century fiction to "harness wonder" included the quixote's ability to baffle, or to bring readers through gauntlets of perplexity and uncertainty.[17]

The historical commonalities between eighteenth-century Britain, the emergent US, and Golden Age Spain all reflect a desire to meet cultural instability with treatments of exceptionalism, particularly as exceptionalism plays a crucial role in the spread of imperial power. Even before Quixote was written into literatures in English, Cervantes was arguably looking ahead to the Americas in imperialist ways. Diana de Armas Wilson makes a compelling case for "the Americanist Cervantes," who, though denied passage, "tried several times to emigrate to the new world," and whose frequent cataloguing and referencing of possibilities (by location) for "Iberian colonial expansion" indicated a serious interest in the Americas.[18] As Wilson suggests, sixteenth-century Spanish debates over "just warfare," slave-trading, and colonization in the Americas recurrently find their way into Don Quixote's discourses and encounters.[19]

Further, from the time of Cervantes to the time of Charlotte Lennox to the time of Washington Irving, each of these writers wrote alongside or in the background of their respective nation's significant imperialist activity. As Clarence Haring observed of Spanish colonialism in the Americas in his pioneering study on the subject, for the Spain of Cervantes's time, "the soldier, the legist, and the priest reigned supreme." In other words, the establishment of the Spanish rule of law and of religion in the American colonies, brought about through military force and administrative virtuosity, was the modus operandi of the Spanish Empire. If *Don Quixote* is permissible as evidence, Cervantes, a soldier himself, certainly understood this. But while Spanish colonizers militarily and administratively brought American cultures more singularly into line with the empire's legal and religious objectives, the tremendous religious, racial, and intellectual diversity in Spain itself nurtured university learning, scientific, mathematical, and medical advancement, and artistic contributors from Cervantes to El Greco to Velázquez during the Golden Age of Spanish art and literature. We must then understand Don Quixote as an imperialist-era character, one who is well versed in the arguments and stakes of Spanish colonialism, as well as the exceptionalist politics that made it possible.[20]

While the "Captive's Tale" interpolated within *Don Quixote* transparently deals with one theater of Spanish imperialism, and one of Cervantes's choice subjects—the Christian captive imprisoned in the Muslim world when a Mediterranean naval battle goes awry—the broader critique of chivalric romance that Don Quixote enacts calls up quite straightforwardly the dated image of the belligerent knight-errant, employed to win foreign lands in battle for the Crown. At its most basic level, then, *Don Quixote* is a direct but ambivalent commentary on Spanish imperial pursuits. Don Quixote is the fulcrum of this ambivalence, or the figure whose orientation toward or in opposition to imperialism helps us discern whether the text is yearning for a return to the Golden Age of Spanish conquest, launching a critique of Spanish imperialism, or doing something else in between.

In light of the Quixote's role in mediating the text's commentary on imperialism, we might also understand the logic of exceptionalism as something historically and recurrently available to be marshaled toward or against imperialist ends. The former being more in line with the kinds of national exceptionalism that justify the "liberation" of foreign peoples and territories through conquest, and perhaps more prevalent in the quixotes-in-English tradition, we might also read British and US quixotes as mediators of imperialist aims and ideologies in much the same way as Cervantes's Don Quixote was for Golden Age Spain.

Fernand Braudel has suggested that Britain's "developing supremacy" as a world economic power "could already be glimpsed" by 1713 and the Treaty of Utrecht, and was "clearly visible by the end of the Seven Years' War." Britain's trading prowess among European nations grew in the first half of the eighteenth century as Britain emerged as a "coherent national market," after which point it was also able to strengthen its geopolitical position against France through the Seven Years' War. Despite the result of the US War of Independence, by the 1783 Treaty of Paris, Britain had established itself "beyond a shadow of doubt" as the dominant nation in the European economy, and the "beating heart of the world economy."[21] Britain achieved its position in this respect not only through vast increases in Atlantic exports from the turn of the eighteenth century to the mid-eighteenth century but also through military success and naval prowess.[22] The emergence of a dominant British state from a struggle with France for control of the Atlantic world-system was thus the result of a gradual buildup in the first half of the eighteenth century, during which the first British Empire—the Atlantic Empire—was prepared to hit its crescendo just before the Revolutionary War and the rise of the US state. Written during a continual series of wars in 1702–13, 1718–21, 1739–48, 1756–63, and 1776–82, much of eighteenth-century British fiction reflected nationalist sentiments placing Britain in opposition to its French rival, or to the French "type."[23] Likewise, Britain's quixotic narratives dramatized internal (national) anxieties over the cost of incessant warfare and the rise of debt and financial economies to pay for this series of wars.[24]

After the US War of Independence and throughout the nineteenth century, Britain would maintain its status as the prevailing world power, shifting its imperial aspirations primarily eastward toward the Indian subcontinent and southward toward Africa. In the late eighteenth century and beginning of the nineteenth century, however, the US would begin to expand westward across the North American continent, most notably through the Louisiana Purchase from France in 1803. But even before expansion, soon after it won independence, the early US sought to centralize its governance, nationalize its debt, and develop itself into a viable geopolitical competitor. Europe's frequent wars produced shortages and created a need for US goods, implicating the US early as an important facet of the global economy.[25]

In this way, the US, recently independent from colonial rule, was primed to behave as an empire in its own right. Here again the logic of exceptionalism is relevant, as the very rhetoric of independence behind which US revolutionaries fought against the British Crown had to be reconfigured and in some cases sanitized when the new nation partook of reexportation from Atlantic islands and transatlantic slave trade, to say nothing of westward expansion across Native American land. Quixotes like Updike Underhill in *The Algerine Captive* comment directly on this predicament and use the logic of exceptionalism to both justify and critique the fundamentally hypocritical notions of English and US freedom through participation in religious persecution and the Atlantic slave trade.

Earlier in the century, writers like Henry Fielding, Alexander Pope, and Jonathan Swift viewed the rise of financial economies in Britain from 1690 to 1740 as disruptive to British industry, values, and patriotism, positioning them similarly with later-century US writers like

Hugh Henry Brackenridge, Tabitha Gilman Tenney, and Royall Tyler against the crude profiteering and opportunism of the rising merchant ranks, who, in both Britain and the US, looked to Atlantic imperialism as a basis for wealth creation.[26] In these eighteenth-century texts, then, the quixotic character played a crucial role as arbiter of the conditions of exceptionalism: When and for what reasons can we sacrifice principle to fuel a larger political, economic, or legal objective?

2

Anatomy of Quixotism

If quixotes play the role of exceptionalists within fiction that allegorizes broader kinds of exceptionalist politics, how then do quixotes come to view themselves as exceptionalists in the first place? Implied here is a related question: What specific characteristics of Quixote made him such a suitable figure for reproducing in fiction the stakes of exceptionalism? Answering these questions requires an understanding of the first principles of character that launch Don Quixote into the adventures that transform him from ordinary hidalgo into literary and cultural archetype. We must get to know Quixote from the inside out. And to do this thoroughly—in light of the prominence Quixote has enjoyed in the English-speaking world—we must follow the construction of the quixote archetype as it migrates and develops from Spain to Britain to the early US. As Susan Manning argues, "Character itself needs in literary contexts to be read as a rhetorical figure," because "literary character reveals itself in patterns of textual relationship."[1] In this brief chapter I provide a collection of patterns that accompany the formulation of quixotic characters across texts and national traditions, a collection of what Manning calls "rhetorical markers of resemblance" that articulate both the character of quixotism and the form of exceptionalism specific to quixotic characters.[2]

That rhetoric is so often the foundation of exceptionalism is deeply relevant to one of the Quixote's fundamental character attributes, a background of socioeconomic advantage, at least enough advantage to spend significant time learning to read imaginatively and literarily. Quixotes exercise imagination in a way that fosters idealism. Quixote is not a wealthy man, but, unlike Sancho, his hidalgo status is enough to afford him the choice of an idle life. Also unlike Sancho, Quixote is learned enough to read beyond the literal (this is perhaps the greatest understatement in all of Quixote studies). Though critics accuse Quixote of reading too literally, what appears at first an overliteral reading of fiction is actually a strikingly imaginative reading of material reality. Quixote does not mis- or overinterpret literatures of chivalric romance in and of themselves. Rather, he accomplishes, for better or worse, the daunting task of conceptually reshaping the material world around him according to fictional representations. This is the work of rhetorical skill and a cultivated literary imagination, one that the pragmatic and unrefined Sancho does not possess. Quixote's ability to realize this fictive world against all counterevidence is a function of Quixote's socioeconomic background as an educated and practiced reader. As we can observe in the original Don Quixote and others in this study, this readerly or literary advantage generates not only pronounced social distinctions between high-minded quixotes and confused commoners but also recurring problems of translation and misunderstanding between quixotes and their picaresque sidekicks. Both of these mutually reinforce the quixote's exceptionalist worldview, providing quixotes with mounting evidence that they are exceptions to those around them.

The rhetorical gap between Quixote and Sancho makes more sense when we account for the distinction between the quixotic and the picaresque. A quixote is a kind of idealist. Though, as I have suggested, idealism alone fails to account for quixotism, idealism is foundational to quixotism. Whereas the picaresque, for example, did not arise as a critique of idealistic fiction, Don Quixote did.[3] Accordingly, Quixote is not merely a dreamer who wants a better life, like so many picaros in the Spanish tradition, but an imaginative figure who pursues an idealistic life through an idealistic vision of the world. The imagination—specifically the literary imagination—is what enables this kind of idealism for quixotes, as the literary imagination supplies and constructs an alternate reality of the possible. Don Quixote comes from a part of Spain that the narrator of his story chooses not to remember, and virtually everything else about Quixote's life is plain, idle, and uninteresting (1.1.25). Without an imaginative and particularly literary outlook, employed, as we all know, in romance reading as an escape from his quotidian humdrum, Quixote could not envision a life in which he renders himself exceptional in a drab and perfidious world.

In addition to this rhetorical power arising from imaginative idealism, however, quixotes do, in some cases, wield socioeconomic advantage and mimetic appeal to gain authority or to influence others.

Quixote is not just an imitator but also a figure capable of inspiring imitation. Quixote's mimetic power is evident when others, despite knowing better, play along with his delusions, speak in the language of romance fiction to mock or humor him, and sometimes find themselves unexpectedly buying into his fantasies. In his landmark study *Mimesis,* Erich Auerbach observes how Sancho learns he can sometimes manipulate his liege by self-consciously imitating Quixote's way of speaking and seeing the world. Sancho convinces Quixote at one point that the three peasant women approaching on donkeys are Dulcinea and her attendants galloping forth on white steeds.[4] Even in such cases where characters understand they are taking advantage of Quixote's foible, their speech and actions are nevertheless imitations of quixotic behavior, which quixotes read as perfectly sensible and in line with quixotic expectations. In other cases, this mimetic appeal of quixotes gets the better of otherwise sound-minded characters, as when Sansón Carrasco, at first only pretending to be a chivalric knight as part of a plot to bring Quixote to his senses, ends up taking enough blows from Quixote in the process that he becomes enmeshed in the fantasy as Quixote's rival, the "Knight of the Spangles," or "Knight of the Mirrors" (2.15.579–81). As Roberto González Echevarría points out, Cervantes's description of Carrasco's reflective armor plays on the word *luna,* used to describe the reflective part of the mirror but also rendering Carrasco a "Knight of the Moons," one moved by imitation to lunacy.[5]

Because quixotes so often find themselves obliged and imitated in these ways, whether in earnest or in jest, real life recapitulates and reinforces the impressions quixotes obtain from chivalric romance. Though it seems counterintuitive, quixotes, in this sense, can be sound reasoners whose expectations develop not purely from delusion but from lived experience and empirical observation. When reality begins to conform plausibly to the quixote's expectations, this reality serves only to bolster the quixote's exceptionalist logic. If the literary imagination convinces Don Quixote that he is an exception in an unjust world, the unjust world, full of pranksters and opportunists willing to mock Quixote through imitation, serves often to affirm this quixotic mind-set.

The exceptionalist attitudes and practices of quixotes I examine in part 2 of this study are derived from a logic trick, the ability to convince oneself that circumstances are such that she or he ought to act and be treated according to a different set of rules from everyone else. If the world around is a den of iniquity, as Henry Fielding's Parson Adams sees it, following the world's rules is the shortest path to damnation. US leaders have applied the same exceptionalist logic to external threats like communism and terrorism to justify military action. What we sometimes take for leadership is the logic of exceptionalism in action. Though scholars of *Don Quixote,* understandably interested in fiction reading as a central trope, typically focus on the ways chivalric romance reading occasions Quixote's renowned case of "turned brain," the act of choosing to make an exception of himself within a larger social or global order is more precisely what transforms Cervantes's Alonso Quijano into Don Quixote. Based on, and perhaps even more fundamental to, the information that Quijano absorbs both from his mundane daily life and from the chivalric romances into which he escapes, the Quixote and quixotism are born of Quijano's unquenchable idealism about the world, and his quite literal desire to do battle with global injustice: "He decided not to wait any longer before putting his plans into action, encouraged by the need that he believed his delay was creating in the world: so great was his determination to redress grievances, right wrongs, correct injustices, rectify abuses and fulfil obligations" (1.2.30).

In this way Don Quixote is created—or rather creates himself—through exceptionalist logic. His laws of chivalry trump the laws and customs of Spain; and, to echo Nabokov's elevation of Quixote "above the skyline of literature," he conceives of himself as fiercely and imaginatively above the dictates of physical reality.[6] The extreme nature of Quixote's exceptionalism even bleeds into what Sancho Panza and others around him understand as the crude laws of human biology, as when Quixote aims to observe the customs of knights-errant, who, he tells Sancho, may choose "not to eat for a whole month, and if they do eat, it must be what they find readiest to hand" (1.10.81). One might understand this behavior as a kind of madness, and largely the result of the combination of Quijano's dull and idle life and his voracious reading of implausibly exciting literature. However, the specific logic by which Don Quixote enters the world is the logic of exceptionalism, the belief in a grander purpose that justifies, quite rationally, elevating the believer above the concerns and limitations of everyone else. More than simple idealism, then, quixotic exceptionalism is founded on a sense of urgency not only to realize an ideal but also to understand oneself as the key to realizing that ideal, as the moral center of some type of reform.

Accordingly, we should note that, however we interpret him, Don Quixote conceives of himself not as a marginal figure, but as a

shining exception in a world of unscrupulous and neglectful characters, murderous villains, and vulnerable Dulcineas. Like picaros—low-
bred tricksters or delinquents who attempt to move upward in social
rank by their wiles—conventional figures of madness or alterity tend
to be marginalized and embattled in ways Don Quixote is not. In an
introductory note to his 1755 translation of *Don Quixote,* Tobias Smollett claims he wants to avoid "debasing [Quixote] to the melancholy
circumstances and unentertaining caprice of an ordinary madman,"
drawing a distinction between madness in general and the *quixotic* madness portrayed by Cervantes.[7] Fittingly, then, Smollett's subsequent
Launcelot Greaves (1760–62) provides a lucid example of this difference
between the exceptionalist quixote and the mad imitator. Launcelot,
accused of imitating Don Quixote, frequently behaves like a madman,
but he retains enough awareness and sense of purpose to identify his
mad imitator and aspiring knight-errant, Captain Crowe, as a misguided impostor.[8] Even where quixotes like Launcelot are mocked and
punished for their exceptionalist deviation from the norm, they do not
internalize these experiences as marginalization but instead take them
as further evidence of the villainy and inadequacy of the surrounding
society (in some cases these quixotes are both reasonable and correct
in their assessments). Edmund Gayton, author of *Pleasant Notes upon Don
Quixot* (1654), affirmed this notion when he suggested that Quixote
"did oblige the places which received him, and left his *Landlords* in debt
to him for his acceptance of their Courtesies."[9] Where Quixote is able
to avoid paying his bill at the inn by invoking the antiquated laws of
chivalry, the picaresque Sancho Panza, whose station does not afford
him Quixote's chivalric privileges, finds himself harrowingly (and comically) tossed in a blanket for attempting to skip out on the bill as well
(1.17.135). In this scenario Sancho participates mimetically in quixotic madness but feels the effects of marginalization as a result. Quixote, on the other hand, moves on from the inn without paying and,
more importantly, moves forward with his understanding—that he is an
exception to the rules that govern common men like Sancho—not only
intact but reinforced by others who play along in jest or exasperation.
As the following chapter demonstrates, even Quixote's British translators, who brought Quixote to the English-speaking world, interpreted
Quixote as an exceptionalist figure, a quality that made him an attractive character to rewrite and reconfigure as the instructive exception
within new literary landscapes.

3

Character and Front Matters

Prefacing his maps of *Don Quixote*'s many European translations, Franco Moretti calls *Don Quixote* Europe's "first international bestseller."[1] Though issues concerning the translation of Cervantes's *Don Quixote* into English in the seventeenth and eighteenth centuries could merit their own books, we still need to understand how Quixote was framed for his British readership to appreciate the extent to which the character of quixotism has always been about the exception. We need to know how translators were reading and thinking about Quixote.

Even as Spain was Europe's dominant power in the early modern period, and one of Britain's major geopolitical rivals, the British were particularly inclined to look to Spain for their literary models.[2] *Don Quixote*'s translation history is also important here because so many eighteenth-century quixotic narratives are also part of the canon of early novels in English and demonstrate as such the connection between quixotism and the emergence of novelistic fiction in the English-speaking world. Taking the translation of *Don Quixote* as an example, Mary Helen McMurran writes, "Translating and originality are not easily distinguished in eighteenth-century fiction, not least because novels did not simply move from the source to target language, and one nation to another, but dangled between languages and cultures."[3] The fact that *Don Quixote* "dangles" in this way means that translating the character of Don Quixote was always going to be an exercise in reframing Quixote's attributes for new national audiences as British writers took Quixote as a basis for novels.

The front matter of seventeenth- and eighteenth-century translations of *Don Quixote* provides remarkable insight into the extent to which British translators and publishers read and understood Quixote not only as an exceptional figure but as a figure whom subsequent translators and authors would make an exception of for their own purposes. In close readings of translators' prefaces, frontispieces, biographical sketches, and other elements of front matter, I link these underdiscussed aspects of the presentation of the Quixote story to the exceptionalist character of quixotism.

In Cervantes's own preface to the reader of *Don Quixote*, as translated into English for the first time by Thomas Shelton in 1612, Cervantes conceives of himself as "in shew a father but in truth a stepfather to Don Quixote."[4] From the beginning we get an author's personification of the namesake character, notably in what we now recognize as a classically Cervantic statement, disavowing paternal right over the character he introduces to the world. Cervantes's Don Quixote, then, was already a degree removed from his roots in his emergence as a character, already part of a chain of authorial reproduction that takes biological reproduction as its metaphor. Though these clever introductory lines are of course those of Cervantes and not his first English translator, Shelton's dedication mimics Cervantes's reproduction metaphor, implying, like Cervantes, a degree of shame for the foibles of his offspring when he writes, "Since it is mine, though abortive, I doe humbly intreate, that your Honour will lend it a favourable countenance, thereby to animate the parent thereof to produce in time some worthier subject."[5] The dedication of Shelton's 1620 translation of the second part of *Don Quixote* continues with this metaphor, characterizing with noticeable sympathy the lineage of his translation as though it were the lineage of the Quixote himself, now with "none of the deformities: But as a bashful stranger, newly arrived in English, having originally had the fortune to be borne commended to a Grande of Spaine."[6] While the birthing metaphor may appear trite, it demonstrates the affinity between textual and biological reproduction in the seventeenth and eighteenth centuries— one that, importantly, implies standards for the quality of lineage—that has been central to the ways early translators understood Quixote. Cervantes framed text and eponymous character as mutual participants in a lineage of reproduction, and Shelton's first English translations picked up on this. From these origins the Quixote was always suitable (I will not say "ripe" or "fertile") for the mimesis and character reproduction we have subsequently witnessed.

The production of Shelton's 1612 translation also plays a part, unlike many subsequent translations, in bringing the reader almost immediately to Cervantes's text and Quixote's story. For example, unlike

Shelton's 1620 translation, the first edition includes no frontispiece (ornate and allegorical frontispieces would become common in late seventeenth-century and eighteenth-century translations; see fig. 2). Shelton's brief dedication in this first edition includes the claim, long since received by scholars with understandable skepticism, that he completed the translation "in the space of forty daies" on behalf of a friend who wanted to "understand the subject" of Cervantes's text.[7] That Shelton also claims that his translation had been set aside to languish after his friend perused it, such that Shelton was not inclined to look it over or edit it further, frames the story of Don Quixote for English-language readers as a work in progress. Shelton himself hopes that "some one or other, would peruse and amend the errors escaped," inviting the criticism subsequent translators would deal Shelton's offering.[8] Here again, from the very origins of the English-language translation of *Don Quixote,* Shelton presents both text and character as open-ended work to which readers are openly invited to respond, if not correct or reconfigure.

John Phillips, nephew of John Milton, produced a translation in 1687 that illustrates how early in the English-translation history of *Don Quixote* elaboration upon and imitation of the Quixote story become part of the translations themselves. Unlike Shelton's austere editions with comparably sparse front matter and illustrations, Phillips's is a handsome folio edition that begins with "Something Instead of an Epistle to the Reader, by way of Dialogue," which takes the form of a conversation between a defender of the translation of *Don Quixote* and a skeptic of the value of introducing Don Quixote to the British readership.[9] Phillips's Dialogue, like Shelton's dedication, assumes a Cervantic tone but also serves as an opening defense of the volume he puts forth. Bemoaning the cantankerous and dissatisfied readers "in this Age," so "inspired . . . with Contradiction and ill Nature," the defender of the volume expects that the translation will be met with poor reviews. His interlocutor fully expects that the volume will experience harsh criticism with difficulty, though the defender calls the book a "book-errant," with "Don Quixote's Lance and Buckler . . . to defend itself." Because the "book-errant," like Don Quixote, is used to being knocked around, it will receive harsh criticism merely as "Unluckie Adventures."[10]

Whereas Shelton's front matter borrowed Cervantes's reproduction metaphor in explaining how it came to be, Phillips's Dialogue takes the book itself as a quixotic figure. This "book-errant" possesses the exceptionalist qualities of Quixote in its ability to forge on amid battles,

Figure 2. Frontispiece, John Phillips translation (1687). (Courtesy of the Cambridge University Library)

rebuffs, and criticism without internalizing the outward skepticism of those who engage with it. In quixotic fashion, Phillips's "book-errant" also justifies itself as an exception to the romance tradition in which its skeptics wish to place it. When the skeptic raises the question, "But why *Don Quixote*? Had you nothing else to trouble your brain with?," the defender responds:

> Distinguish, Sir, you take it for a bare Romance; and I look upon it as a pleasant Story, to shew how vainly Youth mispend their hours in heightening their Amorous Fancies, by reading those bewitching Legends of *Tom Thumb* and *Amadis de Gual* [*sic*]; and Thousands more of that Nature, not worth the naming. Now Instructions are like Pills, for they meet with many humours that keck at their bitterness, unless guilded over with Fable and Fancy. . . . [T]he best way to represent the Deformity of any thing, is to expose it in a pleasing Mirrour.[11]

Though the "book-errant," standing in for Don Quixote as knight-errant, contains what is ostensibly a romance plot, it sets itself up as an exception to the romance tradition by virtue of the fact that, while delighting, it also instructs readers against romantic inclinations. Phillips's Dialogue is also important as an indication that, as early as 1687, one could undertake a translation of *Don Quixote* that not only understood the narrative as instructive satire rather than straightforward romance but could also present it to readers as such with an opening dialogue meant to frame the Quixote story as no simple romance.

Though Phillips's translation occupies a minor role in the history of *Don Quixote* translations, sandwiched between Shelton's pioneering translations in the first half of the seventeenth century and the more popular translations of Motteaux and Jarvis in the first half of the eighteenth,[12] it tells us several very important things about the early British afterlife of Don Quixote. First, with its introductory Dialogue and the addition of illustrations, it is a representative example of the increasing tendency of translations to include illustrations, as well as translators' elaborations on and justifications of the Quixote story. These marketing features undoubtedly helped shape readers' images of the Quixote, as well as, as we see in Phillips's Dialogue, their tendency to read the narrative as either romance or satire. Second, Phillips's translation shows us that, well before the prominent eighteenth-century translations of Jarvis and Smollett, *Don Quixote* could be read and understood by translators as a satire against romance reading rather than as a romance itself. Third, and perhaps most importantly, Phillips's translation provides evidence of a translator's use of the exceptionalist logic of quixotism to introduce the Quixote to British readers, separating the "book-errant" from the romance tradition by proclaiming it a different kind of text whose representations follow a different set of rules, not those of romance but those of satire. For Phillips, the character of quixotism and the character of translation—or at least the justifications for the introduction of both of these to British readers—are linked not only by Cervantic tone but by quixotic logic.

The turn of the eighteenth century witnessed yet greater translational license in Peter Motteaux's popular 1700 offering, which notes on its title page that it was "translated by many hands."[13] Motteaux's translation received ample criticism for its inaccuracy and overreliance on Shelton. Charles Jarvis later took Motteaux's translation to task in his 1742 translation, calling Motteaux's "kind of a loose paraphrase, rather than a translation . . . full of what is called the *Faux brilliant,* and openly carries throughout it a kind of low comic or burlesque vein."[14] A long way from Shelton's sparely introduced attempt at an accurate and serviceable, if flawed, translation, Motteaux's presented the Quixote, as Jarvis suggests, with attention to entertainment possibilities that a more burlesque rendering might provide. Motteaux's translation appeared in several editions, including a fourth, in 1719, after his death, further revised by John Ozell, who published a seventh edition with extensive "Explanatory Notes" in 1743.[15]

By 1711–12, British readers could acquire Edward (Ned) Ward's translation of *Don Quixote* into, as its title page proclaims, "Hudibrastick Verse," referencing what Ward understood as the comparably quixotic *Hudibras* (1663).[16] As Ward's title page suggests, this translation is indeed written in verse rather than prose, straddling the border between translation (conventionally understood) and rewriting or refashioning. Though it would be misleading to suggest that various ways of complicating *Don Quixote* in translation—with translators' notes and prefaces, illustrations, and intentional rewritings and deviations from Cervantes's text—became more prevalent in perfectly linear fashion from 1612 onward, it is important to point out that as the literary marketplace made room for more and more quixotic texts since Shelton's translations, even self-styled "translators" like Motteaux and Ward had begun reinventing *Don Quixote* as much as translating it from Cervantes.

With Charles Jarvis's translation in 1742, however, the desire to translate *Don Quixote* not just appealingly or innovatively but accurately reemerged, but not without complication. Though Jarvis approached prior translations from a metacritical perspective, setting out to correct the various flaws of the translations that appeared before his, he nevertheless leaves one of the strongest editorial marks on our understanding of the relationship between Quixote and Cervantes. The Jarvis translation includes a detailed, allegorical frontispiece illustrated by John Vanderbank and engraved by Gerard van der Gucht. The frontispiece depicts a Herculean figure representing Cervantes, trailed by the nine Muses, approaching a Satyr to receive arms (a great club and a comedy mask) to do battle with a series of fantastical monsters one might find in chivalric romance. A small, shadowlike figure resembling Don Quixote and bearing a lance appears in the background of the image, yielding the central action and, we presume, heroic potential to the authorial figure in the foreground, Cervantes. Unlike Shelton's 1620 frontispiece, in which Cervantes is absent and Don Quixote and Sancho take a far less dramatic center stage in the image, the Jarvis translation starkly indicates that the author is the hero of the narrative, the narrative is a satire, and the world of chivalric books stands trembling before Cervantes while Quixote looks on from the shadows.

Should readers of the Jarvis translation get the impression that this allegorical reading is overwrought, the volume also includes a ninety-page "Life of Cervantes" before we get to the text of *Don Quixote*. Though Jarvis's translator's preface indicates that he possesses the meticulous nature and linguistic skill to correct flaws, misreadings, and exaggerations in prior translations, readers of Jarvis's translation can observe how robustly the volume interposes Cervantes. Jarvis's stated purpose in the translation is to "preserve the wit and genius of the author," yet by the time we get to Jarvis's preface, we have already read the dedication to John Lord Carteret, which would appear more an homage to Cervantes than a dedication to Carteret.[17] Of Cervantes, Jarvis writes:

> For though the Age he liv'd in, is said to be a *Golden* one, very certain I am, that with respect to *Him* and some other well-deserving Persons, it was an Age of *Iron*. The Enviers of his Wit and Eloquence did nothing but murmur at and satyrize him. Scholasticks' incapable of equalling him either in Invention or Art, slighted him as a Writer not Book-learn'd. Many Noblemen, whose Names

but for him had been buried in Oblivion, lavish'd and threw away Parasites, Flatterers, and Buffoons, their whole Power, Interest, and Authority, without bestowing the least Favour on the Greatest Wit of his Time.[18]

In addition to Jarvis's prefatory remarks, his homage to Cervantes, the inclusion of an extensive life of Cervantes, and the Cervantes-centric, allegorical frontispiece included in the edition, Jarvis also took the opportunity to editorialize both Cervantes's text and its knight by providing readers with, as part of his translator's preface, a history of chivalry against which to position Cervantes's satirical intervention. Noting that at first many Spaniards thought Don Quixote's a true history upon the book's first appearance, Jarvis, like translators before him, describes *Don Quixote* as a "work calculated to ridicule that false system of honour and gallantry, which prevailed even 'till our author's time.'"[19] After presenting this brief history of chivalry, Jarvis continues, "Infinite were the mischiefs proceeding from these false and absurd notions of honour."[20] In this way Jarvis is as explicit as he can be about his reading of *Don Quixote* as a text meant to ridicule chivalric romances, taking Don Quixote as the butt of the heroic Cervantes's satire.

Curiously, then, Jarvis's 1742 translation advertises its accuracy in translating Cervantes's *Don Quixote,* but it includes so much framing and prefatory material before we get to the story of Quixote that it constitutes its own kind of translator's intervention. Neither "Hudibrastick Verse" nor a burlesqued translation "by many hands," Jarvis's translation simply piles more original writing on top of the text it renders in translation, participating in the mid-eighteenth-century British literary trend of reinterpreting and rewriting Quixote and his story.

The last of the major eighteenth-century translations, Tobias Smollett's 1755 translation is perhaps the most curious for the ambivalence it signals in its introduction of the Quixote. Like Jarvis, Smollett's translation features an allegorical frontispiece by Francis Hayman (fig. 3) featuring the lady Comedy (signified by the comedy mask) toppling a gothic castle guarded by a recoiling dragon (signifying chivalric romance). Athena shines the light of truth from her shield while monsters cower away from the light. In the background, Don Quixote and Dulcinea ride off into the shadows. Like the Jarvis frontispiece, this one puts the text of *Don Quixote* in the foreground as an agent doing battle

Figure 3. Frontispiece, Tobias Smollett translation (1755). (Courtesy of the Cambridge University Library)

with the corrupting influence of romance fiction, with Quixote himself hidden and subordinated to the scene's central action.

Nevertheless, when Smollett turns to words in his translator's note, he distinguishes Quixote "without raising him to the insipid rank of dry philosopher," or, as I have said, without "debasing him to the ordinary circumstances and unentertaining caprice of an ordinary madman." Compared with the Jarvis translation, Smollett's provides a far less exhaustive "life of Cervantes." Smollett's stated purpose in undertaking the translation reflects this tendency to recognize Cervantes for his creative accomplishment while privileging the character of Quixote: "to maintain that ludicrous solemnity and self-importance by which the inimitable Cervantes has distinguished the character of Don Quixote." Smollett is most compelled by the character of Don Quixote—his "ludicrous solemnity and self-importance"—such that preserving the effects of Cervantes's character rendering becomes his primary objective as translator. Cervantes himself is "inimitable," but the Quixote must be imitated and shared.[21]

These translations are important not only because they introduced British readers to the character of Don Quixote in ways that prefigure Quixote as an exception in eighteenth-century fiction but also because they reflect some of the impressions of Quixote that British writers developed before creating their own quixotes. The history of Quixote's translation into English positions Quixote as both a reproducible character whom translators and writers alike could reinterpret and reconfigure and, by virtue of this, a character primed to represent countless versions of exceptionalism. Don Quixote in translation could slay the monster of chivalric romance, or he could serve as the victim of chivalric romance, its cautionary tale; he could be adopted with reservations and flaws in need of correcting (for Shelton), or with care to preserve his most compelling features (for Smollett); he could be kept in the shadows while the text he inhabits takes faithfully translating Cervantes as its priority, or he could become an archetype, a driving force of novelistic fiction in the eighteenth century.

To acknowledge that Quixote is a major archetype in eighteenth-century literatures in English is a commonplace, just as it is to explain Quixote's broad and variegated influence as a function of the militarily and commercially interconnected Atlantic world. But when we look more closely at the exceptionalist character of quixotism, it becomes evident that the Quixote archetype is not only and generally a consequence of Atlantic maritime interconnectedness but more specifically of what we might call the sociability of the quixote archetype.[22] As we have seen, translations laid the groundwork for the imitation and rewriting of Quixote, which in turn laid the groundwork for what becomes the Quixote's pronounced character reproduction in the eighteenth century.

4

Relational Quixotism

In *Poetics of Character,* Susan Manning makes a compelling case for understanding character as relational, like allegory and metaphor—"intrinsically *relational* forms of ethical representation"—particularly for comparative studies of texts in a transatlantic context.[1] As Manning observes, "Enlightenment teaching described a symbiotic relationship between ethos and character which amounted to a mutually constitutive correspondence of representation and response." Character representations were understood as analogous to human thoughts and actions, such that characters, by relation or analogy, had the capacity to make ethical impressions upon their readers. This relationship of representation and response works, too, because reasoning itself was understood as "comparative, analogical, even tropological, at its core."[2] If reasoning—following Locke's definition in *An Essay Concerning Human Understanding* (1689)—is fundamentally about the similitude or incongruity of ideas in the process of comparison, the acts of writing and reading character are also exercises in reason, in comparative or analogical thinking.

This is particularly important for understanding quixotic characters, not only because there are so many quixotic characters but also because it helps us account for *why* there are so many quixotic characters. Jed Rasula has argued that "*Don Quixote* is incitement to a superfluous yet irresistible abundance which, in the historical span of the rise of the novel, has come to be known as Literature," though I aim to be more specific in this chapter about how and why this incitement to abundance takes place, at least as it concerns quixotic characters.[3] The comparative or relational study of character demands that we assess the similitude of quixotes across texts and national traditions, and understand the character of quixotism not as a collection of allusions within a chain of authorial influence, but as a character canon formed

and strengthened by demonstrations of similitude. Further, the analogical thinking that enables us to argue that a character like Jonathan
Swift's Gulliver belongs in a character canon alongside a character
like Tabitha Gilman Tenney's Dorcasina—when we have no reason to
think Swift's *Gulliver's Travels* was a direct influence on Tenney's *Female
Quixotism*—is what enabled eighteenth-century writers to identify a set
of core attributes in Cervantes's Don Quixote and reproduce them in
quixotic characters who have nothing to do with things like chivalric romance or seventeenth-century Spain. In other words, quixotism
became a widely recognizable mode of behavior from Spain to Britain
to the early US because Quixote made for an easy analogy, adaptable
across languages, cultures, and social and political circumstances. The
quixotic character is an easy analogy because quixotes proceed always
and everywhere as exceptions.

For this reason—the suitability of the exceptionalist Quixote to analogy and adaptation—quixotes are particularly "sociable" characters. In
describing a framework of character "sociability" that recognizes fan-
fiction-like personal investment in the sharing and proliferation of characters—like Shakespeare's Falstaff—across texts, David Brewer notes
that Don Quixote and Sancho Panza were often shared and discussed
in rewritings of their stories.[4] Yet the proliferation of quixotes in the
seventeenth and eighteenth centuries was usually not a proliferation
of Quixote himself—a consistent recapitulation of the same Spanish
knight who, as in Fielding's *Don Quixote in England* (1734), just happens to
travel to the English-speaking world—but of Quixote-types that bring
with them a core set of characteristics anchored in quixotic exceptionalism. For this reason the proliferation of quixotes is indeed "sociable," as
Brewer observes, but cannot be explained wholly by Brewer's model of
character proliferation. The quixote is also, in Brewer's terms, an ontologically specific character type, one who circulates broadly within and
beyond cultures and must therefore be understood as a heuristic problem because of its vast, meme-like reproduction. Once again, however,
the quixote is not always Don Quixote in the way, as Brewer observes,
Falstaff sometimes remains the same Falstaff across different texts.[5] For
this reason Brewer's model of character sociability can help us understand certain aspects of the proliferation of quixotes but does not alone
explain why quixotes proliferate as they do.

Even in their mass reproduction, then, quixotes continually understand themselves as exceptional. As I will argue, Don Quixote has taken

on a character afterlife as an archetype that supersedes his immediate connection to the original Spanish text that produced him. I begin here what will become, progressively, the work of separating Don Quixote from *Don Quixote* as the quixotic figure acquires new meanings and functions in Britain and the early US, and as quixotism emerges as a widespread cultural touchstone in the eighteenth century.

Jorge Luis Borges elegantly explains the process by which Don Quixote became an important and influential character in the English-speaking world in a 1966 lecture on the relationship between Samuel Johnson and James Boswell. We know from Thomas Percy, by way of Boswell's *Life of Johnson* (1791), that the teenaged Johnson was "immoderately fond of reading romances of chivalry," a fondness he "retained . . . throughout his life." Percy also noted that Johnson himself ascribed to "these extravagant fictions that unsettled turn of mind which prevented his ever fixing in any profession."[6] Using this characterization of Johnson as a quixotic figure in relation to his biographer Boswell (who strategically styled himself as Johnson's Sancho Panza), Borges explains Boswell's artful role in creating the character of Johnson in much the same way as Cervantes created the character of Don Quixote. In so doing, Borges emphasizes the process by which the creator of character fades into the background as the character itself becomes increasingly real, and as authors and readers "get to know" the character who develops:

> This is what happens with Cervantes' character, especially in the second part, when the author has learned to know his character and has forgotten his initial goal of parodying novels of chivalry. This is true, because the more writers develop their characters, the better they get to know them. So, that's how we have a character who is sometimes ridiculous, but who can be serious and have profound thoughts, and above all is one of the most beloved characters in all of history. And we can say "of history" because Don Quixote is more real to us than Cervantes himself.[7]

Here Borges acknowledges a reality that many of the early translators of *Don Quixote* acknowledged as well: the character Don Quixote has the capacity to become not *as real,* but "more real" than the flesh-and-blood author who created him. We can take Borges's formulation "more real" to mean that Don Quixote becomes more familiar, more sociable, and more viscerally a part of our lives than does Cervantes.

Borges, like the early British translators of *Don Quixote,* does not labor under Don Quixote's confusion between fiction and reality when he describes Don Quixote as "more real," even if he runs afoul of Bertrand Russell's claim that all statements about characters are false.[8] Rather, Borges gives an account of the unmistakable reality that characters' lives—even as archetypes—mattered to readers who were nevertheless fully capable of distinguishing between the ontological categories of reality and fiction.[9] As Catherine Gallagher notes, "Discussions of the dissimilarities between possible and fictional worlds underscore certain features of characters that can help us understand their emotional appeal."[10] Though, as I have noted, literary scholars have been duly fascinated by the "Cervantic" or "Cervantine" or "Cervantean" qualities of texts, seventeenth- and eighteenth-century readers and translators tended to be more invested in who Don Quixote was, how his mind functioned (or malfunctioned), and what instructive (or destructive) possibilities emerge not only from his life story but from the stories of other quixotes refitted for British and early US readerships. Though quixotes were not usually the subjects of fan fiction in the ways Gulliver or Falstaff were, the tendency of authors to reproduce quixote stories made the quixote-type—if not a singular quixote with a consistent backstory—a recognizable phenomenon in British and early US cultures.

Particularly at stake in this discussion of the character afterlife of Don Quixote is how we understand the eighteenth-century reader's relationship to character, as well as what characters signified to readers. Deidre Lynch's argument that character is in eighteenth-century Britain "a rubric that licensed discussion of the order of things in a conversible, commercial society" helps explain the first element of the importance of character as a political medium that I want to address: literary characters have material, real-world functions as mediators and signifiers of real-world feelings and actions.[11] The second important element of character that I want to establish here relates to Brewer's analysis of character as the primary participant in "social canon" formation.[12] Lynch is interested in the possibilities characters generate for readers to insinuate themselves in imaginative but controlled ways into their broader commercial societies, as a means of coping with the demands of an "economy of prestige."[13] Brewer is interested in the social "feedback loop or bandwagon effect" by which "characters come to seem more socially canonical and desirable as they came to seem more common and used by all, which in turn enhanced their value and publicity."[14] Both of these analyses are relevant for what happens to the quixote in the eighteenth century, even as, in the case of quixotes, it is the archetype, and not the selfsame Don Quixote, who generates social interest.

The widespread reproductions of the quixote character in eighteenth-century writing emphasized the very characteristics that readers valued. As Lynch has shown, eighteenth-century characters became "valued for their indescribability, their exceptionality, and their polyvalence," traits that enabled a vast multiplicity of readers to cultivate their own senses of interiority through characters and to use representations of carefully and skillfully crafted characters to establish themselves as exceptions to the sort of "undiscriminating" readers who reveled in mere caricature or burlesque.[15] The "indescribability" of the quixote stems not merely from Quixote's peculiar strain of madness but also from the fact that quixotic characters could be reactionaries (Washington Irving's Died-rich Knickerbocker) or radicals (Charles Lucas's Marauder), gentry (Smollett's Launcelot Greaves) or clergy (Fielding's Parson Adams), women (Tabitha Gilman Tenney's Dorcasina) or men (Royall Tyler's Updike Underhill). This variety has certainly given way to the problem of the quixotic character's polyvalence, as well as the exceptionality of the quixote as a slippery character who eschews definition and trans-gresses the conventional boundaries of genre, nationality, and political ideology. Accordingly, readers could scour the depths of these quix-otic characters almost endlessly, without fixing immediately on a sin-gular, quixotic "type" that might short-circuit the reader's imaginative social self-positioning through "deep" character exploration. In other words, quixotic characters were ideally suitable for the kinds of social and interpretive reading practices that were central to how eighteenth-century readers apprehended character.

We can see further how the reproduction of the quixotic character throughout the eighteenth century—whether read roughly as a "type" or perused case by case for the "depth" of the individual quixote—also reflects what Lynch identifies as an important "shift in the economy of characteristic writing." This shift—from reading character for clearly legible "types" to reading character as part of a signifying system increasingly reliant on particulars and fine detail—arose from print-culture-related anxieties about the "copy theory of knowledge" that "postulated a mimetic relation between ideas and the external objects of sensation that ideas imagined."[16]

If, as Lynch posits, the "enhancement of communications technologies in the early modern period" and the heightening of commercial print culture meant that "an unprecedented attention to fine detail" was required of readers to differentiate between originals and copies, then the "newly intense emphasis on uniform reproduction" that results is especially relevant to the reproduction of quixotes in eighteenth-century fiction.[17] Translating the Quixote meant at once grappling with questions of accuracy and precision in translation and the question of cultural fit, or how to introduce Quixote such that the Quixote's particular characteristics would be legible to a British readership. As the early translators indicate, portraying the character of Don Quixote accurately, with precise attention to his humor-generating and sympathy-generating foibles and mannerisms, was sometimes in tension with framing the Quixote such that British audiences could relate to him.

Further, as British authors began to adopt the quixote for their own narratives, this tension between faithful and legible imitation gained increasing importance. Authors like Henry Fielding and Charlotte Lennox gave ample indications that characters like Parson Adams and Arabella were to be read and understood as spin-offs of Don Quixote, yet these characters also took on, quite ostentatiously, the language and mannerisms of British types in British settings. In Henry Fielding's dramatic rendering of the Quixote story, *Don Quixote in England* (1734), for example, Sancho Panza tells us he is "so fond of the English rost beef and strong beer, that I don't intend ever to set my Foot in Spain again."[18] Not coincidentally, the question of whether English roast beef or Spanish mutton is the more desirable food comes up as well in eighteenth-century English translations of *Don Quixote*, particularly in Smollett's satirical translator's notes on the proportion of beef to mutton in a Spanish dish whose translation was under dispute.[19] In these ways, translating the character of Quixote and his supporting cast meant simultaneously coding the Quixote for more local sensibilities while decoding Cervantes's Quixote from a British perspective. This coding-decoding dynamic also enabled quixotic figures to embody and critique national stereotypes (England as a stout, "rost beef" society, for example), feeding into larger commentaries on nationalism and international relations.

Here again we get the impression that the project of rewriting the quixote is an inherently paradoxical endeavor, fraught with inconsistencies and plagued by tensions and hybrid identities. Nevertheless, if we consider the great reproduction of quixotes that ensued in literatures in English from 1612 to 1815 as at least partly a manifestation of the successful translation of the quixotic character type, we see that quixotic characters have been able to transcend authors' and readers' scruples about inconsistency, tension, and cultural hybridity. The quixotic character possessed traits that made it particularly attractive to eighteenth-century British readers who looked to literary characters as vessels for positioning themselves within a society under the considerable influence of commercial imperatives, and the more specific socioeconomic demands of prestige and individuation.[20]

Here we can observe that Lynch's argument about the role eighteenth-century characters played in social self-positioning in the world is consistent with Manning's understanding of eighteenth-century character as relational and analogical, an occasion for readers to engage in ethical reasoning with and through fictional characters. Further, "characters are not ontologically different because they inhabit possible, rather than actual worlds to which novels merely refer," writes Gallagher. "They are different because they are 'constructs of textual activity.'" It is precisely the fictionality of characters that enables an "inviting openness" that draws us to them.[21]

To caution against the misunderstanding that *all* eighteenth-century readers clamored voraciously for more iterations of their favorite characters' stories, Brewer cites Samuel Johnson's famous rhetorical question, "Was ever yet any thing written by mere man that was wished longer by its readers, excepting Don Quixote, Robinson Crusoe, and the Pilgrim's Progress?"[22] Notwithstanding Johnson's justifiably sound and thus heavily weighted reputation as an eighteenth-century reader, we might nonetheless attribute this list of exceptional texts to Johnson's idiosyncrasy. Yet it would be an understatement of comical proportion to suggest at this point that *Don Quixote,* named here as one of the texts that even Johnson wanted more of, did indeed deliver more. Don Quixote became something of an eighteenth-century literary meme who generated increasing cultural capital with each new reproduction of a quixote-type character.

In Brewer's assessment of the comments of a sample, flesh-and-blood eighteenth-century reader on Smollett's rewriting of the quixote story in *Launcelot Greaves,* we see that (in the reader's words) "the novels in which these characters are to be found . . . will furnish perpetual amusement." Further, this amusement is particularly special because Launcelot

Greaves and his squire, Timothy Crabshaw, "resemble" Don Quixote and Sancho Panza "without imitating, and remind us of what imparted exquisite enjoyment, without diminishing their own novelty."[23] If we consider the anxieties translators of the original Quixote faced—anxieties produced by the mutual but at times conflicting desires to represent accurately and to represent in ways new audiences could relate to—we see that this concern becomes further complicated by the benefits that accrue to those who can imitate, but not slavishly. Translating the quixotic character for the British reader also meant making the character paradoxically novel and familiar. The Quixote, then, was a character to whom British readers related in large part because of the many translations and reconfigurations of his story available to them. But Quixote was also highly legible and reproducible because these translations and reconfigurations perpetuated both the sociability of the quixotic character and the many stories of these characters as representatives of a highly visible character canon. Brewer takes Shakespeare's Falstaff as the "inexhaustible" character of his study, but we can see just as well how the quixote archetype proved just as inexhaustible.[24]

Brewer offers a parallel discussion of first principles of character as a way of confronting what I would refer to as Brewer's "Multiple Falstaffs Problem," whose analogue here is obvious. In the face of the confusion wrought not just by multiple and vastly differing representations of a character type but also by inconsistencies, gaps, and mysteries within singular portrayals of character, looking to what we might call first principles of character is a method that, in Brewer's words, "offers a superior means of dealing with the conflicting emotions which a character like Falstaff inspires."[25] I argue likewise that operating from first principles of character is useful for unpacking this range of inconsistencies we tend to find in quixotes, who represent character inconsistencies to readers not in spite of the fact that they are types and not a singular character with a consistent backstory but because they are types. The crisis of meaning surrounding the term "quixotic"—the problem with which I began this study—is evidence that the very character inconsistencies that Brewer identifies in singular characters who appear across texts are only magnified in dealing with character archetypes who appear across texts.

Rather than spinning wheels in the muddied waters of the conflicting character positions offered by the seemingly endless reproduction of versions featuring these inexhaustible characters and character archetypes, finding in the end that, unsurprisingly, these versions provide little intellectual consistency, we should acknowledge and confront the deracination of the inexhaustible character.

This deracination, what Brewer terms the "character migration" that occurs when readers imagine characters' lives "extending off-page in ways which suggest their fundamental independence and detachability," might also apply to the act of *writing* inexhaustible characters.[26] When so many prominent authors reconfigure the Quixote in new narratives, they necessarily lend both "independence and detachability" to the new quixote, who then becomes a participant in something larger than Cervantes's original. Though scholars have been quick to label this larger thing a genre, it is more accurately a character canon, made coherent not by the formal or stylistic elements of genre, but by the reproducible elements of character.

In other words, authors, too, were crucial participants in character reproducibility. Brewer is attentive to the role of readers in perpetuating characters' "off-page" lives; however, some very prominent authors— Fielding, Smollett, Sterne, Lennox—would copy just as blithely in writing a kind of quixote fan-fiction.[27] Questions over who wrote the character with more faithfulness, nuance, or originality played out not just between authors and readers but among very prominent authors themselves. Rewriting a common character type with *authority* meant that the quixote was not only part of the social formation of the character canon "from below" but also a legible signifier that appealed in both Britain and the early US to a privileged and often politically connected group of authors who used the quixotic figure as a vehicle for political and ideological positioning. The quixotic character certainly took on meaning to readers of fiction looking to reap from character the individual benefits made available by character reading in general, but the quixotic character also took on an important role "from above" as an icon of social commentary and political maneuvering.

PART II

The Character of Exceptionalism

5

Gulliver and English Exceptionalism

I begin part 2 of this book—a series of case studies in quixotic exceptionalism—with a study of English exceptionalism in Jonathan Swift's *Gulliver's Travels* (1726). The logic of state exceptionalism—that a state should act and be treated differently from other states on account of its claim to moral leadership in the international community—is likely familiar to those who have read about or experienced the widespread effects of American exceptionalism. The prominence of the idea of American exceptionalism is both a boon and a drawback for understanding how quixotes embody, and are sometimes used to challenge, exceptionalist politics. On one hand, as I argued in part 1, the logic of American exceptionalism is similar to that of quixotism: in both cases, exceptionalism is a mind-set or an attitude reinforced and perpetuated rhetorically. On the other hand, the exceptionalism of quixotes is akin to but not identical to state exceptionalisms like American exceptionalism. Quixotes like Gulliver (and his US analogue, Updike Underhill, treated in the following chapter) do not necessarily embark on rhetorical or propaganda campaigns aimed at convincing others of their exceptionality. They have already prevailed upon themselves in believing in their exceptionality, a consequence of which is, as we will see throughout part 2 of this book, that others frequently imitate quixotism, even without buying into it.

For this reason quixotic figures like Gulliver have been potent vehicles for critiquing state exceptionalism, because such figures embody and illustrate the naïveté of state exceptionalism, or the tendency to believe in the superiority of one's nation even in the face of compelling counterevidence. Because quixotes like Gulliver are already convinced of their exceptionality, and—unlike those who intentionally promulgate the myth of state exceptionalism—feel no urgency or imperative to convince anyone else of what is for them self-evidently true, they are perfect foils for the ideology of state exceptionalism. As such, they draw our attention to the frequently unexamined assumptions of state exceptionalism.

Further, because the quixote is a distinctly transatlantic character archetype, a literary history of quixotes is crucial for understanding the transatlantic history of American exceptionalism. Understanding American exceptionalism, in other words, necessitates understanding its roots in English exceptionalism in the eighteenth century. The quixote, shipped across the Atlantic from its inception in seventeenth-century Spain and published more widely in English in the eighteenth century than in its original Spanish, carried notions of state exceptionalism from England to the early US.[1] Gulliver's quixotic exceptionalism is an indispensable part of the transatlantic histories of both quixotism and state exceptionalism. Yet at this point we might wonder, What is quixotic about Gulliver?

Two contextual aspects of *Gulliver's Travels* make it a particularly useful case study in quixotism. First, like *Don Quixote, Gulliver's Travels* was met with widespread interest and imitation. Within two years of the first publication of *Gulliver's Travels,* English and Irish readers could peruse a half dozen printings and as many imitations. Overall, scholars have counted more than sixty responses to *Gulliver's Travels* by the end of the eighteenth century, eighteen of which are rather direct imitations, "attempting to reproduce something of its style, intent, and design."[2] As with the quixotic, then, what counts as "Gulliveriana" is subject to difficult questions of allusive, thematic, and stylistic imitation, such that a taxonomy of responses to *Gulliver's Travels* is at once useful and limited. A character study of Gulliver as quixote can address both the question of what constitutes Gulliveriana and what constitutes quixotism, locating in Gulliver the attributes of Quixote.

Second, Gulliver, like Quixote, is one of what David Brewer might term "inexhaustible" characters. As Jeanne Welcher tells us, "Gulliver achieved a further destiny [beyond *Gulliver's Travels*] that, while characteristic of myth, is rare in literary fiction." Gulliver is a character who "stepped off the printed page and assumed an extra-literary existence," a description very similar to that which Brewer calls the "off-page" lives of inexhaustible characters.[3] As with Don Quixote, people know roughly who Gulliver is without having read the book. We might consider, then, whether Gulliver's inexhaustibility is related to Quixote's, given what Gulliver and Quixote have in common.

In addition to these contextual elements that Gulliver shares with Quixote—Gulliver is a popularly reproduced character beyond Swift's original rendering, and consequently Gulliver enjoys an "extra-literary existence"—we can also observe more immediate character commonalities between the two. Gulliver is raised like a quixote and behaves like a quixote; but in turning away from England and the human race in the land of the Houyhnhnms, he also undergoes a quixotic conversion, a moment at which he realizes that the idealism that guides his exceptionalist way of proceeding in the world is empty or flawed. The test of quixotic conversions—which frequently appear in quixotic narratives of the long eighteenth century—is not simply if the quixote disavows the particular brand of idealism that drives him, but if he disavows the exceptionalist worldview. Don Quixote's deathbed conversion—his rejection of the chivalric idealism by which he lived—is among the most challenging and disappointing moments for readers of Cervantes's original (2.74.976–77). But it also provided authors of subsequent quixotic narratives with a potent literary device, a means of signaling a narrative's political or satirical intervention according to the tone with which the narrative treats the moment of quixotic conversion.[4] If we are disappointed that the quixote has renounced quixotism, there must have been something good or useful in the quixotic mind-set; and if we are relieved that the quixote has come back to earth, the narrative has accomplished a critique of quixotism. Gulliver's conversion to the Houyhnhnm way of life is just such a pivotal moment and helps us gauge the extent to which quixotism is a valuable heuristic with which to read and understand Swift's critique in *Gulliver's Travels*.

To be clear, literary scholars generally have not associated Gulliver with quixotism, though we know Swift started and abandoned a translation of *Don Quixote* in the 1730s.[5] If Swift had Cervantes in mind when he was writing *Gulliver's Travels*, he certainly refrained from the kinds of straightforward allusions to *Don Quixote* that we see in Fielding, Lennox, Sterne, and Smollett. The idea of Gulliver as quixote is not entirely without precedent, however. When *Gulliver's Travels* was published in 1726, *Craftsman* editor Nicholas Amhurst compared it with *Don Quixote*, hinting at the relationship between quixotic protagonist and object of critique when he commented on "the same Manner that *Cervantes* exposes Books of *Chivalry*, or Captain *Gulliver* the Writings of *Travellers*."[6] In more contemporary readings of *Gulliver's Travels*, however, comparisons between Gulliver and Don Quixote are rare, overshadowed by historicist preoccupations with Swift's political life.[7] Frequently lost amid this diligent historicizing about Swift are his characters, who amount to more than mere stand-ins for the nonfictional victims of Swiftian political satire. We can read Gulliver as a quixote even as Swift chose not to allude to Quixote directly, as Gulliver proceeds with an exceptionalist disposition fundamental to quixotes. In these ways *Gulliver's Travels* anticipates the development of the quixotic as a political concept in eighteenth-century literatures in English that transcends directly or immediately allusive ties to *Don Quixote*.

As I have suggested, Swift gives no overt indication in *Gulliver's Travels* that *Don Quixote* was a literary source for his narrative, either by title (as in Charlotte Lennox's *The Female Quixote*), front matter (as in Henry Fielding's *Joseph Andrews*), or direct thematic allusion (as in Laurence Sterne's *Tristram Shandy*). As Christine Rees suggests, however, Swift, a master of weaving together the comic and the ironic, was certainly an admirer of Cervantes.[8] While we do know that Swift was very familiar with *Don Quixote*, no statements or correspondences of Swift's tie *Gulliver's Travels* directly to *Don Quixote*. This lack of overt paratextual evidence—overt in such a way as to link the two texts in a chain of authorial influence—has led critics away from prominent elements of *Gulliver's Travels* that, wittingly or not for Swift, are strikingly quixotic.

At the outset of *Gulliver's Travels,* we learn that Gulliver comes from the lower noble ranks, having been raised on his father's "small estate in Nottinghamshire" and having received an education at "Emanuel-College in Cambridge."[9] Like Don Quixote, a hidalgo, Gulliver's family estate is not adequate to provide the kind of lifestyle he seeks, so he undergoes a practical education with a desire to embark on an itinerant life. As Frank Boyle notes, "When his father's land cannot support him through his university studies, he turns or is directed to the New Philosophy's most practical discipline, medicine, and to sea as a ship's surgeon."[10] Though not educated specifically in literature or in the romance tradition, he does, after becoming an apprenticed surgeon, spend allowances sent from his father on "learning Navigation, and other Parts of the Mathematicks, useful to those who intend to travel, as [he] always believed it would be some time or another [his] Fortune to do" (15).

The word "Fortune" here—and throughout *Gulliver's Travels*—is telling. Of course Gulliver seeks a material fortune with each maritime adventure, but his belief that travel is his destiny takes the form of idealism. As Amhurst recognized in his 1726 review, Gulliver's is a quixotism of travel. Gulliver's affinity with travel is both reinforced and made literary by the fact that, in addition to writing a book of travel in *Gulliver's Travels,* he also delighted in reading them in his youth, before his traveling imbued him with a sense that his accounts of the lands he visits are the only true accounts, or that his vision is self-justifiably true: "I have perused several Books of Travel with great Delight in my younger Days; but, having since gone over most Parts of the Globe, and been able to contradict many fabulous Accounts from my own Observation; it hath given me great Disgust against this Part of Reading, and some Indignation to see the Credulity of Mankind so impudently abused" (272).

In addition to his travel reading in youth, Gulliver is a bookish type more generally, passing his "hours of Leisure" amid his earlier travels in reading the best Authors, ancient and modern; being always provided with a good Number of Books" (16). Although Swift makes passing and comedic reference to the pitfalls of romance reading while describing the cause of the fire in the Lilliputian queen's apartment—"by the Carelessness of a Maid of Honour, who fell asleep while she was reading a Romance"—we receive no indication that the practical Gulliver reads romances himself (49). However, Gulliver's continual tendency toward "service" and courtly manners—as when the Brobdingnagian queen takes interest in him, and he vows that "if [he] were at [his] own Disposal, [he] should be proud to devote [his] life to her Majesty's Service"—is reminiscent of Don Quixote's imitation of chivalric code (91). Both Gulliver and Quixote overcompensate with affectatious politeness for a lack of access to the lifestyles of high-ranking aristocracy and court life.

Gulliver's "quixotism of travel" is also, beyond its literary manifestation in his travel narrations, highly romanticized. Gulliver recapitulates the belief that traveling is his "Fortune to do" each time he returns to England from a journey that, however fascinating and adventurous, proves also perilous. Like Quixote, harsh reality is not only incapable of curing Gulliver's quixotism but likely to reinforce and propel it. After the voyage to Lilliput, Gulliver's adventure in Brobdingnag begins with what becomes a familiar line of justification for Gulliver throughout his travels: "Having been condemned by Nature and Fortune to an active and restless life; in two months after my return [to England], I again left my native country" (75). Gulliver leaves for Brobdingnag on account of his "insatiable Desire of seeing foreign Countries" (71). After returning from Brobdingnag and before embarking on a trip to Laputa in part 3, Gulliver ends part 2 with an admission that "my Wife protested I should never go to Sea any more; although my evil Destiny so ordered, that she had not Power to hinder me; as the reader may know hereafter" (137). At last, after returning home for the third time after yet another long and dangerous journey, and finding his "Wife and Family in good health," Gulliver remains home with his family "about five months in a very happy Condition" before leaving a final time for his most fateful journey to the Country of the Houyhnhnms, his wife "big with Child," musing, "If I could have learned the Lesson of Knowing when I was well" (203, 207).[11]

In each of these passages Gulliver behaves as if compelled by a force greater than his own will, such that travel becomes not just an itch in need of scratching but a romantic call of duty. Against the rational understanding that his perpetual journeys could at some point estrange him from family and country, Gulliver chases a romantic ideal as if duty-bound to fate or destiny, travel being his "Fortune to do" (15). Just as Don Quixote's romantic idealization of knight-errantry renders him duty-bound to its conventions, Gulliver's romantic idealization of the traveling life causes him to understand his recurrent journeys as pre-ordained and necessary, to be carried out above the needs and desires of his wife and children, and those who would advise him to remain at home after testing his "Fortune" so many times, each time narrowly escaping an unfortunate end.

Though Gulliver shares with Robinson Crusoe the need to travel despite the protests of his family, it is less his faith and industrious-ness than his tendency to romanticize and aggrandize his desire that propels each journey. And just as a profound sense of justice propels Don Quixote, Gulliver's voyages also become more about just gover-nance and ways of living than simply collecting curios from foreign lands and amassing a fortune in trade. Because of Swift's wry portrayal of Gulliver, critics tend to overlook the extent to which Gulliver's deep-est existential entanglements—his argument with the Brobdingnagian king and his struggle to embrace and then separate from the ways of the Houyhnhnms—center on justice in living and in governance.

Gulliver's idealism morphs gradually throughout Swift's narrative into a full-on quixotic quest for a utopian ideal (which he eventually finds, though perhaps without the results he desires, in the land of the Houyhnhnms).[12] As the narrative progresses, Gulliver develops greater vocabulary and facility in his criticisms of the political systems and ways of life most familiar to him, this progression hitting its nationalist peak in Gulliver's conversation with the King of Brobdingnag, and its culmination in the outright rejection of his own nationality upon returning from the Country of the Houyhnhnms.

At the very least, then, we can build a circumstantial case for reading Gulliver as a quixote, and taking the quixotic as a framework for understanding Gulliver's actions and Swift's satirical performance in *Gulliver's Travels*. Gulliver comes from a socioeconomic background that allows for both education and quixotic idealism, and his education is inextricably connected with the obsession (or call to duty) that he develops (travel). As with Don Quixote, this obsession is both literary (insofar as it relates to the reading and writing of travel narratives) and romanticized (insofar as it is understood as a function of his destiny). The telos of this romanticized obsession with travel is a utopian ideal, or the discovery of a land, culture, and political system capable of addressing the cumulative set of problems that Gulliver registers with the known world (Europe). When Quixote looks around his native Spain and witnesses social and legal systems incapable of providing justice, he sets out to provide justice his own way. When Gulliver witnesses in travel all the ways his native country is comparatively unjust and unscrupulous, he feebly attempts to bring the Houyhnhnm way of life back to England.

In light of these conditions, Gulliver also constructs and exposes exceptionalist arguments throughout his travels, culminating in a moment of quixotic conversion at the end of the narrative—what Michael McKeon calls "a decisive island conversion"—that reinforces rather than extinguishes his quixotism.[13] While *Gulliver's Travels* is certainly Cervantic in its many moments of comic irony, its protagonist is also quixotic in his brand of exceptionalism, his tendency to continually separate himself from the reality of his parochial worldview, or to simultaneously defend and expose the flaws of his nation and national identity. Gulliver illuminates England's flaws even to himself as he defends them to foreign peoples. In Gulliver we see the beginnings of an eighteenth-century quixotic exceptionalism, a belief in one's moral superiority arising from literary idealism in the face of counterevidence.

Part 1 of the *Travels* has been the subject of extensive commentary on the Lilliputians as political allegory for English court society, but it also reflects Gulliver's chivalrous mind-set. In part 1, Gulliver proceeds with a removed, anthropological perspective on the world around him. He engages with the Lilliputians not with the imperialist air of Robinson Crusoe, but with a sense of bewilderment. And he finds occasion to

behave deferentially, to bow, or to indicate courtly respect for his foreign hosts.[14] Among the relatively tiny Lilliputians, Gulliver expresses
gratitude for being released from captivity in a graceful and deferential
manner: "I made my Acknowledgements, by prostrating myself at his
Majesty's Feet" (39). And, as Neil Chudgar has pointed out, Gulliver
proceeds mainly with gentleness, which he largely shares with those
around him.[15] Gulliver's mannerisms in Lilliput are chivalric, awk-
wardly formal gestures of the sort that a lower-ranking noble like Gulliver or Quixote might expect when in the company of court (given that
Gulliver's social standing precludes any familiarity with court life in his
own country).

The changes Gulliver experiences in part 2 of the *Travels,* in Brobdingnag, best illustrate his quixotic exceptionalism. In Brobdingnag,
the sheer size of the inhabitants forces Gulliver into a bellicose mode—
as a quixote reacting to giants—and his chivalric quixotism turns defensive. From their size and appearance to their politics, as we learn once
the king engages Gulliver in conversation about the land from which he
came, the Brobdingnagians magnify Gulliver's quixotism by rendering
him defensive, just as Don Quixote's forthrightness becomes more pronounced when interlocutors question or challenge his worldview. No
longer capable of seeing himself as an exceptional figure on account of
his size, Gulliver's exceptionalism pivots to national pride. As Gulliver
writes of his first encounter with the Brobdingnagians in part 2: "In
this terrible Agitation of Mind I could not forbear thinking of Lilliput,
whose Inhabitants looked upon me as the greatest Prodigy that ever
appeared in the World; where I was able to draw an Imperial Fleet
in my Hand, and perform those other Actions which will be recorded
for ever in the Chronicles of that Empire, while Posterity shall hardly
believe them, although attested by Millions" (78).

By the time Gulliver makes it to Brobdingnag, a separate, oppositional sense of England and its national politics and customs emerges
more saliently, forcing Gulliver to defend his Englishness while at the
same time reckoning with its flaws. Part 1 is not without humorous
comparisons to Gulliver's native land—the "peculiar" manner of Lilliputian writing is "aslant from one corner of the Paper to the other,
like Ladies in *England*"—though part 2 is the site of Gulliver's pivotal
interactions with the Brobdingnagian king, in which Swift positions a
fuller, comparative portrait of Gulliver's impression of England against
Brobdingnagian ideals (51).

Early interactions with the Brobdingnagian king depict Gulliver as a patriotic traveler, one who leaves the homeland and finds abroad nothing but confirmations of the superiority of his own nation. Gulliver gushes "a little too copious[ly] in talking of [his] own beloved Country; of [English] Trade, and Wars by Sea and Land, of [English] Schisms in Religion, and Parties in the State." The king's counterperspective leaves Gulliver at a loss, compelling him to defend England and broader Europe with exceptionalist arguments (96). When the king prompts Gulliver to give an account of his native England, Gulliver provides a list of superlative descriptions: "the Fertility of our Soil"; "an illus-trious body called the House of Peers" (as well as "that extraordinary Care always taken of their Education," and their "Valour, Conduct, and Fidelity"); the House of Commons "*freely* picked by the People them-selves, for their great Abilities, and Love of their Country, to represent the Wisdom of the whole Nation," among others, along with a summary of English history, military and otherwise. The king's series of ques-tions and points of contention—asking about the qualifications of new Lords, the potential for political corruption and conflicts of interest, the existence of national credit and national debt, among others—lead him to conclude "the Bulk of [English] Natives, to be the most pernicious Race of little odious Vermin that Nature ever suffered to crawl upon the Surface of the Earth" (116–21).

Confronted with such judgments, Gulliver finds himself "forced to rest with Patience, while [his] noble and most beloved Country was so injuriously treated" (122). Ashamed to admit his inability to offer a substantive counterargument to the king, Gulliver, "heartily sorry as any of [his] readers can possibly be, that such an Occasion was given," admits in this attempt to excuse himself, that he "artfully eluded" many of the king's questions "and gave every Point a more favourable turn by many Degrees than the strictness of Truth would allow" (122). Gulliver begins to construct an exceptionalist argument against the accusations of the Brobdingnagian king in the absence of a substantive one, alleg-ing that Brobdingnag, unlike Europe, is too isolated to have knowledge of such things as cannons (widely known and understood in Europe) or to have "reduced *Politicks* into a *Science,* as the more acute Wits of *Europe* have done" (124). Gulliver laments the possibility that "a confined Edu-cation" and a "certain narrowness of Thinking," such as those which he ascribes to the king in the absence of a solid counterargument to the king's critiques of English society, "be offered as a Standard for all

Mankind" (122). In other words, whereas Gulliver's single-mindedness is cosmopolitan, the king's is parochial. This is exceptionalist logic.

Gulliver's inability to defend his country before the king—his arguments in this endeavor "failed of Success"—renders him vulnerable to the kinds of utopian notions that he will eventually embrace wholeheartedly among the Houyhnhnms in part 4, leading ultimately to his quixotic conversion. Even before the Brobdingnagian king successfully makes his arguments against Gulliver's account of Englishness, his first encounters with the king produce in Gulliver a critical outlook on his own country, along with seeds of doubt over his previously unquestioned patriotism and English identity:

> But, as I was not in a Condition to resent Injuries, so, upon mature Thoughts, I began to doubt whether I were injured or no. For, after having been accustomed several months to the Sight and Converse of this People, and observed every Object upon which I cast my Eyes, to be of proportionable Magnitude; the Horror I had first conceived from their Bulk and Aspect was so far worn off, that if I had then beheld a Company of *English* Lords and Ladies in their Finery and Birth-day Cloaths, acting their several Parts in the most courtly Manner of Strutting, and Bowing and Prating; to say the Truth, I should have been strongly tempted to laugh as much at them as the King and his Grandees did at me. (97)

When the king forces Gulliver to think critically about both the practices of his native country and the ways his perspective, frequently changing amid his travels, can affect how he views England and his English identity, Gulliver doubles down on the single-mindedness of English (and European) exceptionalism. Thereafter he is hurdled with fragile nationalist baggage and magnified force into his quixotism of travel, believing still that, despite his willingness to bend the truth to skirt the Brobdingnagian king's criticisms of England, his destiny is not an English utopia, but a utopia abroad. After his time in Brobdingnag, before setting sail yet again for Laputa, Gulliver writes: "I could not reject [Captain William Robinson's] Proposal; the Thirst I had of seeing the World, notwithstanding my past Misfortunes, continuing as violent as ever" (141). In this moment, Gulliver is compelled by his quixotism of travel above and beyond whatever concerns he might have acquired from experience about the dangers of travel to his physical—and ultimately to his ontological—condition.

We can observe how the anthropological quixote of part 1 becomes a quixotic exceptionalist in part 2, paradoxically defending his own nation as a utopia only after departing from it to seek knowledge and better opportunity abroad. In the same vein of Swiftian irony, Gulliver extols that presumed characteristic of Europe—a broad range of knowledge, derived from intercultural relations and experience—that he seeks for himself through *leaving* Europe, indulging his quixotism of travel.

The English exceptionalism that Gulliver puts forth to counter the Brobdingnagian king's critiques posits both the demonstrably false notion (falsified by the very presence and experience of Gulliver in a foreign land) that England "and the politer Countries of Europe are wholly exempted" from the prejudices of limited knowledge, as well as the ideal of universal knowledge through travel. Gulliver constructs an ideal (universal knowledge through travel) while positioning himself as an example of this ideal. This is precisely how Gulliver's quixotism of travel works: it is the exceptionalist melding of the European ideal of universal knowledge with the itinerant quixotic ideal of universal knowledge through travel. Gulliver's quixotism becomes in part 2 of the narrative a more traditional Anglo-European idealism—for Gulliver, a form of exceptionalism stemming from his nationalism and naïveté—to which Gulliver holds fast, despite the skillful counterarguments of the Brobdingnagian king. By the end of part 2, we have witnessed Gulliver's display of quixotism, marked by his nationalist defense of England and wider Europe as particularly enlightened nations. As a quixote of travel bearing nationalist baggage, Gulliver has witnessed realities that contradict his idealisms about both travel and England, yet he clings to these idealisms.

After witnessing the Laputan dystopia in part 3 and returning home to England once more with a travel idealism that has not flagged, but has become stronger, Gulliver sets out in part 4 and arrives in the Country of the Houyhnhnms, a utopian land ultimately responsible for Gulliver's final moments of quixotic conversion, not from mad quixote to rational English citizen, but from an apologist for a fictive vision of England and Europe to an apologist for a foreign utopia. Gulliver's quixotic conversion is complex, less a rejection of quixotism than a substitution of one quixotic ideal for another. In this sense, Gulliver is the gullible character par excellence, an engine of satire because he fails to learn that his quixotism of travel and his exceptionalist predisposition are what continually land him in trouble.

On the brink of quixotic conversion, Gulliver is clearly impressed by the rational horses, their innovative child-distribution policies, their stoic attitude toward death, and the absence of words in their language to express *"the thing which is not,"* or "any thing that is *evil,* except what they borrow from the Deformities or ill Qualities of the *Yahoos*" (223, 257). Gulliver expresses his utopian vision of the Houyhnhnms in his description of his own life while among them: "I enjoyed perfect Health of Body, and Tranquility of Mind; I did not feel the Treachery or Inconstancy of a Friend, nor the Injuries of a secret or open Enemy" (258). While in the land of rational horses, Gulliver also begins to speak more critically of his native country, explaining wars resulting from "the Corruption of Ministers," and the soldier as "a *Yahoo* hired to kill in cold Blood as many of his own Species, who have never offended him, as he possibly can" (228–29). These impressions lead to Gulliver's final conversion in the land of the Houyhnhnms, at which point Gulliver admits that "those excellent *Quadrupeds* placed in opposite View to human Corruptions, had so far opened my Eyes, and enlarged my Understanding, that I began to view the Actions and Passions of man in a very different Light; and to think the Honour of my own Kind not worth managing," resolving then "never to return to human Kind" (240).

The Houyhnhnms ultimately force Gulliver, by edict, to return home anyway. When he does, his wife and children, and the rest of his own species, repulse him. Converted, he still looks to re-create a utopian existence back in England. Whereas Don Quixote begins with idealism and concludes with a remorseful pragmatism upon his deathbed, Gulliver's quixotism progresses in the opposite direction. Having gotten into travel for pragmatic purposes before realizing it was "his Fortune to do," Gulliver's quixotism of travel finally upends his entire life. He purchases two horses upon returning to England, whose smells he finds comforting, and with whom he "converse[s] at least four Hours every Day," never rides, and considers partners "in great Amity" with himself and each other (271). When he launches what appears to be a final apologia for England, its government and its occupants—a seemingly out-of-place vestige of his preconversion sentiments in part 2—we can comfortably read these notes with irony (275). In the elusive, mocking tone of Morus's final comments at the end of *Utopia* (1516), Gulliver writes of his previous denouncements of European colonialism: "This Description, I confess, doth by no means affect the *British* nation, who may be an Example to the whole World for their Wisdom, Care, and

Justice in planting Colonies" (275). After this passage he goes on to affirm the psychological conditions of his utopian conversion, attempting to "apply those excellent Lessons of Virtue which [he] learned among the Houyhnhnms" in slowly conditioning himself to tolerate his family and, perhaps, "a neighbor *Yahoo*" (276).

In Gulliver's relation of his travels we can see, then, a progression of quixotism and the ways this progression alters his quixotic exceptionalism. Gulliver embarks on his travels under the inspiration of a romanticized, quixotic ideal—the ideal of the life of travel, understood as his absolute destiny. He derives this destiny from a childhood fascination with books of travel, and the pursuit of a travel-oriented education. Despite early encounters with the Lilliputians and the Brobdingnagians—including an ability to appreciate some of the foreign things he witnesses—his quixotism of travel carries with it at first an idealistic belief in the supremacy and utopian potential of his native English culture. Gulliver encounters difference and is fascinated by it, yet his quixotism prevents him from dwelling on the wonders of Lilliput or Brobdingnag or developing a critical outlook on his own country. After passing through Laputa and its neighboring lands intrigued and questioning but still unmoored from his default nationalism, he undergoes a form of quixotic conversion in the Country of the Houyhnhnms, through which his quixotism remains, but its focus shifts. After living among the rational horses, Gulliver continues to embrace the cultural model of the Houyhnhnms, even as they evict him from their society, and even though his own family, still healthy and loyal, had long since awaited his physical and psychological return.

This progression of quixotism not only illuminates aspects of Gulliver's character—his anthropological aloofness, his failure to compromise grand ideologies for smaller bits and pieces of useful knowledge he picks up amid his travels, and his stubborn inability to learn the flaws in his worldview through experience—but also directs our attention to one of the most critically underdeveloped yet important implications of Swift's narrative. In Gulliver's meandering and sometimes self-contradictory quixotism, Swift shows us how exceptionalism operates as apologia for both nationalist (Gulliver in Brobdingnag) and utopian (Gulliver among the Houyhnhnms) ideologies, the combination of which is the logic of what we can call eighteenth-century English exceptionalism. Further, Gulliver's shift from exceptionalist notions about his own nation to an exceptionalist pursuit of utopia abroad provides a conceptual map for the historical transformation of forms of English patriotism into utopian visions of Anglo-America into nascent American exceptionalism.

This mode of exceptionalism—the shielding of one's idealistic worldview from the scrutiny and harsh reality of the surrounding world—is expressly linked with quixotic qualities and characters in eighteenth-century prose fiction, from Gulliver's contorted argument with the King of Brobdingnag, to Parson Adams's shock and dismay at England's treatment of the poor in Henry Fielding's *Joseph Andrews,* to Arabella's insistence that her lowly gardener is really a gentleman suitor in disguise in Charlotte Lennox's *The Female Quixote.* The fictive and fantastical elements of quixotism make possible each quixote's resistance to surrounding realities and are as such the sine qua non of quixotic exceptionalism. Quixotic exceptionalism in fiction reflects the wider state exceptionalisms at work in British domestic and foreign policy, which constitute Britain as the world's freest and mightiest nation, despite the abundance of domestic problems we see fictionalized in *Gulliver's Travels* and elsewhere.

Though quixotes were increasingly understood, through the middle of the eighteenth century, as heroic visionaries rather than foolish objects of satire, Gulliver's character progression preempts this shift, inviting our consideration of a third possibility for understanding quixotism. Whether Gulliver's quixotic naïveté, idealism, and stubbornness frame him as an admirably determined dreamer—a gentle and well-meaning hero—or, perhaps more likely, the misguided butt of the joke who continually fails to learn his lesson, Gulliver's quixotic characteristics underlie his exceptionalism, which is in either case central to the social and political interventions of *Gulliver's Travels.* For it is not only the allusions to persons and policy issues that Swift pillories that define his political intervention in *Gulliver's Travels* but also the manner in which Gulliver frames these issues. Gulliver's quixotism leads him to willfully ignore arguments that he acknowledges to be superior to his own, to prioritize affinity over reason (whether identifying with the English or the Houyhnhnms), to estrange his family, and to repeatedly jeopardize his life. Gulliver's exceptionalist justifications for each of these decisions undoubtedly say as much about fractious, vitriolic party politics, political corruption, militant nationalism, utopian beliefs, and misplaced social and domestic priorities as do Swift's more minute political allusions throughout *Gulliver's Travels.*

As we can see, then, Gulliver bears the core characteristics of Quixote in his upbringing in the ranks of the lower nobility, his literary education, his propensity for reading travel narratives and idealizing a life of travel, his belligerent defense of the worldview these produce, and his quixotic conversion from one form of idealism to another. Above all, perhaps, Gulliver's exchanges with foreign Brahmins and potentates reflect an idealism in search of just governance and an end to needless warring, factionalism, and disputation, or an improved human condition that Gulliver's family back in England can only interpret as a form of madness.

To be precise, it is not only idealism but an exceptionalist worldview that drives Gulliver. Until his conversion in the land of the Houyhnhnms, he argues for the exceptionality of the English way of life even as the Lilliputians had already demonstrated the pitfalls of so much of it, and even as the Brobdingnagian king put forth counterarguments that Gulliver could not refute. Afterward, that very exceptionalist mind-set enables Gulliver to identify with the Houyhnhnms despite his physical resemblance to the reviled Yahoos. That exceptionalist mind-set arose from his reading of books of travel that idealized England and wider Europe's place in the world, and this is precisely why Amhurst took *Gulliver's Travels* for a Cervantic satire on travel writing. In the end, because Gulliver's exceptionalism proves catastrophically malleable, allowing Gulliver to turn entirely away from the English society he first defended as exceptional, *Gulliver's Travels* offers an important illustration—and simultaneously an important critique—of English exceptionalism in the early eighteenth century.

6

Underhill and American Exceptionalism

Gulliver's Travels shows us how quixotic characteristics can enable a satirical critique of national exceptionalism, a character strategy that informs
our understanding of Royall Tyler's rendering of quixotism in *The Algerine
Captive* (1797). *The Algerine Captive* resembles *Gulliver's Travels* most nearly in
its capacity to bring national exceptionalisms into conflict for satirical
purposes. By sending Gulliver off to foreign lands, Swift engages in
a simple but highly effective comparative strategy, taking up international difference as a critical mirror in much the same way that authors
of other quixotic narratives (Fielding, Brackenridge, Lennox, Tenney)
engage their quixotes in more localized encounters with difference.
Though the exceptionalist framework remains the same for quixotic
narratives set primarily within national borders as for those whose quixotes venture beyond them, the latter provides the eighteenth-century
author with greater freedom, in many cases, to construct an imaginary
other that local readers are likely to find especially aberrant, producing
in readers many of the same effects Gulliver experiences himself: anxiety, shock, wonder, and delight.

Swift clearly takes this liberty in *Gulliver's Travels*, in its depiction of
a series of fantastical characters and nations. Tyler's *The Algerine Captive*,
on the other hand, constructs as other the inhabitants of the Barbary
Coast, largely through Tyler's borrowing from other travel narratives
and contemporary Barbary accounts. Both Swift and Tyler use quixotism to reflect a traumatic image of foreign cultures ironically back onto
their own societies. Both writers avail themselves of a form of comic
irony that situates their quixotes as absorbers of satire and its consequences, leading readers through the narrative with the awareness that
they are in on the joke with the author, but the quixote is not. We can
witness this commonality, for example, in Tyler's Swiftian catalogues,

which appear in moments of heightened irony, as when his narrator dramatizes the colonial pursuits of the first US "settlers," who "crossed a boisterous ocean, penetrated a savage wilderness, encountered famine, pestilence, and Indian warfare" to secure their places in US history.[1]

Though Tyler draws his Algerian figures very loosely from second-hand information about an existing culture, the fact that most early US readers would not have had any firsthand (or even, necessarily, second-hand) experience of the Barbary Coast enables Tyler to color his Algerines with a fantastical quality. In so doing, Tyler also brings in elements of *Don Quixote*, specifically from Cervantes's fictional account in *Don Quixote* of his actual enslavement in Algiers. As María Antonia Garcés has shown, Cervantes was himself an Algerine captive between 1575 and 1580, abducted, like Tyler's quixotic protagonist, Updike Underhill, by Barbary pirates during his service in Mediterranean military campaigns against the Turks.[2] Cervantes retells parts of this experience in Algiers in part 1 of *Don Quixote* in "the captive's tale" (1.39.360). Tyler, who had previously reworked the Barrataria episode from part 2 of *Don Quixote* into a three-act play featuring Sancho Panza, *The Island of Barrataria* (ca. 1808–15), employs in *The Algerine Captive* several of Cervantes's themes and references from "the captive's tale" to form parts of Updike's account of enslavement in Algiers.[3] Both Tyler's Updike and Cervantes's captive struggle to purchase their freedom with the aid of sympathetic Algerians and fellow slaves; both reference the gruesome punishment of impalement for those caught in escape attempts; and both treat religious difference between the Algerian Muslims and the Christian captives as a means of interrogating national (and religious) loyalties and identities. Though some of these similarities are circumstantial—common not only among *Don Quixote* and *The Algerine Captive* but also among a wider range of captivity narratives—others provide more telling links between the two texts. The captivity tale predates *Don Quixote* within the Spanish tradition and certainly flourishes in varying forms in eighteenth-century Anglo-American traditions ("Indian" captivity narratives, Barbary narratives, slave narratives). But *The Algerine Captive*'s captivity-narrative elements arguably owe much to Cervantes in particular. Tyler, who had never traveled to Algiers, borrowed much of his fictional account of the Barbary Coast not only from contemporary captivity narratives but also from Cervantes's "captive's tale" in *Don Quixote*.[4]

In terms of its influences, *The Algerine Captive* draws most legibly on travel writing, the quixotic narrative tradition, the captivity narrative tradition, and the novel. Cathy Davidson has called it "broken-backed in its odd conjoining of apparently inconsistent parts," noting that it "verges into a captivity tale . . . to register the full horror of slavery" by way of a "travelogue of the protagonist's disconnected life."[5] Nancy Armstrong and Leonard Tennenhouse have addressed the captivity-tale elements of *The Algerine Captive,* arguing that the cosmopolitan inflection of the Barbary narrative best characterizes the early US novel, given the preoccupations of early US writers with questions of, as Bruce Burgett has put it, "not . . . nationality, territoriality, and citizenship," but "civility, commerce, travel, and ethnographic description."[6] Of these acknowledged influences, the quixotic influence is most crucial for our understanding of *The Algerine Captive*'s pivotal ending, the conversion of protagonist Updike Underhill from globe-trotting American malcontent to "worthy FEDERAL citizen" (225). To account for Tyler's controversial ending, and thus to reexamine the political implications of Updike's experience in captivity, we need to read *The Algerine Captive* with particular attention to the bearing of Updike's sustained quixotism on his final conversion. In so doing, we can demonstrate the role of quixotic exceptionalism in affirming the ideal of national superiority while at the same time, as does *Gulliver's Travels,* calling our attention precisely to the process of creating such an exceptionalist outlook. Reading *The Algerine Captive* with *Gulliver's Travels* in mind provides a clearer view of how English exceptionalism in the time of Swift was recapitulated as American exceptionalism in Tyler's late eighteenth century.

Updike behaves very much like a quixote throughout both of the novel's seemingly inconsistent volumes. Though volume 2 of the *The Algerine Captive*—the volume that treats Updike's captivity in Algiers— was critically dismissed by Tyler's contemporaries as inferior to volume 1, recent critics have focused on volume 2 as the primary site of "the political implications of the whole novel."[7] However, it is volume 1, a chronicle of Updike's travels and travails throughout the US, which introduces Updike as a quixote and sets the stage for his frequently overlooked quixotic behavior as a captive in volume 2. As Updike's mother remarks in volume 1 after the family minister attempts to recruit young Updike into the academy, "the boy loves books" (25). Updike's quixotic bookishness and comic fascination with Greek and Latin give rise to a string of social and professional blunders in the US, leading Wood to dub him a "classical quixote."[8]

Exhibiting a marked genre-switch both formally and thematically, volume 2 affords Tyler's captive much less freedom than volume 1 to travel the countryside in quixotic fashion. Nonetheless, the quixotic episodes of volume 1 are not wholly disconnected from the captivity saga of volume 2. Once in captivity, Updike imagines that among his "grossly illiterate" lot of fellow slaves is "a Spanish Don with forty noble names" (119). His fantasy is a thorough recapitulation of the story of Cervantes's captive in *Don Quixote*, who absconds with the aid of his opulent master's beautiful Muslim daughter, Zoraida:

> I fancied my future-master's head gardener, taking me one side, professing the warmest friendship, and telling me in confidence that he was a Spanish Don with forty noble names; that he had fallen in love with my master's fair daughter, whose mother was a christian slave; that the young lady was equally charmed with him; that she was to rob her father of a rich casket of jewels, there being no dishonour in stealing from an infidel; jump into his arms in boy's clothes that very night, and escape by a vessel, already provided, to his native country. I saw in imagination all of this accomplished. I saw the lady descend the rope ladder; heard the old man and his servants pursue; saw the lady carried off breathless in the arms of her knight; arrive safe in Spain; was present at the lady's baptism into the catholic church, and at her marriage with her noble deliverer. (119)

Just as Updike reimagined the captive's escape from slavery in *Don Quixote*, Tyler reimagined quixotism in Updike, whose fanciful thinking propels both his physical adventures in volume 1 and his psychological adventures in captivity in volume 2. Critical tendencies to mark the end of the "quixotic" volume 1 as the end of Updike's quixotism have obscured the extent to which Updike remains quixotic throughout the novel, and throughout its quixotic conversion scene. Though the fragmented, seemingly inconsistent structure of *The Algerine Captive* has given critics difficulty in assessing its parts as a unified whole, its quixote consistently defies the structural changes imposed upon him.

Updike is discovered by a minister to be fit for a scholar, educated in Latin, Greek, and the classics, made a schoolteacher, and subsequently chased out of a number of New England locales for his classical education, pedantry, and high-mindedness. In a Gulliverian turn, he then turns practical and studies to become a physician, finding similar dissatisfaction with repressed, vulgar, and uneducated Americans first in New England and then in the US South. Frustrated, he quits the US for England and takes up a physician post aboard a slave ship, which Tyler ironically names *Sympathy*. Marooned on the Barbary Coast thereafter, Updike is captured and made a slave himself in Algiers. After spending much of volume 1 drifting from failed occupation to failed occupation in his native country, Updike spends volume 2 narrating his experiences as a slave and a practicing physician in Algiers.

Tyler's narrator introduces his adventures by way of an ancestor, Captain John Underhill. Updike spends the first three short chapters of his account explaining the circumstances of his ancestor, as he tells us, "one of the first emigrants to New England," who undergoes a persecution saga of his own before we get to Updike's story (11). Captain Underhill, who "had early imbibed an ardent love of liberty, civil and religious, by his service as a soldier among the Dutch," finds himself exiled from his Massachusetts settlement under John Winthrop because of his attitude of religious tolerance, and charged with "adultery of the heart" for gazing upon a woman who was illicitly wearing "a pair of wanton open worked gloves, slit at the thumbs and fingers, for the convenience of taking snuff" (11, 15). The banished captain resettles in New Hampshire and is elected governor there before the Massachusetts government claims jurisdiction over New Hampshire too, forcing him to relocate to Dutch-settled Albany. There he is granted a tract of land by the Dutch for his services in battles against Native Americans (20). The captain dies without capitalizing on his land grant, which sets up Updike's future encounter with unscrupulous land speculators in Hartford who attempt to purchase and then sell Updike's ancestral claim to the land with full knowledge that no such land, or no such title, formally exists.

The introduction of Updike's ancestor into the narrative provides a historical context against which we can consider Updike's experiences, then his postconversion sentiments. Like his ancestor, Updike moves from state to state in his own country, having difficulty finding a place to settle in which his ideals are taken seriously, or in which he can find tolerable acceptance. Once captured in Algiers, he struggles to reconcile his Christianity with the Muslim faith of the Algerians, as well as his naïveté with the artful traders looking to capitalize on his circumstances. As John Engell has notably pointed out: "The two great tests of Updike's captivity, his debate with the Mollah and his dealings with the son of Abonah Ben Benjamin, parallel the adventures of his ancestor, Captain John Underhill. The Mollah, like Winthrop and his followers, tries to enslave a man to a sectarian religious hypocrisy. The young Jew, like the English Land-Speculators of the frontier, promulgates slavery for the sake of greed."[9] Tyler familiarizes readers with a narrative history of persecution in the US and abroad that repeats itself across generations from one Underhill to the next, introducing a pattern of circumstances and behavior that Updike will quixotically fail to acknowledge. As he endures escalating hardship in his travels, he increasingly romanticizes these histories of persecution, leading to a quixotic conversion scene in which his account of life in the early US becomes, seemingly, mere nationalist apologia.

Updike has been the subject of the typical quixotic conversion debate, the debate over the extent to which the end result of quixotism—whether the quixote remains quixotic or converted—reflects a critique of the quixotic mind-set itself or a critique of the society or societies the quixote inhabits or passes through. As we will see in *Joseph Andrews* and *Modern Chivalry*, quixotes often produce double-edged critiques of both quixotic behavior and the quixote's surrounding circumstances through degrees of difference between quixote and society. *The Algerine Captive*'s cosmopolitan outlook modifies this critical framework by setting up layers of difference (between quixote and society, between one society and another) but demonstrating *similarity* among them. With a narrative strategy similar to that which Swift deploys in *Gulliver's Travels*, Tyler's narrative treats difference as a mirror, gaining critical traction by demonstrating counterintuitive and sometimes shocking commonalities between generations, characters, and societies otherwise presumed radically different. The novel's final conversion scene, however, can lead us to mistake cross-cultural similarity for the minimization or elision of difference and thus to misread Tyler's ending as an endorsement of nationalist unification projects in the early republic.

The Algerine Captive ends with a fairly traditional quixotic conversion scene. Updike finally escapes captivity, finding his way back home to the US. Upon landing on home soil after the harsh circumstances of his captivity, he declares that he had been "degraded as a slave, and was now advanced to a citizen of the freest country in the universe." Once embattled in and disdainful of his US surroundings, in which he was a disrespected teacher and unsuccessful doctor, the restored Updike vows "to contribute cheerfully to the support of our excellent government, which I have learnt to adore, in schools of despotism; and thus secure to myself the enviable character of an useful physician, a good father and worthy FEDERAL citizen" (225). A straightforward reading of Updike's closing statements suggests that he has learned the error of his ways in a sort of trial by fire and demonstrates remorse for having thought his circumstances as a US citizen so unfortunate before having been swept up and cast into the cold reality of slavery in a foreign land. Now, we might suppose, the quixote has been converted and restored, a "worthy FEDERAL citizen," in solidarity with his nation and national government, who, in writing his memoir, hopes that his "fellow citizens may profit by [his] misfortunes" (225).

Even those who have called attention to quixotic influence in *The Algerine Captive* have largely ignored or minimized Updike's quixotism as it relates to his final conversion. A number of critics have shown fundamental disagreement over how to read Updike's experiences in captivity and subsequent quixotic conversion, a testament, perhaps, to Tyler's artful awareness and subversion of his own authorship. As Edward Larkin notes, Tyler was "a once staunch Federalist who famously and unsuccessfully courted John Adams' daughter," a figure whose political orientation has left his novel open to political allegory critiques not unlike those so frequently applied to Swift's *Gulliver's Travels*.[10] Nonetheless, Davidson prudently urges us to consider that, though Tyler himself was a Federalist, he was considered relatively moderate and evenhanded in both his personal and political life.[11] Wood cautions further against "the tendency to over-identify Updike with his Federalist creator Royall Tyler."[12] The potential for misreading Tyler's novel by overassociating Tyler's Federalist politics with those of his narrator is considerable.

In a reading of *The Algerine Captive* that frequently aligns Updike's politics with Tyler's, Larry Dennis suggests that Updike is indeed changed by his experiences as an Algerine slave. For Dennis, Updike's sense of the redemptive potency of his "inherent romantic qualities[ ] is cruelly shattered by the squalor and wretchedness of the real situation" in Algiers. In such a reading, then, slavery in Algiers is a pivot point for Updike toward what might be understood as "successful" quixotic conversion, as well as a buildup toward Updike's comments in the final conversion scene, in which, for Dennis, "there is no distance . . . between the persona's perspective and the real author's."[13] In other words, Updike's conversion is the primary means by which Tyler emphasizes the importance of national solidarity. Without aligning

Updike's politics with Tyler's so directly, Davidson has taken a similar view on Updike's conversion, claiming that "for Underhill, to travel is to see different things, but, more importantly, to sojourn for six years in Algiers is to see things differently. The protagonist learns much from his captivity." Additional scholars have taken up the view that Updike undergoes a serious transformation in captivity and thus that we should read Updike's final narrations as representative of Tyler's "republican values of individual responsibility, individual conscience, and individual action within and for the good of the commonwealth."[14] Wood suggests that the "upbeat mood and Quixotic undertones of Underhill's American quest are swiftly dissipated in the face of the diabolical slave trade he encounters along the Ivory Coast."[15] Similarly, Joseph Schopp writes that Updike "shows that his own captivity has taught him the lesson of the 'inalienable birth-right of man.'"[16]

Each of these readings adheres to what Stephen Shapiro calls a "nationalist imaginary" preoccupation, for which the assumed novelistic aim is to address anxieties over national identity and (dis)unity amid the instability of the early republic.[17] A "nationalist imaginary" reading presupposes that if Updike is truly reformed and converted after enslavement in Algiers, this is the case because the quixotic dissatisfaction with his own nation that led him into greater trouble abroad is unacceptable for those invested in metanarratives of unification and nationalization in the early US. Accordingly, Updike's quixotism must be "dissipated": the quixote must be reeducated and converted, through harsh treatment on foreign soil, from disaffected and defected critic to penitent patriot, a "worthy FEDERAL citizen."

Contrarily, others have read Updike's changes after captivity primarily as rhetorical ones, unsupported by Updike's actions. The naïve rambler who expects better of his own country finds his medical abilities respected for the first time as a physician, although still a slave, in Algiers. He remains as gullible as ever throughout his captivity as well, believing in self-interested frauds who claim to be able to deliver him to freedom. And in his poignant exchange with the Algerian Mollah, who offers to make him a free citizen of Algiers in exchange for religious conversion, Updike, like Gulliver before the Brobdingnagian king, retains his quixotic (religious) idealism, even as he fails to justify his Christian faith coherently to the Mollah, and even as he is cast back into slavery. Observing these factors, John Engell reads irony in the constancy of Updike's worldview as a "free" US citizen and a slave in

Algiers, understanding Updike's seeming inability to surrender his idealism as Tyler's means of commenting at a distance on various modes of "slavery" in the US republic:

> The lessons of *The Algerine Captive* are at once more harsh and more subtle than previous critics have noted. Were the United States to be made of "worthy FEDERAL citizens" like Updike Underhill, the country would quickly descend into slavery, taking the very path followed, quite innocently, by Tyler's narrator. Readers, if they are to be true worthy citizens, must, like Captain Underhill and Benjamin Franklin, gauge the limits of human goodness and the potential of human depravity. . . . They must see that the American citizen of 1797 or of any age can, by staying at home, become an Algerine Captive.[18]

Engell points us to a counterintuitive comparison of US and Algerian forms of oppression, understanding the central problem of *The Algerine Captive* as one of rigid insularity, or Updike's inability to move beyond his single-mindedness to address observably exigent problems. Engel understands Updike's conversion scene as ironic because Updike has demonstrably failed to learn from his experiences by the novel's end; yet the role that quixotism plays in Updike's naïve constancy goes unregistered in the critical interventions of Engell and others. Edward Watts, who identifies the "genre-switch" of Updike's conversion scene not as quixotic, but as "resembl[ing] a sermon in which the homily is republican," has similarly found Updike's conversion scene evident of "Tyler's irony" in closing with a protagonist who "teaches imitation, not freedom."[19] Watts similarly shies away from any discussion of the quixotic and its significant influence on Tyler's novel, specifically on Updike's imitative behavior. Though these critics reject certain versions of the "nationalist imaginary" preoccupation by arguing that Updike's newfound prudence and nationalism after being enslaved are not a genuine, Federalist push for national unity but instead an ironic jab at discourses of lockstep unification or a somber warning against nationalistic single-mindedness, these readings nonetheless recapitulate the "nationalist imaginary" construction by assuming the primacy of questions of US citizenship and nationality in Tyler's novel. However, *The Algerine Captive* actually assumes a much more global scope of concerns and influence, particularly via its quixotic influences, which call our attention not so much to the "local" categories of citizenship and national identity as to the potency of quixotic imitation beyond nationality and across national borders.

Updike might be considered a *student* of imitation as well, spending much of his narrative under the tutelage of preceptors and coming out of it at the end mimicking the life trajectory of his ancestor Captain John Underhill, who flees his native England in search of freedom and a better life only to arrive in a state of persecution. By affirming, upon his return home, a form of US nationalism based on "uniting... federal strength to enforce a due respect among other nations," Updike rearticulates the US split from its "parent" country, but in the very terms of transnational self-fashioning that made the early US almost at once a liberated colony and, like its former colonizer, a colonial force (226). The different (but corresponding) stories of Updike and his progenitor Captain John Underhill fictionalize in many ways the relationship between the early US, which Shapiro rightly identifies as a "re-export republic," fully engaged in the lucrative Atlantic economy of the late eighteenth century and growing into its ambitions as an international power, and its English parent.[20] While Tyler uses lineage and ancestral influence to give Updike's behavior and adventures a historical reference point, he simultaneously lifts Updike and his ancestor out of national (US) context, placing them instead in a cosmopolitan world of transatlantic trade and cross-cultural exchange.

We can observe the beginnings of *The Algerine Captive*'s global scope of concern even before we get to the narrative itself, in a telling preface written under the Updike persona after he has returned from captivity and begun to embark on the writing of his adventures. The preface concerns itself with three primary observations: first, that in the time Updike was away, the US had developed as a reading nation through increased literacy and the formation of "social libraries" for those interested in reading for pleasure rather than instruction; second, that this newfound interest in novels, romances, and travel narratives has resulted in, lamentably for Updike, the sale and consumption of books "not of our own manufacture," that is, from overseas; and third, that because these books are foreign and fanciful, they are problematic for young US readers. As Updike warns, as though he were the author of a quixotic narrative rather than a quixote himself, "if the English Novel does not inculcate vice, it at least impresses on the young mind an erroneous idea of the world, in which she is to live. It paints the manners, customs, and habits of a strange country" (5–6).

In addition to the particularly Cervantic undertones of Updike's preface—its allusions to the potential of European novels and romances to corrupt one's sensibility or lead one down a dangerous path of fancy—the preface positions Updike's own narrative in comparative terms. The preface justifies the split structure of *The Algerine Captive*, the first section intended to "display a portrait of New England manners, hitherto unattempted," and the second section aimed at portraying Updike's "captivity among the Algerines, with some notices of the manners of that ferocious race, so dreaded by commercial powers, and so little known in our country" (6–7). Updike's positioning of his narrative account as a necessary "New England" addition both to domestic US literature and to an international literary conversation on Barbary narratives and Atlantic trade demonstrates his narrative's global and comparative outlook, which is only reinforced by continual references to the world beyond the US and ample narrations of international travel. Where Updike's preface takes nationalist stances, we should read these, as with his final conversion scene, with irony. As though he were one of the European novelists he addresses in his preface, Updike allures the provincial reader with tales of high-seas adventure, English hypocrisy, and orientalist ethnography, "paint[ing] the manners, customs, and habits of a strange country," all while cautioning against the "dangerous" curiosities that compel one to pick up a European novel or board a transatlantic vessel. Always prominent in the narrative, however, is the Atlantic trade system in which the US is a crucial participant. Updike criticizes the transatlantic book trade, apprehends slavery in the US South, and gains passage to England aboard a slave ship not long after he identifies the South as "the high road to fortune" (74). As with the entrepreneurial inflection of *Gulliver's Travels,* the engines of the Atlantic economy power along the plot in *The Algerine Captive.* Gulliver's quixotism of travel is frequently accompanied by not-so-subtle indications that overseas travel is also a means of accumulating wealth and of bringing the goods and curiosities of foreign lands back to England for profit.

Given these observations, there remain arguments that *The Algerine Captive* fails to substantively engage with issues arising from US transatlantic relationships. Gesa Mackenthun, who reads the former-slave Updike's ready-made capitulation to the notion of a free and unified US upon his return to native soil as a demonstration of the novel's willful amnesia over US participation in slavery, argues that early US political discourse was mostly focused on domestic, rather than transatlantic or global, issues.[21] In this sense Tyler's tidy ending—through Updike's quixotic conversion—would certainly seem to indicate that for the US in the late eighteenth century, tidying up, or smoothing over the striations of national difference and polyvocality under the banner of Updike's "by uniting we stand, by dividing we fall" aphorism, may indeed have been more important as a domestic goal than taking on the issue of transatlantic slavery (226). But in its ancestral preoccupations and purposive discussions of difference between Algerian, US, and English literatures, customs, religions, politics, and societies, *The Algerine Captive* is indeed, as Armstrong and Tennenhouse suggest, cosmopolitan in its scope, engaging rather clearly with US identity as a transnational and transhistorical phenomenon.[22] Mackenthun—for whom "Updike finds himself happily reconciled with his nation and family, his abolitionist designs . . . evaporated from his consciousness"—cleverly calls attention to the novel's "double semantics of slavery," alleging that Tyler has his narrator forget about his prior abolitionist tendencies, even after the abject experiences of being aboard a slave ship and being enslaved himself, because of domestic pressures to affirm a national discourse of unity.[23] But such an interpretation, like others focused on the "nationalist imaginary," relies on a straightforward reading of the quixotic conversion scene—a reading that, as I have suggested, is at least questionable.

Attention to *The Algerine Captive*'s quixotic elements helps both to illuminate and to call into question each of these "nationalist imaginary" readings, which proceed from two basic formulations. The first of these formulations is that, as Mackenthun argues, Updike turning his back on his prior abolitionist position and giving himself over to a Federalist, nationalist politics of unity at the end of the novel is to be read straightforwardly as evidence of the narrative's willful amnesia (with regard not just to slavery, but to the rest of Updike's unfulfilling US past as well). Taken at face value, Tyler's wholesome ending certainly suggests as much; however, taken as quixotic conversion, it becomes clear that Updike's closing sentiments are not reliable intimations, but quixotic formulations derived from a demonstrable pattern of quixotic behavior. The second basic formulation of "nationalist imaginary" readings is that, given the first formulation, *The Algerine Captive* ventures beyond US borders as a travel narrative and a captivity tale only to focus our attention back onto questions of US national identity. If, in other words, Updike's alacrity in rejoining his native country tells us reliably that all else, including slavery, is mere afterthought in light of his full and committed reinstatement into US citizenry, then *The Algerine Captive*'s comparative structure and transnational narrative engagement are not genuinely comparative, but simply means of reinforcing an a priori nationalist position.

I have already mentioned that reading Updike's final remarks as a quixotic conversion calls into question a number of straightforward "nationalist imaginary" readings. Additionally, by fashioning Updike as a quixote, Tyler gives us cause to reexamine Updike's travels as genuinely comparative—that is, as a means of deemphasizing the nationalistic concerns that Updike parrots upon return to native soil, emphasizing instead the importance of understanding the early US as part of a larger, interconnected world. The quixotic narrative has historically taken on a similar comparative function in its migration to the early US, placing quixotes in a multitude of locales and social situations to test, as Eve Tavor Bannet has argued, the "cultural fit" of foreign customs and behaviors in societies largely shaped by "transnational codes" of behavior.[24] For the early US, the quixotic narrative is somewhat like Gulliver himself: a foreign thing brought within national borders that arouses curiosity among the locals just as it finds itself prodded and tested by their difference.

The problems of unity and national identity favored by "nationalist imaginary" readings arose, then, not simply through an oppositional relationship between early US citizens and foreigners but rather through the ways various transnationally circulated behavioral codes were understood or misunderstood by "consumers" of literatures and fashions across the Atlantic. Taken this way, in light of the quixotic narrative's considerable role in early US testing and trying-on of foreign customs and behaviors, Tyler's "New England" account of the Barbary Coast can be understood as a legitimate comparative intervention into the Atlantic cultural economy by way of a mock-nationalistic quixote, an unworthy global citizen, who travels the world but learns little from the experience. In quixotic fashion, then, *The Algerine Captive* teaches us that the steadfast insularity brought about by unreflective nationalism is a significant barrier to cross-cultural understanding.

As I have suggested, critics reading Updike's comments upon his return to America have disagreed plausibly over issues of narrative distance and irony in Updike's conversion moment; however, these readings have not taken into account the literary lineage of quixotic conversion as it relates to the global scope of *The Algerine Captive*'s concerns. Taking Updike as a quixote whose precepts are by definition imitative or derivative—part of a quixotic lineage—a straightforward reading of Updike's stock, nationalistic comments at the end of the novel becomes less tenable. Even critics who read *The Algerine Captive* as a quixotic narrative have neglected to focus on the quixotic nature of Updike's homecoming and conversion.

Placing *The Algerine Captive* rightfully within its lineage of quixotic narratives highlights Updike's entrée into a story of his own through the idealized history of another, and thus the mimetic imperative that operates within Updike, the quixote. Beyond his itinerancy, his penchant for classical learning, his idealism, and his naïveté, Updike remains throughout the novel a fervent imitator of a fictive model of US history and identity, which is derived from and evinced in his romanticized account of his noble ancestor's struggles. After including in his narrative the text of a letter from his ancestor explaining the circumstances of his persecution, Updike colors our impression of Captain John Underhill's founding, proto-US society with the following quixotic apologia: "Whoever reflects upon the piety of our forefathers, the noble unrestrained ardour, with which they resisted oppression in England, relinquished the delights of their native country, crossed a boisterous ocean, penetrated a savage wilderness, encountered famine, pestilence, and Indian warfare, and transmitted to us their sentiments of independence, that love of liberty, which under God enabled us to obtain our own glorious freedom, will readily pass over those few dark spots of zeal, which clouded their rising sun" (18–19). We can observe how closely this resembles Gulliver's utopian apology for English colonialism: "This Description, I confess, doth by no means affect the *British* nation, who may be an Example to the whole World for their Wisdom, Care, and Justice in planting Colonies" (275).

Traveling throughout the US, Updike draws his disdain for many of those around him from such idealized impressions of his ancestral and national histories, or, in other words, from his quixotic tendency to cling to an antiquated and romanticized model, despite having knowledge and experiences to the contrary. When Updike first takes up his post as headmaster at a country school, he vows to be "mild in [his] government, to avoid all manual correction," expecting "by these means to secure the love and respect of [his] pupils" (31). In the spirit of early US republicanism, he believes, like Brackenridge's Captain Farrago, in an orderly system of governance that absorbs dissent smoothly and without violence, until he is met with the cold reality of a beating by a parent after deigning himself to administer a beating of his own to a misbehaving student. When he decides to venture to the South to practice medicine, he does so conceiving of the South as "the high road to fortune," believing southerners to be "extremely partial to the characteristic industry of their New England brethren." He seeks, like his ancestor, the free and industrious US of national folklore. At the same time, he leaves his native New England on account of "the illiberality and ignorance" of its people, the shortcomings of New Englanders that Captain John Underhill witnessed generations prior (74). Yet it is Updike's "New England conscience"—the idea of liberality—that later results in his astonishment over the harsh treatment of a southern slave at the hands of a highly respected parson, and eventually his disenchantment with the South (80). Nevertheless, after Updike ventures to foreign lands, he takes with him the mythical sense of US identity that he has seen disproved with his own eyes and evaluates other societies against the US ideal rather than his own experience. Shortly after leaving for London in disgust over his own country, Updike lambastes England as a place of "hereditary senators, ignorant and inattentive to the welfare of their country, and unacquainted with the geography of its foreign possessions" (86). He denounces Thomas Paine as boastful, "his bodily presence . . . both mean and contemptible" (88–90). And once aboard the slave ship *Sympathy,* he laments the conditions under which the slaves are kept, expressing thoughts, the ship's captain suspects, that derive from "*some yankee nonsense about humanity*" (99).

Each of Updike's criticisms of foreign societies and practices is born of a US-styled ethos of freedom, justice, and humanity that both Updike and his ancestor fail to find on home soil. He likewise continues to vaunt, while abroad, a crude brand of American exceptionalism that betrays the material truth of his reasons for leaving first New England, and then the US altogether. Once in captivity, delivered to the Algerian Mollah for his first consultation and finding the Mollah in lavish circumstances, Updike observes that "in all countries, except New England, those, whose profession it is to decry the luxuries and vanities of this world somehow or other, contrive to possess the greatest portion of them" (128). Updike keenly observes hypocrisy in the colonizing English "boasting of the GLORIOUS FREEDOM OF ENGLISHMEN" and the Algerian Mollah's adornments, yet he fails to make comparable connections between the notion of freedom and enterprise in New England that he continually lauds and the illiberal treatment of his ancestor; or between the southern parson's hard usage of an African slave and the Christian morality that Updike defends to the Mollah (86). Justifying the Christian Bible to the Mollah, he argues: "We have received it from our ancestors, and we have as good evidence for the truths it contains, as we have in profane history for any historical fact" (132). Like Gulliver before the Brobdingnagian king, his arguments falter, but his resolution remains. For Updike, the evidence of mythical histories trumps the evidence of experience in much the same way as, for any quixote, the evidence of *histories*—romances, novels, fictions, and travelogues—trumps that of physical reality.

It is crucial to bear in mind, then, that in dealing with Updike we are dealing with a quixote, one whose nationalist sentiments are inherited from those of the times of his ancestor even as, like his ancestor, his own experiences would belie such sentiments. Based on the idealized version of US life and identity that Updike borrows from his ancestral past, coupled with the contradictory realities that Updike illustrates for us throughout his travels and dealings with global difference, we can read the glaring irony in Updike's closing remarks, and therefore the irony in Tyler's quixotic conversion scene, as primarily a function of Updike's quixotism. Rather than simply eliding the various forms of oppression in the US, from religious persecution to slavery, upon Updike's return and conversion, Tyler gives us a quixote whose frequent blunders and romanticized worldview continually draw our attention to the process of elision. In giving us the parallel histories of the Underhills cast through the lens of the quixotic, *The Algerine Captive* reminds us not merely that "free" US citizens can be persecuted at home just as one could be in the Barbary Coast, but that the quixotic inheritance of the idealized past can be highly influential beyond national boundaries and throughout global experiences. As Tyler's novel exhorts, knowing, or even living, a transnational history of oppression, for Updike and for the upstart US, is rarely enough to prevent history from being repeated.

The Algerine Captive's ability to draw our attention to this process of eliding or apologizing for acknowledged problems within and between nations is comparable to that of *Gulliver's Travels* to highlight the process of Gulliver's quixotic shifts of national loyalty. Each of these narratives engages with powerful notions of national (or transnational) exceptionalism, or in both cases the quixotic tendency to read myths of nation or national identity as though they were Don Quixote's chivalric romances. *The Algerine Captive* starkly conveys this mode of quixotic exceptionalism by the fact that Updike reflects on texts of his ancestral past to forge his image of a national present, such that his romanticized history becomes like a chivalric romance, with his ancestor Captain John Underhill situated as the heroic knight in a time when such mythical heroism is alleged (by Updike) to have been common among those fighting for pre-Revolution liberty.

When Armstrong and Tennenhouse emphasize the suitability of the Barbary narrative for early US writers focused on the place of the US in the wider world, they might also acknowledge that exceptionalism of the sort that Updike practices is a likely by-product of the early US novel's tendency to "imagine a community in cosmopolitan terms."[25] In other words, the very building blocks of such cosmopolitan imaginaries, which for Armstrong and Tennenhouse are remarkably resistant to critics' nationalization attempts, are "national" affinities and characteristics. In a world in which, as with Updike in captivity in Algiers, characters are "defined, not so much by their nation of origin, or home, as by their encounters in a world produced by the circulation of goods and peoples," such global encounters are bound to produce exceptionalist justifications for observed differences that cannot be explained outside the framework of the nation, the "national culture," or national identity.[26] Even in *Gulliver's Travels,* in which national differences are sometimes overshadowed by (and other times conflated with) typological differences among fictitious, rational, humanoid beings, exceptionalism operates centrally as a means of negotiating difference.

In *Gulliver's Travels* and *The Algerine Captive,* quixotic exceptionalism takes the form of romantically seeking out difference only to define one's own identity position as superior in opposition to another. Notwithstanding their thirst and opportunity for travel, and for the acquisition of novel experience and perspective, Gulliver and Updike struggle to learn much at all from their conversations, adventures, and near-death experiences. In each of these instances of quixotic exceptionalism, the

quixotes ultimately struggle to find satisfaction, or to find their quixotism vindicated. Gulliver retires from his travels in a state of loneliness,
spending more time in the stables conversing with his horses than with
his human family. Updike, full of patriotic zeal, returns after an ironic
conversion scene to the very country that drove him into the shackles
of slavery abroad. Captain John Underhill's willingness to overlook the
"dark spots of zeal" in favor of the "glorious freedom" US citizenship
supposedly affords him echoes in Thomas Paine's ironized "boasting of
the GLORIOUS FREEDOM" of the English, aligning English exceptionalism
with American exceptionalism as related phenomena with not only a
shared logic but also a shared set of narrative strategies in eighteenth-
century British and US novels (18–19, 86).

7

Adams, Farrago, and Civic Exceptionalism

We have seen that Gulliver and Updike function as vehicles for critiques of national exceptionalism on both sides of the Atlantic. But exceptionalism also operates *within* national borders and among citizens and subjects negotiating local or domestic policy. National exceptionalism—particularly in English and US historical contexts—is largely a function of more local forms of exceptionalism that reinforce notions of the superiority of a system of governance, whether the legalistic republicanism of the early US or the "glorious freedom" of the English that Updike ridicules and Gulliver exposes as lacking. This chapter focuses on what we might call civic exceptionalism, or the popular belief that local systems of government and spheres of public political activity are inevitably and ultimately just, despite counterevidence.

Two eighteenth-century novels in particular adopt the quixotic exceptionalist motif to address civic exceptionalism through illustrations of political and economic tumult at home. Henry Fielding's *Joseph Andrews* (1742) and Hugh Henry Brackenridge's *Modern Chivalry* (1792–1815) engage explicitly with civic issues and problems—charity, poverty, social and legal order—on two sides of the Atlantic, though with a stark awareness of the interconnectedness of the Atlantic political economy in the eighteenth century. Fielding presents his quixote in *Joseph Andrews*, Parson Adams, as a representation of measure and sanity in an English society gone mad, a society in which the clergy have abandoned their charitable duties, and another parson mistakes Adams's copy of Aeschylus for a pilfered sermon. In many ways, Adams's England in *Joseph Andrews* looks a lot like Brackenridge's US in *Modern Chivalry*, which features a similarly bookish quixote, Captain John Farrago, who struggles to understand why his crass, illiterate sidekick, a crudely stereotyped Irishman, Teague O'Regan, commands so much more respect among angry and unlettered US citizens than the effete and learned captain.

Adams and Farrago find their societies bewildering, largely because both men generate their expectations of political reality from exceptionalist myths. Adams expects a deeply moral, Christian society that cares for its poor and its young, whereas Farrago expects the high-minded, legalistic discourse that underwrites US founding documents to sufficiently curb excesses of self-interest and political fervor among the populace. Both quixotes respond to the bewilderment of mismatched expectations and experiences by adopting an exceptionalist outlook. As moral and political visionaries, they alone can forge a path to enlightenment, if only they can convince everyone else to follow along. The tragicomic fact that Adams and Farrago, convinced of their visionary qualities, nevertheless struggle to gain a following creates a scenario that forces readers to evaluate whether quixotism is a form of madness or of exceeding rationality in these novels.

Joseph Andrews and *Modern Chivalry* both foreground the problem of quixotism as a conflation of madness and rationality, a problem of how to tell whether madness is the exception, or the very rule that governs the societies Adams and Farrago occupy. Another way of understanding this problem is as a problem of fictionality, or of whether reading quixotic madness against societal madness in these novels can help us determine whether the quixotic worldview is meant to be antiquated fiction or an incisive reading of immediate societal realities.

This method of investigating the counterintuitive relationship between madness and rationality—a relationship structured like the counterintuitive relationship between exception and rule that Agamben illustrates—is certainly pertinent to Cervantes's Don Quixote, whose ostensible madness is not without ample moments of reason and good sense. After having taken him home at the close of part 1, the priest and the barber evaluate a bedridden Don Quixote at the beginning of part 2:

> He gave them a warm welcome, they inquired after his health and he provided a well reasoned and elegantly expressed account of his progress. And as the conversation developed they came to the subject that is sometimes called reason of state and methods of government, and they all corrected this abuse and condemned that one, and reformed one custom and forbad another, and each

of the three men turned into a new legislator, a present-day Lycur-
gus or a modern Solon; and they subjected society to such radical
reforms that anyone would have thought they'd taken it to a forge
and brought away a different one; and Don Quixote spoke with
such good sense about every subject they discussed that his two
examiners reached the firm conclusion that he was fully recovered
and of sound mind. The niece and the housekeeper were present
at the conversation, and they were tireless in thanking God for
having restored their master to his senses. (2.1.488)

Through this passage we can make sense of Fielding's portrayal of Parson Adams, a sensible, educated, and socially engaged quixote who
also appears mad and disconnected from his surrounding reality. That
Don Quixote's madness is so well disguised by his reasonable speech
with regard to the well-being of the state—"correcting" and "condemning" abuses and "reforming" nation and custom—is pertinent in light
of Adams's quixotic efforts to reform the fallen society around him as
a lone knight of moral fortitude. Notably, after his assessors deem him
sane and rational, Quixote proceeds almost immediately to talk further
of "His Majesty" proclaiming "all knights errant wandering in Spain
must assemble in Madrid" to fight off the Turks, declaring ultimately,
"A knight errant I shall be until I die" (2.1.490). Quixote continually
defies hard definitions of madness and rationality, occupying the paradoxical state of rational madness that Fielding later picks up on in his
rendering of Parson Adams. This brings us to a pivotal question: Are
Adams's moments of incisive, even visionary rationality a function of a
prosocial form of quixotic exceptionalism, or are they the fictive dress
in which Fielding disguises and mocks Adams's madness?

Reading the politics of quixotism in such scenarios that demand consideration of whether the quixote or the society is truly mad is important in the context of eighteenth-century understandings of madness as
a kind of social disease. Michel Foucault, for example, took particular
interest in Don Quixote as a representation of early modern madness.
"In the landscape of unreason where the sixteenth century located it,"
writes Foucault, "madness concealed a meaning and an origin that were
obscurely moral; its secrecy related it to sin."[1] Foucault understands
Quixote's madness as a kind of tragedy, an irredeemable sense of
demise (in this sense, Quixote's deathbed renunciation of his quixotism
is simultaneously a pathetic and redemptive gesture). By the eighteenth

century, for Foucault, understandings of madness in Europe undergo a shift, characterized by a returned association of madness with morality, and a fear of madness as a social disease capable of transcending the individual case: "The unreason that had been relegated to the distance of confinement reappeared, fraught with new dangers as if endowed with a new power of interrogation. Yet what the eighteenth century first noticed about it was not the secret interrogation, but only the social effects: the torn clothing, the arrogance in rags, the tolerated insolence, whose disturbing powers were silenced by an amused indulgence. . . . [T]his was the first time since the Great Confinement that the madman had become a social individual."[2] This characterization of madness as a social danger—an "arrogance in rags"—that announces itself in tatters recalls Cervantes's description of Don Quixote, who appears battered and gaunt, especially after his more extreme bouts of quixotism result in physically destructive bouts with others (1.37.348; 2.64.928). Comparing the ragged appearances of quixotism and of extreme piety, Quixote describes the life of knight-errantry, from the experience of "[his] own sufferings," as "hungrier and thirstier, more wretched, ragged, and louse-ridden" than the life of "a cloistered monk" (1.13.98). Quixote—himself the "Knight of the Sorry Face"—also apprehends a "madman," the "Ragged Knight of the Miserable Face," dressed in "a ragged suede jerkin" and "muttering words that were incomprehensible" (1.23.195–96). In eighteenth-century Britain, the quixotic narrative modified this image of the quintessential seventeenth-century madman, Quixote, to address perceived social ills associated with emergent fears of societal madness, which Foucault describes as "formulated in medical terms, but animated, basically, by a moral myth." Concern over the social implications of madness created a desire for "a political and economic explanation . . . in which wealth, progress, institutions appear as the determining element of madness."[3]

Adams is perhaps the quintessential quixote of eighteenth-century Britain, given that his madness is not only moral and social in its scope of concerns but distinctly religious as well (recalling Don Quixote's comparison of the knight-errant and the cloistered monk). As Foucault notes, citing case instances from the *Encyclopedie*: "For a long time doctors were suspicious of too strict a devotion, too strong a belief. Too much moral rigor, too much anxiety about salvation and the life to come were often thought to bring on melancholia."[4] Adams's religious quixotism presented as a form of madness, in his brooding over sermons and scriptural passages, preoccupation with classical texts as gateways into religious and moral learning, and tendency to understand his sermons in the way Don Quixote understands his chivalric romances: with the expectation that such myths are not the exception, but the norm.

Yet, as with Quixote, Adams's mode of quixotic madness is especially unsettling because it is so frequently couched in the language of reason, understanding, and scripture. In this way Adams embodies a societal understanding of madness in eighteenth-century Britain that not only associated madness with questions of moral and religious well-being but was also vested in concerns about madness as social contagion. As Parson Adams wanders through the English countryside with sermons in hand and a command of language and classical scripture that appears foreign to his interlocutors, Fielding raises questions about the quixote's liminal role as a figure of madness and, simultaneously, of moral fortitude. For this reason simple madness is not an adequate framework for understanding the impact of quixotes like Adams, who, in accordance with Smollett's insistence that Quixote is no ordinary madman, set themselves up as exceptions to mad societies.

The societal madness and breakdown surrounding Fielding's quixote have been a subject of considerable attention. Contending that "*Joseph Andrews* is about the absence of charity in eighteenth-century England," Christopher Parkes demonstrates how Fielding conveys through characters like Lady Booby and Peter Pounce some troubling, if exaggerated, English notions of dealing with poverty, including putting the poor to pasture, as one would a horse, because of the abundant grazing fields and freshwater streams available throughout the countryside.[5] Similar moments of absurdity and of victimization of the disadvantaged populate Fielding's novel, from Joseph's reluctance to give up his borrowed breeches at gunpoint before being beaten nearly to death on the occasion of one of multiple roadside attacks (as he would not be able to make good on his word to return the breeches to the original lender) to the macabre pursuit of Parson Adams by, as Fielding writes, "a great Hunter of Men" on horseback, in the tradition of ferreting out and hunting wild game.[6]

Though Fielding portrays Adams, in his "simplicity," as outmoded and distant from the unquestioning perfidy of so many of those with whom he comes into contact on the road, the degree to which Fielding casts his English society as madly corrupt and uncharitable, if not at times sociopathic, renders Adams a figure of measure by comparison.

Walter Reed calls Adams "a Quixote of ethical rather than aesthetic precept."[7] And Martin Battestin famously sees Adams as a "moral yardstick" for the times "in his bewildered exposure to the vanities of the age: the levees of great men, country hunting matches and horse races, drums and routs, beaus and coquettes."[8] But to avoid simply recasting eighteenth-century England in Adams's moralistic terms, it is necessary to consider how socioeconomic developments reinforced Fielding's portrait of English madness and disorientation.

As Judith Frank observes, "Work on both the satire and the fiction of [the eighteenth century] has tended to focus on the transition from patrician culture to a culture dominated by the logic of the market, or what Michael McKeon has described as the tension between aristocratic and progressive ideology."[9] Recalling Fielding's uncharitable clergymen, Parkes calls attention to the ways the workhouse movement and Poor Laws reform, aimed at systematizing care for and control over the poor, allowed clergy to abandon more localized charitable endeavors under the pretense that other state provisions were available.[10]

In addition to substantial changes in the handling of the English poor, the last decades of the seventeenth century and the first of the eighteenth century witnessed debates over the impact of financial markets (the "financial revolution" of William III, the nationalization of debt, and the creation of the Bank of England in 1694), debates over the shift from the land-based accumulation of wealth to credit-based speculation. Michael Gilmore describes this shift as the installation of "a system of public credit and national debt . . . created in order to underwrite commercial expansion and the wars with France," which included, in the first two decades of the eighteenth century, the War of the Spanish Succession (1701–14), and, by the time of the publication of *Joseph Andrews,* the War of the Austrian Succession, including the transatlantic King George's War (1740–48). Emphasizing the destabilizing nature of this shift, Gilmore writes: "While real wealth in land was taxed to pay off interest on the debt, stockjobbers and speculators were amassing fortunes by manipulating worthless paper. Scandals like the South Sea Bubble of 1720, when the stock climbed astronomically and then abruptly plunged, strengthened the conviction of the landowners that the new economic order was unstable, irrational, and a menace to civic health."[11]

The early century rise of finance economies was an antecedent to a related but different phase of societal change, which emerged in the

wake of Walpolian policies and the opposition to Walpole as representative of a legacy of materialism and self-interest. Contributing to
this emergent sense of societal madness and cynicism in the 1730s was
Walpole's reputation for covering up corruption, and an attendant lack
of trust in public figures.[12] This notion of mistrust in the mid-1730s,
leading up to the publication of *Joseph Andrews,* only compounded prior
skepticism, generated from the fallout of the South Sea Bubble, about
the direction in which British society was heading. Consequently, as
Christine Gerrard writes, "larger patterns of deception, enticement, and
moral metamorphosis" were behind what Walpole's opposition believed
were "people's changed moral behaviour in Walpolian Britain."[13]

Fielding was very much an active participant in the discourse of
opposition to Walpole and adhered to the political view that, amid a
morally deteriorating society, there were yet sly and powerful figures,
like Walpole, who aimed to lead people ever-further astray. Curiously,
one of Fielding's satires on Walpole, published in the *Champion* on
December 13, 1739, portrays Walpole as a magician who, lurking in a
pastoral setting, lures passersby into complicity by taking them by the
hand and giving them a "gentle squeeze" (a sinister image of the "invis-
ible hand" decades before the publication of *The Wealth of Nations*).[14] Parson Adams, hardly a Walpolian figure, is nonetheless something of a
mystic in the eyes of the uneducated and uncharitable country masses in
Joseph Andrews, his quixotism in a society gone morally awry contributing
to his liminal status as both a sage and a dunce. Adams, a moral idealist
critical of the idealization of self-interest, complicates the notion that
when Walpole fell, cynicism reigned, idealism vanished from British
society, and Britain entered, in the midcentury, an antiquixotic phase
of national politics. The seeming "irrationality" and instability of financial markets, joined with marked shifts in the loci of personal versus
social responsibility and the prominent Walpole-opposition's notions
of a regressive "moral metamorphosis," make Adams's England indeed
a world of particular uncertainty.

As Battestin argues convincingly, and Fielding illustrates transparently in his portrait of Adams the parson, Adams is an "imitator of
Christ."[15] Fielding drew his basis for Adams's character from a series of
homilies that stress "the depiction of the good man as hero."[16] Rendering Adams a quixote, then, fits into a lineage of quixote criticism that
reads the quixote as the hero and protagonist of the quixotic narrative,
and the surrounding "world of windmills" as the villain, or the object

of quixotic satire.[17] Adams's relative sanity, stemming from his moral and ethical grounding, is perhaps the foundation of his quixotic heroism; though it is not necessarily, as we can observe, without its complications. His litany of comic overreactions, from flinging his beloved copy of Aeschylus into the fire at Fanny's slightest disturbance to the entreaties to others in dire peril to "repose thy Trust in the same Providence, which hath hitherto protected thee," depict a figure detached from and anachronistic within a mad society, yet neither wholly sane nor wholly heroic, thereby (122). Attentive to the world before his eyes, Adams recognizes exigent social problems and courageously attempts to engage them; yet his orientation, vaguely nostalgic, is also to a world very distant from the one he occupies, rendering his precepts for the most part ineffectual. The breakdown of stable notions of sanity and madness Adams exemplifies points to an important facet of quixotic exceptionalism: the line between visionary and revisionist. Again, is Adams's way of perceiving the world around him an inventive fiction, or an incisive reading of a mad society?

Crucial to our understanding of Adams's moral function in Fielding's novel is the way Adams avails himself of quixotic exceptionalism both to position himself as an objective onlooker above his society and to cast his surrounding society as mad and unscrupulous, despite his own anachronistic worldview.[18] In this way Adams collapses his liminal position into a fundamentally quixotic position, his quixotism effectively obviating the problem of difference (and distance) between himself and the characters he encounters on the road and ultimately justifying his function as a humorous, at times ironic, but not unserious critic of the provincial worlds he passes through. That is, the difficulties Adams encounters are never enough to puncture his quixotic worldview or his belief that he understands the path to righteousness more clearly and acutely than anyone else, such that his comic and aberrant behavior is wholly justified.

Being too literate to be accepted and understood by even the magistrates and clergy with whom he comes into contact, Adams understands himself as an exception to the rule of moral and societal decay. From this position, the likes of Joseph and Fanny, however skeptical at times of his seemingly irrational moral fastidiousness, nonetheless consider that Parson Adams must be possessed of a higher-order understanding.

The sidekicks who accompany Adams are not beholden to his worldview and moral outlook merely out of duty or class-based obligation (despite the fact that Joseph and Fanny are both of the servant ranks, they are not Adams's servants), but because they place some degree of faith in his moral precepts and his conduct as an exemplar of charity, justice, and good sense. Adams's quixotic ability to draw Joseph and Fanny into his ways of thinking and acting—even when immediately harsh and dire circumstances give them pause—is predicated on his characteristically quixotic eloquence, learnedness, and convincingness as a quixotic visionary. He can rope Joseph and Fanny into his way of seeing the world by claiming a position of intellectual and moral superiority, which, for the young couple amid the throes of love and adventure, is especially compelling.

Nonetheless, the class difference between Parson Adams and his sidekicks is not irrelevant to the dynamic between these characters, nor is it irrelevant to Adams's quixotic claim to exceptionalism. Adams's learnedness relative to Joseph and Fanny is largely a function of his social rank as a member of the clergy, just as the class and social roles of Joseph and Fanny demand that they maintain a degree of humility and respect for the likes of Adams. This makes both doubly susceptible to Adams's quixotism. Though Sancho Panza is something of a picaresque figure—an opportunist—who sees in Don Quixote a means toward a better (or at least more exciting) life, with promises of land, riches, and political power, Joseph and Fanny are morally involved sidekicks to a morally preoccupied quixote. Adams's quixotic exceptionalism flourishes in this scenario.

After wagging his finger at Joseph and Fanny for their violent reactions to situations of real danger, questioning their excessive passion and attachment to worldly things and finding their faith in divine will insufficient, Adams struggles to practice as he preaches. In the most pronounced example of Adams's exceptionalism in this regard, he begins to "stamp about the Room and deplore his Loss with the bitterest Agony" while under the (false) impression that his son has drowned (270). This is the cruelest joke Fielding puts Adams through, though it reflects the exceptionalist logic by which quixotes see themselves as superlative adherents to the path of justice while finding errors in the comparable behavior of others.

Quixotic narratives often end with scenes of mixed resolution that ostensibly restore quixotes to comfortable and respectable places in society, though only after they realize and take responsibility for their follies and renounce their quixotism. Both Gulliver and Updike undergo quixotic conversions of their own, though with mixed results. At the end of *Joseph Andrews* we find Adams endowed with a solid annual salary and joyously marrying Joseph and Fanny, though in the final few pages of the novel Adams remains the butt of Fielding's jokes, accidentally spurring his horse and being thrown from it, chastising Mr. Booby and Pamela at the wedding for "laughing in so sacred a Place, and so solemn an Occasion," and overindulging in so much "Ale and Pudding" as to have "given a Loose to more Facetiousness than was usual to him," remaining at the novel's close a kind of comic anachronism (300–302). The ambiguity created by writing the quixote as both a comical figure for readers to justifiably mock and a sympathetic figure whose behavior and worldview raise questions about the surrounding society with which the quixote is largely incompatible is part of a narrative strategy that enables writers to make subtle and multifaceted social critiques through quixotes.

Though Fielding's treatment of Adams is not without irony in the novel's closing moments—the parson is still shown preaching solemnity to guests at the wedding who simply wish to share in the joy of the occasion—we also get the sense that, even for his quixotism, Adams is vindicated in marrying the two beleaguered young lovers. In the primarily comical and upbeat final scenes of *Joseph Andrews,* the microcosm of British society over which Parson Adams loosely presides is indeed, as Ruth Mack attributes to Arabella's vision in *The Female Quixote,* "a better reality," a harmonious and virtuous segment of a nation portrayed otherwise as burdened by social and financial waywardness.[19] That Adams ultimately avoids conversion from his moral quixotism by the novel's end vindicates his exceptionalism while leaving open the question of its broader efficacy.

Further, without attention to Adams's quixotic exceptionalism—how Adams as a liminal figure in relation to the surrounding society he aims to critique is fundamentally quixotic—we can easily lose sight of the fact that Adams's moral bearing is not only a "yardstick," as Battestin suggests, demarcating the dated from the new, but an idealistic vision, or a quixotic attempt to reinstitute the moral codes of the past. As a quixote, Parson Adams is, likewise, an imitator of the past, a misplaced romantic, and a driving force of precisely the kind of pious self-regulation that is to the inhabitants of Adams's provincial England what chivalry is to those who mock Don Quixote for scrupulously sitting vigil over his arms before he is to be "knighted" by the confounded innkeeper (1.3.36). Readings that minimize the quixotic risk missing connections of this sort, connections that can alter our understanding of well-studied motifs—morality, charity, chastity—in well-studied novels like *Joseph Andrews*.

Hugh Henry Brackenridge's rambling *Modern Chivalry* is, like *Joseph Andrews*, a commentary on issues of explicitly public political concern, including, as in *Joseph Andrews*, issues of perceived societal madness, civic well-being, and government reform. Published initially in two parts in 1792, *Modern Chivalry* was eventually revised to include two more parts (in 1793 and 1797, respectively), a revision in 1805, and a final revision in 1815. Brackenridge's ranging narrative, closer in length to Cervantes's *Don Quixote* than the other early US quixotic narratives, features a bookish statesman-quixote in Captain John Farrago, who departs from his Pennsylvania farm to travel on horseback throughout the frontier. Captain Farrago's Sancho Panza is an Irish immigrant, Teague O'Regan, whom Brackenridge illustrates as a rough, heavily ethnicized stereotype of a servant-rank Irishman. In their travels throughout the frontier, the educated and articulate Farrago attempts to persuade a series of uneducated frontier mobs of his political philosophies and recommendations for good governance and an engaged and productive citizenry, while Teague takes an entirely different approach to public life. As Farrago struggles to gain popularity with the citizens of the frontier on account of his high-mindedness and patriotic idealism, the uneducated, incurious, and unceremonious Teague eats, drinks, and womanizes his way into the hearts and minds of frontier settlers, schoolmasters, clergy, and politicians. Teague is eventually elected to Congress, which Farrago takes as a heavy slap in the face.

While its explicit treatment of domestic political concerns makes it unmistakably Fieldingesque, *Modern Chivalry* engages more directly with questions of representative democracy than does *Joseph Andrews*. The first of the expressly quixotic narratives in the early US, *Modern Chivalry* emerged during a period in which the US underwent something of its own quixotic phase in its efforts to build and justify narratives of American exceptionalism.[20] The US in the late eighteenth century looks strikingly similar to Parson Adams's early eighteenth-century England.

Like eighteenth-century England, the early US was influenced by Walpolian financial ideas, mainly through the intermediary of Alexander Hamilton, the first US secretary of the treasury. Linking aspects of

Hamiltonian economics with economic trends in Augustan England, Gilmore describes "a kind of social madness in which 'imagination governs the world'"; thus, parts of *Modern Chivalry* satirize "the epidemic of fantasy produced by Hamilton's financial program," portraying the early US as "the very antithesis of a sane society." The transatlantic financial currents that brought a brand of financial economics to the US also roused more than a modicum of Oppositional spirit in Brackenridge, whose *Modern Chivalry* aligns significantly, in its US context, with the sentiments of an English landed gentry who opposed Walpolian programs that heavily taxed their land to finance national debt.[21] Only for Brackenridge in *Modern Chivalry*, Hamiltonian economics represented both a failure and abandonment of popular sovereignty, in that irrational, mob thinking among the populace was responsible for electing the wrong leaders, who in turn failed to serve the best interests of the people.

Approximately a half century after quixotic narratives began to flourish in Britain, alongside comparably radical social and political changes, the post-Revolutionary US embraced the quixotic narrative. Calling attention to the transatlantic potency of "imitative genres," Eve Tavor Bannet writes:

> The publication of successive translations, imitations, abridgements, and adaptations of Cervantes' early sixteenth-century novel throughout Europe and on both sides of the Atlantic made quixotism itself a transatlantic and transnational genre. In this respect, quixotism was comparable to the circulation and adoption in different parts of Europe and America of other genres, such as the romance or the sentimental novel. Quixotism itself therefore bears witness to the importance of genre, and of its diverse methods of transplantation in making Atlantic literary cultures more alike.[22]

Picking up on the transatlantic relevance of the quixotic narrative and, perhaps more importantly, reconstructing the character models of Cervantes, Fielding, and Swift to create a quixotic narrative for the early US, Brackenridge was also attuned to the role of imitation in the nascent republic's relationship with Britain. *Modern Chivalry* imitated British imitations of *Don Quixote* as a means of addressing and engaging the early republic's considerable set of transatlantically informed challenges, intervening in early US discourses of growth, prosperity, and national self-fashioning and producing a quixote in Captain Farrago whose quixotism attenuates the force of his social insights.

As with *Joseph Andrews*, *Modern Chivalry* confronts the question of whether quixotic behavior is visionary or revisionist by positioning the mad quixote against an even madder society. Occupying a society that is "the very antithesis of sane," Captain Farrago, despite his quixotism, can actually appear rational and deliberative. Joseph Harkey urges us to note that "the frontier society, not Farrago, is mad in *Modern Chivalry*." Similarly, between Captain Farrago and his servant Teague, in contrast to Don Quixote and Sancho, the captain represents the "rational minority," while the servant is, like the mass public, fickle and "impetuous."[23] Farrago goes to lengths to remove himself from the opinions of the masses—"it is of little, or perhaps no consequence to me, what my stile is amongst men"—and spends much time in the novel in distant observation and reflection over mob scenes, tarring and feathering, and chasing and shouting, all of these quite often surrounding the exploits of his servant Teague, whom Davidson rightly calls "the id" to Captain Farrago's ego, "provid[ing] most of the adventures which keep the novel going."[24]

Nonetheless, in situations in which the quixote can seem more rational than his attendant, or than the society that sets the standards for his madness, notions of rationality-by-degree are particularly difficult to pin down. Farrago rationally sees danger in the frontier mob mentality, yet it is the impetuous Teague who, unlike Sancho Panza, capitalizes on mob tendencies. And as Teague appears to learn something from his exploits—that his behavior is capable of producing favorable results—Farrago works himself into endless frustration over his inability to fruitfully assess the people with whom he comes into contact on the road, as well as his uneducated footman's continual success. Teague initially struggles to make sense of Farrago's elegant philosophical pronouncements, though he barely concerns himself with them; and this is the very attitude that makes him more successful in his political operations than his learned employer. In this sense, Teague is himself an ambivalent figure, lacking the first-instance skepticism and general common sense of Sancho Panza, yet politically shrewd in his own way.

Farrago treads a similar line. Wendy Martin identifies his strange "inversion of values," by which the mad quixote represents and identifies with "sanity in a society where profit takes precedence over knowledge."[25] In a moment of radical self-awareness similar to Launce-lot Greaves's defense of his own brand of quixotism, Farrago makes a claim to his sanity by way of his own madness, bemoaning: "I am shut up here as a mad man, in a mad place, and yet it appears to me that I am the only rational being amongst men, because I know that I am mad" (385). In complicating his quixote's relationship to the society he occupies, Brackenridge, like Fielding, opens up space for a double-edged satirical critique: the politically elusive and ambivalent Brackenridge pillories not just the uninformed, unreflective mob but also the pedantic and distrustful Farrago, all while undermining the general credibility of rhetorical claims about madness and sanity.

As with Parson Adams, Farrago's liminal position between sanity and madness relies upon a play of relativity. Despite Farrago's attempts to socialize Teague, to dress up his person and his manners in the image of a gentleman before he is to assume a government post, Teague appears obstinately antimimetic. When Farrago has a serendipitous encounter with his former servant after having let him go so that he may take up his newly acquired government position, Teague has bartered away the horse that Farrago had given him (Teague having been no longer a footman) for a watch, despite that Teague does not know how to tell time.[26] Teague's decision to trade the horse for the watch is a mark of his general disinterest in adopting the oft-mounted Captain Farrago's means of travel, and with that Farrago's knightly and gentlemanly visage. It also bespeaks Teague's appreciation of the surface-level requirements associated with political success, a property that distinguishes him from Farrago in an important way: the rational and practical Farrago lends his former footman a horse for transportation—the gift equivalent of an unglamorous but necessary political pronouncement—and Teague exchanges the horse for an object of no practical use to him, other than to give him what he understands as the appearance of an important political figure. Moments later, in stark contrast to his apparent social advancement, Teague is ready to strike Farrago's replacement servant, Duncan, with his cudgel, forcing Farrago to pacify the two.

Teague, a crudely stereotyped Irishman not altogether different from his Scottish counterpart Duncan, embodies all that is appetitive, impetuous, ignorant, and hot-tempered—a polar opposite of the refined, calculating, and articulate Farrago. Yet where Farrago's words ineffectually wash over his interlocutors and observers (as do Don

Quixote's in his many moments of pontification), Teague proceeds through the novel in episodes of relative success, effortlessly winning the favor of both crowds and women. Teague's success frustrates Farrago, who is continually confounded by it. As Bannet writes: "In *Modern Chivalry*, complete unwillingness to imitate either classical or English models is used to characterize the Pennsylvania backcountry. Brackenridge ironically dramatizes Franklin's dictum that America is 'the best poor man's country in the world,' by showing Teague . . . being offered every manner of opportunity in the new world. Meanwhile, his master, Captain Farrago, repeatedly tries to distract attention from Teague to himself by explaining to local communities what he has learned from books."[27]

The diametric distinctions between the captain and his servant operate against the backdrop of Brackenridge's fictional frontier society—a society much more like Teague than Farrago—and are critically significant beyond the terms of the disparate relationship between Farrago and Teague, quixote and sidekick. To the extent that Farrago lays claim to sanity by his relative thoughtfulness and measure, he is, as he laments, a madman shut up in a mimetic world, a world in which the impetuous circuitously mimic one another. Farrago's reluctance to participate in this mimetic cycle renders him, rather than Teague, the antimimetic figure, or perhaps the wrongly mimetic figure.

Though quixotes are imitators of a given model (and in many cases flawed imitators whose readings are too literal), they are also, paradoxically, antimimetic in relation to the "sane" worlds that they inhabit. Teague resists Captain Farrago's attempts at socialization, believing (perhaps correctly) that his demeanor, as well as his ability to mimic the mobs, is the foundation of his success. Captain Farrago's measured distance from the crudely mimetic world around him is central to his quixotism. Once he develops a taste for a given model, the scope of his mimesis is stubbornly narrow. He is mad in his inability to mimic a model that would bring him success (like that which his footman enjoys), yet in that same inability he is also sane, possessed of an understanding that if all were to fall into the mimetic cycle in which the mobs participate, the country could not survive, much less get off the ground.

Farrago is, like Parson Adams, part visionary who sees beyond the fray of profiteering and unenlightened self-interest, and part revisionist whose precepts seem no longer applicable to rapidly changing social landscapes. It is this mode of quixotism—the reasoned aloofness, the visionary outlook—set against the semi-fictional background of a "mad" midcentury Britain or early US, that makes *Joseph Andrews* and *Modern Chivalry* such compatible narratives for understanding how quixotism operates within public discourse. It is important to note, once again, that this form of aloofness is an essential precondition for quixotic exceptionalism, in this case the elevation of the quixote above the very concrete social problem of his obsolescence. For Farrago, reticence in the face of a seemingly ill-advised mob populism—an antimimetic quality—demonstrates one of the primary ways that quixotes preserve quixotic idealism, despite social forces acting to bring the quixote back to the reality that others practice. Quixotism entails the obstinate belief in one's own approach and worldview, despite concrete evidence of its falsehood or inadequacy.

In the case of *Modern Chivalry,* Farrago's ambivalent yet steadfast belief in the myth of American exceptionalism reflects much of Brackenridge's own political career, as well as the complicated stakes of Brackenridge's politics. Brackenridge, born in Scotland in 1748 and transplanted with his family to Pennsylvania as a child in 1753, was among the most legally and politically engaged of the prominent early US writers. He attended the College of New Jersey (present-day Princeton University) with the poet and polemicist Philip Freneau and the coauthor of the US Constitution and fourth US president, James Madison, where the three founded the American Whig Society, a group of playful polemicists established to counter the Cliosophic (Tory) society. Though Brackenridge was himself an especially complicated political figure, evinced by his bipartisan efforts and negotiations to end the Whiskey Rebellion in 1794, his evenhandedness in critiquing both mob mentality and detached plutocracy in the early republic, his career as a highly respected and politically savvy judge, and his affiliation with Madison and the Princeton Whigs reflect his seminal role in shaping the guiding principles of US governance in the eighteenth century.

By the turn of the nineteenth century, during the period in which Tabitha Gilman Tenney wrote *Female Quixotism* and the partisan divide between Federalists and Democratic-Republicans heated up, Madison and Thomas Jefferson were aligned against the Hamiltonian Federalists with a brand of republicanism that Brackenridge, Freneau, and Madison helped shape at the College of New Jersey. Brackenridge would go on to practice law and serve as a magistrate and a justice of the Pennsylvania Supreme Court. He was also the founder of the Pittsburgh Academy (present-day University of Pittsburgh) and the *Pittsburgh Gazette* (present-day *Pittsburgh Post-Gazette*). This diversified background of legal and political involvement, educational stewardship, and experience on the western Pennsylvania frontier primed Brackenridge to make *Modern Chivalry* one of the early republic's most ideologically capacious and subtle quixotic narratives.

As I have suggested, Farrago's quixotism, in many ways responsible for his lack of social and political success, takes the form of an aloofness—an especially reasoned, learned, even patrician approach to political dialogue—that frequently resembles the quixotism of Fielding's Parson Adams in its ambitions to alter the political and moral landscape of his surrounding society. Farrago's experiences call into question the myth of American exceptionalism in ways analogous to how Parson Adams ruptures easy notions of a morally upright, Christian England. Brackenridge coauthored, with Philip Freneau, a 1772 version of "The Rising Glory of America," a poem that trumpeted American exceptionalism in the years approaching the Declaration of Independence.[28] Farrago is a quixotic visionary in the mold of John Adams, Thomas Jefferson, James Madison, and to an extent Brackenridge himself, an educated and legalistic proponent of the notion that US exceptionality is a function of its culture of letters.

John Adams advocated this very notion of American exceptionalism in a project that prefigured the "triumph of the West" attitudes expressed in Freneau and Brackenridge's "The Rising Glory of America." As Michael Warner observes, John Adams took an opportunity amid the rising tide of Revolutionary spirit in 1765 to pen a "history of the West" in the *Boston Gazette*. "It tells modern history as a story of human self-determination rising through reflection," observes Warner; "its history of self-determination yields a protonationalist consciousness of America; its history of reflection takes the form of a history of letters." Warner's account of this early, adept, and successful attempt at national mythmaking is telling in its two crucial observations: first, that John Adams wrote an account of Western history, including US history, specifically to answer the challenges and uncertainties of a tumultuous time, a history in which "the Puritan colonists emerge as the heroes in a political history of enlightenment"; and second, that this work takes as central an intellectual history, a history of "reflection," or "a history of letters."[29] This notion of intellectual reflection is of particular importance in the case of Fielding's and Brackenridge's quixotes, both of whom fashion themselves as aloof, reflective, and ultimately visionary, a pair of quixotic exceptionalists who derive their senses of exceptionalism from the source-texts of national exceptionalist mythology (for Parson Adams, scripture, and for Captain Farrago, the founding documents of the US republic).

We should also note that Farrago travels along the margins of the early republic, through frontier towns and among people constituted as marginal in relation to political elites concentrated in cities like Benjamin Franklin's Philadelphia, in states like Thomas Jefferson's Virginia, or in regions like the Northeast, the Federalist stronghold of John Adams. Farrago avails himself of the freedom to venture between and around these iconic sites of dominant US historical narrative, primarily encountering not the statesman types whose erudite writings, potent rhetoric, and patriotic idealism Farrago takes for his own dominant narrative of US political progress, but temperamental frontier mobs. Farrago derives his quixotic idealism in large part from "classical" notions of early US political identity, traveling as such to discover an idealized early republic and preach idealism where it is lacking.

Like Parson Adams and Updike Underhill, Farrago is caught in a dilemma over social and political trends that diverge from his quixotic understanding of an ideal society, forced to contend with the fact that as a reformer he looks more like an anachronism. He cannot effect change as he would like because the datedness of his precepts, manners of communication, and means of relating to those around him render him a confounding and disquieting figure in the eyes of others. In short, the change the quixote would like to see has already passed him by. Parson Adams desires a society that resembles a willing and able congregation that adheres to less cynical religious models—charity, chastity, piety—but applies Enlightenment notions of rationality, whereas Farrago wants to inject the order and relative stability of the colonial US into the post-Revolutionary US project of self-governance. The former laments the descent of rationality into a philosophical justification for the naked pursuit of self-interest. The latter, whose sense of a more refined, reflective, and "gentlemanly" social order is decidedly pre-Revolutionary, is constantly stymied by the Revolutionary fervor of frontier mobs.

The quixote's claim to exteriority—for Don Quixote, to be in the business of knowing everything; for Parson Adams, to understand the roots of wickedness in his society but not in himself; for Captain Farrago, to distinguish himself from his peers through his measured and sane realization of his own madness—is a central distinction between the quixote and the picaro, or the exceptionalist and the delinquent. Responding to changes around them without adopting compatible (that is, new) models to imitate, and having to navigate their liminal positions as outmoded visionaries, Parson Adams and Captain Farrago illustrate a fundamental feature of quixotic exceptionalism. Their insights are based on aberrant (in this case antiquated) models, and their inability to signal and adapt to changes—their quixotic refusal to mimic, as Bannet argues, the right models—binds them to the political realities of the societies in which they live, their visionary qualities notwithstanding.

Brackenridge's choice of the quixotic narrative for a social critique of the mythical claims of early US self-fashioning emphasizes the quixotic tendency toward aloofness and visionary status, and its prominent role in the construction of national identities and myths. The quixotic narrative framework itself gives authors like Brackenridge the model for a quintessentially Cervantic authorial distance, enabling them to address performatively the very process of myth construction, or of layering stories upon stories to the point at which the originator—the author—has become buried beneath the layers. This quality of the quixotic narrative has made it an attractive form for writers engaging expressly with political themes, and produces in the quixotic narrative as such its own mimetic appeal. Further, the quixote, a figure whose exceptionalism engenders both a disconnectedness from broader society and a consequently visionary tendency, is well equipped to be a purveyor of myths, intentionally or otherwise.

Cathy Davidson reads the duality of both Brackenridge's objects of critique and Farrago's inability (an inability often shared with Parson Adams) to practice as he prescribes as a prime example of "the double perspective of the picaresque and its reliance on contradictory rhetorical strategies."[30] Yet here what is perhaps more illuminating than the *picaresque* (polyvocal, rambling, contradictory) qualities of these novels, or the correlatives of these qualities in nationalist discourses, is the *quixotic,* idealistic claim to aloofness and to sanity in relation to a world gone mad, a claim, in other words, to exteriority and to a transcendent truth.

The discursive correlative of this claim lies at the heart of mythmaking in the early US, through the emergence of a class of quixotic elite, like John Adams, whose skillful rhetoric was tailored to cut through US polyvocality and produce an exceptionalist national identity, a "history of the West" that emphasized triumphs of Christianity, rationality, legalism, and liberalism. The aloof and morally resolute Parson Adams, observing injustice and iniquity all around him, could well have become John Adams's Puritan colonial hero had he tired of wayward England and boarded a ship to the US. The equally aloof Captain Farrago, by contrast, is aware of the instability of his own footing and is as such the early republic's discursively disruptive figure par excellence, Parson Adams's US foil.

8

Arabella, Dorcasina, and
Domestic Exceptionalism

Travel and civic engagement are not the only ways quixotes participated in the politics of exceptionalism during the eighteenth century. Because quixotism was from its beginnings a mode of behavior
grounded in the literary imagination and the problem of fictionality,
quixotes were well positioned to address eighteenth-century anxieties
about the real-world effects of reading the wrong fiction. As we know,
women—particularly young women—bore the brunt of such anxieties, given widespread impressions of women's supposedly heightened
capacities for inauspiciously fanciful reading. Novels like Charlotte
Lennox's *The Female Quixote* (1752) and Tabitha Gilman Tenney's *Female
Quixotism* (1801) concerned themselves primarily with the ill effects of
romance reading on young, provincial women. This was the case even
as, at least in Britain, provincial men were more likely than provincial
women to buy and read novels, including novels written by women.[1]
Novels like *Joseph Andrews* and *Modern Chivalry* treat quixotic reading
practices as comical but ultimately incisive critiques of mad societies.
"Female quixote" novels do likewise, reconfiguring the "domestic" in
the domestic scene from a description of national politics "at home" to
a description of the politics of the home; yet the politics of the home in
female quixote novels tell us as much about wider national politics as
do novels featuring rambling, male quixotes.

The capacity of the politics of the home—as treated in female quixote novels—to illuminate national politics is understandable in light of
what Michael McKeon identifies as women's ambivalent relationship to
the public sphere. On one hand, the Habermasian notion of the public sphere was always utopian, predicated on universal access that was

nevertheless, in reality, "constrained by the same factors—education and the ownership of property—that define the actual reading public."[2] Given that the female quixotes under consideration in this chapter do not have control over the property they stand (conditionally) to inherit, and given that both female quixotes possess a wealth of literary knowledge, the literary public sphere becomes the venue through which female quixotes participate in public life. As McKeon observes, "The literary public sphere seemed to document, indeed to constitute, the public reality of humanity itself, to give voice to private individuals in their universal capacity as human beings."[3] As readers of female quixote novels witnessed quixotic heroines shaping their immediate social and political environments through quixotic exceptionalism—which created in these novels an extreme version of the literary public sphere that brought its notional effects into line with reality—they could imagine themselves gaining similar access to public life through what McKeon calls the literary public sphere. In this way the domestic scene in female quixote novels addresses the impact of civic issues within and beyond the domus, as the domestic exceptionalism of female quixotes renders reading a powerful means of shaping the social worlds quixotes occupy.

Understandably, then, scholarship on female quixote novels tends to focus on the prospects in such novels for the advancement of women and women's domestic living conditions. But these novels also reflect two important and underacknowledged aspects of eighteenth-century quixotism. One, that while female quixote novels portrayed emancipatory prospects for educated, wealthy women, the societies in which these novels were published showed very little tolerance for disruptions of social class or rank. Two, that when female quixotism crossed the Atlantic from Britain it maintained its class stringency and reproduced British notions of social rank even in a US society with a very different class structure. Many of the same questions about women's access to the public sphere in the eighteenth century—questions about literacy and property ownership as barriers to access—apply to commoners as well.[4]

Exceptionalism is the logic that enables the transatlantic portability of class structures in female quixote narratives of the long eighteenth century. Because Lennox and Tenney both write female quixotes whose sense of superiority allows them to shape the decisions of more powerful people (men) while bringing their less powerful—and less educated—female servants along for the ride, quixotic exceptionalism confuses class relations in both novels. For Lennox's quixote, Arabella, an obsession with French romances creates expectations that, as in those romances, the ladies' maids should also be women of the court, not lower-rank servants. And for Dorcasina, Tenney's US-bred quixote, the class dynamics of British amatory fiction prove a perplexing guide to life on the Pennsylvania frontier. Because Arabella and Dorcasina treat their maids in one moment as more knowledgeable about French romance or British amatory fiction than they each prove to be, and in the next moment like ignorant, impudent servants for their lack of knowledge and decorum, historical differences in class relations between Britain and the early US become less pronounced in these novels. A form of domestic exceptionalism—whereby female quixotes simultaneously reconfigure domestic politics for themselves according to their own sets of rules, while holding in place the old rules that govern their servants' conduct, drives the class dynamics in these novels.

We can observe the considerable implications of quixotism for understanding class dynamics—reflections of the classed nature of the traditional Quixote-Sancho relationship—by considering the role of domestic servants in female quixote narratives. This is the case because, in the domestic setting, the Sancho figure takes on greater political significance than it has out on the road. Due to the prominent roles of ladies' maids in perpetuating their mistresses' amorous fantasies in the European romances that Lennox and Tenney parody in their "female quixote" novels, female quixotes' maids tend also to play very important roles as managers of and participants in quixotic fantasy. For this reason, the female quixote novels of Lennox and Tenney, typically discussed in terms of the empowerment of their quixotic heroines, also invite consideration of how representations of female domestic servitude intersect with the wider (and justified) critical tendency to read the quixotic imagination as a means of feminine empowerment in these texts.[5] In other words, the similarly conflicted roles of ladies' maids in *The Female Quixote* and *Female Quixotism*—roles that involve sustaining verbal and physical abuse by and for their mistresses to accommodate a liberating quixotic fantasy—bring each servant character to the forefront of her narrative as a subjugated counterheroine who upholds traditional socioeconomic distinctions, then fades into the background while her mistress challenges gender conventions.[6]

Perhaps to an even greater degree than itinerant male quixotes like Fielding's Parson Adams or Brackenridge's Captain Farrago, and certainly more out of the necessity imposed by the conventions of domesticity, Lennox and Tenney's female quixotes rely on their socioeconomic advantage (and thus their servants) to interact with the worlds around them. Their servants receive and deliver romantic correspondences, guardedly supply compliments and carefully constructed comments to sustain and legitimate their mistresses' fantasies, and become wholly enmeshed in quixotic escapades. This occurs, more often than not, by the quixote's mandate and against the servant's better judgment. The quixote and her servant develop a degree of codependency and participate in a cyclical power transaction, the quixote wielding social authority to get her servant to do her romantic dirty work, and the servant mimicking the quixote as a stand-in or a double within the quixotic fantasy to remain within her mistress's good graces, or to prevent the higher-rank quixote from falling into greater trouble. Through this dynamic—and under the added pressure the strictures of domesticity impose on the servant-quixote relationship—female quixote narratives become especially useful texts for examining comparative class dynamics across the Atlantic.

This is important because the comparative study of class in eighteenth-century British and early US novels is often a fraught endeavor.[7] One problem is that treating eighteenth-century British domestic servants as members of a common social class reflects an incomplete understanding of just how fluid was the domestic servant's identity and relationship to the employer family. "Treating domestic workers as an identifiable and stable class," writes Kristina Straub, "does not get at the knotty connections of contract, kinship, and affiliation that crisscross the British household at that time."[8] Another is that Britain and the US not only differed significantly in the ways that they conceived of class or social strata, but they also lacked an overarching sense of "class" society as we understand it today, or as it emerged in its modern (and primarily Marxian) incarnation in the nineteenth century.

Unlike in the US, where Tenney's quixotic heroine, Dorcasina, is compelled to imitate what she understands as the manners of Britain's "genteel" classes, Lennox's Britain certainly had an aristocracy, and Lennox's quixote, Arabella, would have been part of it. As G. E. Mingay's oeuvre comprehensively demonstrates, however, provincial England of the mid-eighteenth century was better classified by "ranks" of merchants, yeoman, clergy, landed gentlemen, and the like, than by broad "classes" with concomitantly broad "class" affinities. As Mingay notes, "The word 'class' in the sense in which it is now commonly understood first came into use in the latter eighteenth century."[9] Arabella's status as the heiress of a considerable country estate—not merely the holdings of a yeoman farmer or successful merchant—affords her significant and multifaceted socioeconomic advantage over her servant.

In the early US, class difference was certainly an operative aspect of daily social relations, though, as Ronald Schultz notes, US society was not "thoroughly class-dominated," as "inequalities of power in all of its aspects took on many forms."[10] The plantation regions south of the Pennsylvania-Maryland border, influenced by the English planta-tion complex of the colonial period, maintained perhaps the only "well-articulated and centralized class system in early America," while the rural Pennsylvania in which Dorcasina's estate is set in *Female Quixotism* had a much less definitive class structure and relationship to the plantation complex (as evidenced, in part, by Dorcasina's stated opposition to the use and ownership of slaves by a southern suitor, Lysander). By the 1780s, at which point "changes in trade, credit, and productive strategies" led to the gradual emergence of a capitalist system and, by the antebellum nineteenth century, capitalist class relations, rural regions in Pennsylva-nia and the Northeast witnessed "class dominance" in sporadic areas.[11]

Related to these regional differences in class structure and coherence, the early US differed significantly from Britain in its legal treatment of servants. Whereas England legislated punitive "master and servant" laws that "reduced to a single legal relation the heterogeneous man-ual labor statuses of early modern England," grouping domestic labor-ers, outdoor servants, and apprentices generally as "servants," the US witnessed no such laws until the first half of the nineteenth century.[12] In Dorcasina's Pennsylvania, disciplinary laws regarding "servants" applied only to indentured servitude, and certainly not to domestic ser-vants like Dorcasina's Betty.[13] Outside the plantation region, the early US adopted very little of the British system of socioeconomic rank, and its class relations were qualitatively different from those of its British forbear. While acknowledging the existence of something like class in the US, Marx downplayed its social impact, arguing that because of rapid change and high turnover in class "membership," the US had no "fixed" classes.[14] In *Democracy in America* (1835), Tocqueville similarly emphasized the notion of upward mobility and fluctuation in class membership in the US, suggesting that almost everyone who lived in the US, including those who inherited wealth from prior generations of workers, tended to work for a living.[15]

Instead of relying on overbroad and anachronistic class descriptors (lower, middle, upper, aristocratic; proletarian, bourgeois, and so on) to explain the social relations and power dynamics at work between mistresses and maids in quixotic narratives from both sides of the Atlantic, we can turn to the specific power dynamics between quixotes and maids as a way of understanding how quixotic exceptionalism in novels of domesticity was key to reproducing class structures across the Atlantic. Accordingly, my readings of *The Female Quixote* and *Female Quixotism* focus on the power dynamics of class in the contexts of societies that did not necessarily behave like "class societies" in the postindustrial sense, comparing these power dynamics with social conditions in eighteenth-century Britain and the early US to gain a clearer understanding of what it meant for Lennox and Tenney to represent quixote-servant relationships as they did. The following readings of *The Female Quixote* and *Female Quixotism* illustrate a process by which the exceptionalism of female quixotes compels servants to imitate their quixotic behavior without fully understanding the logic or purpose of quixotism. This in turn produces highly mimetic servant-mistress relationships that show us how class operates in these narratives.

The Female Quixote contains myriad mimetic relationships. At one level, Arabella mimics the romantic conventions she draws from her store of European romances. At another, as Thomas Schmid observes, Arabella mimics masculine authority in the process of deriving her authority from the power men grant her over them.[16] At a third level, Arabella's suitors mimic Arabella's mimicked romantic conventions. And at yet another level very different from the prior three, Arabella's maid, Lucy, mimics Arabella's romantic actions and mannerisms by serving as a surrogate Arabella when Arabella's romantic austerity prevents her from having direct contact with male suitors. This third level of mimesis differs because the primary practitioner of mimicry is a servant who, though perhaps at times compelled by the romantic nature of Arabella's constructed narratives, is also moved to mimicry through acts of Arabella's authority over her.

Arabella's ability to ensnare supporting characters into her imaginative world, whether by the authority of her social position or by fantastic wiles, merits careful consideration. As Eve Tavor Bannet argues, Arabella possesses "Don Quixote's amazing ability to make everyone imitate his chosen model."[17] And as April Alliston argues of quixotes, "having introjected their own romance ideal of a character, they

violently project that ideal onto the quotidian world around them, trying to force others to act out their fantasy."[18] Being in a position of
social disadvantage in relation to her male suitors, Arabella affects
their behavior and exercises considerable agency through her ability to
inspire imitation. Though Glanville refuses to read the romance novels
that Arabella recommends to him and believes that Arabella is "gov-
erned by . . . antiquated Maxims," he nonetheless remains "resolved to
accommodate himself, as much as possible, to her Taste, and endeav-
or[s] to gain her Heart by a Behavior most agreeable to her" (45–46).
Glanville's rationale for this devotion, which overtakes his sound reasoning that Arabella is reading more into the situation than is there
in reality, is both because he is "passionately in Love with her" and
because he admires the "Wit and Delicacy" with which she makes her
romantic pronouncements (45–46).

Glanville's admiration of Arabella's "Wit and Delicacy" suggests
that Arabella indeed possesses a particular set of qualities—her attitude, her intellect, her care and adeptness with words—that makes her
capable of inspiring the imitation of her suitors. His love for her, which
he professes quite early in the novel, not long after he first becomes
acquainted with her, is highly romanticized; he develops passionate
love based on a series of trivial interactions with Arabella that adhere
to the romantic modes of courtship that Arabella prefers. As her interactions with Glanville suggest, Arabella's source of power over those
otherwise more powerful than her is indeed not simply her romantic
idealism but her mimetic appeal.

However, in the situations in which Arabella's mimetic appeal operates alongside the influence of Arabella's social advantage, not in the
context of her femininity but in the context of her wealth and status—in
other words, in those situations in which Arabella interacts with Lucy,
a *woman* of lower social standing—mimesis is not merely a function of
Arabella's appeal but also of her authority. Arabella's projection of her
quixotic ideal onto Lucy is indeed a terrifying practice. Though at times
Lucy's alacrity in delivering Arabella's letters or inquiring after Arabella's
affairs bespeaks a form of emotional or at least fanciful investment in
Arabella's romantic saga, a tendency to become swayed by Arabella's
mimetic appeal, readers are often privy to Lucy's stated fear of upset-
ting her mistress, her frequent acquiescence on account of this fear,
and her occasional questioning of her mistress's motives while simultaneously carrying out her mimetic tasks. While Glanville acquiesces

to Arabella's romantic models, even while questioning them, primarily because he is in love with her, Lucy acquiesces in large part because of the gravity of Arabella's reproachfulness and haphazard behavior, being in a social position in which, unlike Glanville when he has had enough, the decision to quit Arabella's company and simply walk out of the house might have realistically meant walking out of her job as well. Though the servant market in mid-eighteenth-century Britain was such that demand for domestic labor was high, and servants could realistically leave a household and find a new contract with another family with relative ease, rural domestics like Lucy would have had fewer prospects than urban servants in London, which Daniel Defoe glibly called a "paradise for Servants."[19] Further, as Kristina Straub has shown, the complex status of the eighteenth-century servant as both employee and intimate part of the family would have put a servant like Lucy in a difficult position with respect to demands like Arabella's.[20]

Arabella demands that Lucy partake of her romantic fantasies from the very beginning of the novel, when Arabella has her first encounter with a suitor from London, Mr. Hervey. Arabella orders Lucy not to accept correspondence from Mr. Hervey, at the same time expecting that Lucy will deliver some news of the London gentleman's interest. Arabella's unpredictable behavior—her charges to refuse correspondence from Mr. Hervey, then her constant expectation that Lucy indulge her desire and bring Mr. Hervey's letters anyway—is the novel's first occasion for verbal abuse. When Lucy reports that Mr. Hervey kissed his own letter to Arabella that Lucy returned to him, thinking it Arabella's reply, Arabella erupts: "Foolish Wench! . . . How can you imagine he had the Temerity to think I should answer his Letter?" (14). As the situation escalates and Arabella imagines that a woeful Mr. Hervey might attempt suicide after having been deprived of a response letter from his inamorata, Lucy finds herself both confused and compelled by the possibility: "Lucy now began to think there was something more, than she imagined, in this Affair. Mr. Hervey indeed, in her Opinion, had seemed to be very far from having any Design to attempt his own Life; but her Lady, she thought, could not possibly be mistaken" (15).

These brief intimations of Lucy's reasoning, reminiscent of Sancho Panza's tentative protests when Don Quixote sees giants for windmills or advancing armies for shepherds, abound in Lennox's novel and provide considerable insight into the complexity of Lucy's position relative to her mistress. On one hand, Lucy relies to an extent on her own judgment and rightly apprehends a disparity between her own rational, if uncertain, perceptions and Arabella's far-fetched yet gravely asserted suppositions. On the other, despite the accuracy of her own judgment, Lucy concludes that "her Lady . . . could not possibly be mistaken" (15). Lucy reaches a similar conclusion later in the novel when Arabella suspects that the gardener, Edward, might be a gentleman of high quality in disguise. When Arabella shares these thoughts with Lucy, Lucy replies: "Truly, Madam . . . I never took him for any body else but a simple Gardener; but now you open my Eyes, methinks I can find I have been strangely mistaken" (24). At these important junctures, after having been harshly reprimanded for relying on her own (accurate) judgments already, Lucy is compelled to partake of Arabella's fantasies not just because of Arabella's dramatization and mimetic appeal but also because Arabella, doubly aristocratic-minded as a landed heiress and imitator of high-bred French heroines, is in the social position to mandate fantasy in place of material reality. Like Sancho's opportunistic suspension of disbelief, practiced in the hope of obtaining islands, riches, or a new and more adventurous life from Don Quixote's pursuits and conquests, Lucy tries to adopt Arabella's way of seeing things to avoid rebuke and participate as best she can in quixotic adventure. By the force of Arabella's passionate mandate, Lucy is entered into a mimetic world in which her actions, emotions, and beliefs come to either mirror or stand in for those of her mistress. Lucy neither understands nor benefits from Arabella's exceptionalist reasoning.

We can observe this at the height of Mr. Hervey's courtship, when Arabella decides to write him a letter to pardon him from his supposed, self-inflicted death sentence. Only instead of writing the letter herself, or even having Lucy take dictations in her mistress's name, Arabella hands Lucy a handwritten note and makes Lucy copy it. The result is a letter from Lucy, addressed to "the unfortunate Lover of her Lady." Lucy's letter begins, "My Lady, who is the most generous Person in the World, has commanded me to tell you . . ." and proceeds with Lucy—not Arabella—at the center of Arabella's fantasy, standing in for her mistress as the speaking subject of Arabella's letters (16).

The mimetic joining of Arabella and Lucy—the voicing of Arabella's words in Lucy's name and the casting of Lucy's actions in Arabella's name—binds Lucy to the consequences of Arabella's whimsy, but without the degree of agency that Arabella deploys in creating and perpetuating her fantasies. After Arabella's behavior leads Mr. Hervey to lose interest in her and retreat back to London, it is Lucy who stands in for her mistress to assume the blame. Mr. Hervey, "not acquainted with Lady Bella's Foible . . . concluded her Fears of him were occasioned by her Simplicity, and some Misrepresentations that had been made her by Lucy, who, he thought, had betrayed him" (21). In the end, Arabella is presumed innocent in her alleged rural simplicity, and Lucy falls victim to her surrogate role in the ordeal.

In addition to Lucy's mimicking Arabella's words and actions, Lennox's novel is littered with instances of Lucy (and other female servants) shadowing Arabella's movements and mimicking Arabella's thoughts and emotions. Lucy "always thought as her Lady did"; and when Arabella walked in the garden with Glanville, "Lucy, and another Attendant, always followed her" (26, 46). Perhaps the most pronounced of these examples comes when Arabella believes she is about to be abducted and elicits Lucy's mirrored emotional response to the melodrama. When Lucy fails to show bravery in the face of her mistress's imagined danger, Arabella excoriates her: "Weak-souled Wench! . . . How unfit art thou for Accidents like these! Ah! had Cylenia and Martesia been like thee, the fair Berenice, and the Divine Princess of Media, had not so eagerly intreated their Ravishers to afford them their Company in their Captivity!" (93).

Arabella's allusion here to seventeenth-century romances, in which female attendants were themselves of aristocratic birth, raises yet another mimetic issue. Through Arabella's mimicking of romantic conventions and simultaneous insistence on differentiating herself and the noble-born attendants of seventeenth-century romances from the lower-born Lucy, she demonstrates the perceived trouble—in Gillian Brown's terms, the quixotic fallacy—of taking romance for reality.[21] Lucy, an undereducated servant, always fails to be the aristocratic attendant of seventeenth-century romances, though Arabella insists on the paradox of Lucy being both at once. If romance is itself a mimetic genre, capable of inspiring imitation (courtly behavior, abduction scenes, complicity between lady and lady-attendants)—and Lennox was clearly addressing this possibility—then Lucy must grapple with a double and self-contradictory mimetic imperative: play the surrogate mistress and the aristocratic lady-attendant at the same time, in fulfilment of her responsibility as a servant and her mimetic attraction to Arabella's fantasies.

Still fearing the "ravishers" and drawing Lucy into her dire fiction, Arabella charges her servant to suffer the consequences of her own imagination. Lucy, mimicking Arabella's fear and moving in close to Arabella, becomes Arabella's unfortunate double, in accordance with Don Quixote's pronouncement, "*quando caput dolet*" (2.2.499).[22] When the two women decide to escape the room, head through the garden, and set out for refuge at Lucy's brother's farm, Lennox's use of pronouns makes it particularly difficult to follow which woman is Arabella and which is Lucy: "Lucy, upon whose Arm she leaned, perceiving her fainting, screamed out loud, not knowing what to do with her in that Condition: She placed her upon the Ground; and, supporting her Head against that fatal Stump, began to rub her Temples, weeping excessively all the time. Her Swoon still continuing, the poor Girl was in inconceivable Terror: Her Brother's House was now but a little Way off" (95). These mimetic vignettes effectively bring Arabella and Lucy ever closer and ever less distinguishable from one another in descriptions of Arabella's imaginative world; however, the crucial authority distinction remains: whereas Lucy is pulled into her mistress's fantasies to bear the harsh consequences with little power or awareness to opt out of them, Arabella is the sovereign impetus for their escapades. And, just as Arabella brings about these escapades, she too assumes the power to end them, as she does at the novel's end when she admits to the folly of her quixotic behavior.

Arabella experiences at the end of the novel "violent" emotions of shame and regret for her behavior, behavior that, notably, Lennox is careful not to vindicate (383). Arabella apologizes to Sir George and gives herself over to Glanville for marriage with an air of humility that would seem to betray her independence, and likewise her prior desire "to live single, not being desirous of entering into any Engagement which may hinder [her] Solicitude of Cares" (41). Nevertheless, in the mimetic circle of exchange between Arabella and Lucy, Arabella is in the end enlightened, redeemed, and married, while Lucy disappears, as servants do, quietly into the background.

After observing how Lucy is abused, ridiculed, terrorized, and blamed during the course of her mimetic role-playing in Arabella's fantasies, we can see more clearly how mimesis can take unfortunate turns in Lennox's text. Playing the part of the incredulous Sancho Panza willfully laying aside his doubts to follow his Quixote into a costly skirmish, Lucy seeks Arabella's approval and kind treatment by modifying her own thoughts and behavior to mirror those of her mistress. Arabella continually responds with demands and derision, reaffirming her superiority according to the servant-mistress relationships in her romances. In this sense, the relationship between Lucy and Arabella is one of constant, self-perpetuating struggle—Lucy's struggle to ingratiate herself by mimicking Arabella, and Arabella's struggle to differentiate herself by rebuking Lucy. The struggle comes to an end by relegating Lucy to the background.

Lennox's novel restores Arabella by its end, and in so doing affirms a number of its core principles (most notably the virtue of reason) while complicating others (the virtues of female independence and imagination). However, Lucy, who played an instrumental role in Arabella's imaginative affairs, remains a vestige of all that Arabella cast off.[23] Between Arabella and Lucy—two subjects in mimetic struggle—the former is the face of redemption in the text, while the sacrifice of the latter accompanies an abandoned sensibility, perhaps even the abandonment of Arabella's imaginative independence. Because Lucy—Arabella's double and the primary instrument of Arabella's imaginative affairs—is abandoned in this way, Arabella can be restored. Despite Lucy's prominent role in Arabella's fantasies, we do not expect Lucy—a servant, a dispensable double—to be redeemed alongside her mistress.

Like *The Female Quixote,* Tenney's *Female Quixotism* features a relationship between its quixote, Dorcasina, and her servant, Betty, which is heavily defined by mimetic acts. These mimetic acts are a function of Dorcasina's exceptionalism, her ability to treat Betty at once as a friend and a subordinate, an educated quixote on her level and a buffoon who fails to make sense of quixotism. Betty's forced mimetic behavior is at times very similar to that of Arabella's Lucy; however, the nature of Betty and Dorcasina's relationship produces for the most part a different read on mimesis, one in which Betty does not always mimic Dorcasina but sometimes is made to mimic *for* Dorcasina. This difference is predicated on Betty's rather explicit objection to her lady's behavior and her consequent refusal to consent to that behavior through mimicry. But as the novel develops and Dorcasina's fantastic indulgence intensifies, it is ultimately Dorcasina's influence over her servant that obviates Betty's initial withholding of consent and compels Betty into mimetic participation.

Whereas Lucy rarely voices dissent to her mistress out of both a fear of admonishment and a tendency to become emotionally absorbed in her mistress's affairs, even in those cases in which the narration tells us that Lucy is skeptical, Betty initially takes considerable liberty with

Dorcasina in letting Dorcasina know when her words or actions sound or appear ridiculous. Tenney indicates at the beginning of her novel that Dorcasina has the capacity to view Betty as a companion as much as a servant. We are told that Dorcasina considers Betty "indispensable; for it would be entirely out of character, and setting aside a most essential circumstance in the life of a heroine, not to have had either a friend to whom she could confide the secret of her love, or a maid who could be bribed by an enamorato, to place a letter in her way, and then confidentially assert that she knew not from whence it came."[24] The duality of this servant-friend relationship, the "friend" component ostensibly more pronounced at the beginning of Tenney's novel than in all of Lennox's, greatly informs the nature of Betty's subjection.[25]

Because Betty protests throughout Dorcasina's episodes, we get at times a more vivid, realist sense of Betty's confusion over Dorcasina's exceptionalism than we do of Lucy's confusion over Arabella's. Dorcasina's treatment of Betty serves as a reasonably accurate gauge of the extremity of Dorcasina's immersion in fantasy, and the progression of this immersion sets up a series of cruel and violent mimetic acts. As Dorcasina becomes increasingly consumed by her fantasies, she becomes decreasingly tolerant of Betty. When Dorcasina is overcome with anxiety over the news that Lysander, a slave-owning gentleman from Virginia, will be visiting her estate and will have the opportunity to be her first suitor, her first scruple over their prospective marriage is his possession of slaves. As Dorcasina troubles herself over how she might persuade Lysander to free his slaves, Betty provides an immediate reality check: "'Tis pity you should make yourself so uneasy beforehand; perhaps you and the young gentleman won't fall so violently in love with each other as you imagine; and perhaps you will never become his wife" (9). We can imagine how offensive Betty's blunt wisdom might be to a quixote; but, while Dorcasina is dismissive of these words, she is not at this point derisive toward her servant.

Similarly, when Dorcasina first expresses her love and admiration for her next romantic object, O'Connor—a fraud and convicted criminal who tries to con Dorcasina into marrying him in the hope of taking possession of her valuable estate—Betty immediately sees through the con and lets Dorcasina know what she thinks:

> "Well, my mind of him," said Betty, "is, that he is a bold, impudent fellor, to go for to talking about love the first time he seed

you; and as he has been walking in the grove for some days, I suspects that he is after no good, and that he is no better than he should be. As to what you say of his warm manner, compared with Lysander's, you never heard him talk of love, he only writ you a letter; perhaps his talk about it would have been as lively as this forward fellor's, who nobody knows." (28)

Betty gives Dorcasina innumerable warnings about O'Connor, but as Dorcasina's infatuation intensifies, Betty's protests are met with condescension, ridicule, and outright coercion. In spite of her reasonable appeals, aimed at protecting Dorcasina from a series of pranksters and con men with designs on her wealth, Betty descends into a passive role in Dorcasina's adventures. After she witnesses Dorcasina make several clandestine appointments with the unknown and untrustworthy O'Connor, Betty remonstrates with her mistress, accusing her of drawing her romanticized image of O'Connor from books rather than reality. When Betty continues her protests, noting that real people "don't so easily die of love," Dorcasina, piqued by the amorous possibilities on the horizon and deluded about O'Connor's background and integrity, delivers a telling line: "Those are the ideas, Betty, of vulgar minds; they know nothing of that pure, refined passion, which, absorbing every faculty of the soul, swallows up all concern except for the beloved object" (33).

As quixotes do, Dorcasina mistakes her delusional "passion" for love, which indeed "swallows up all concern" for those around her. Betty slinks off after these words "in silent dejection" and under the impression that she offended Dorcasina "by the liberty she had taken" in communicating her doubts about O'Connor (33–34). This is the most prominent indication we get early on in Tenney's novel that Betty feels she has crossed the line with her mistress and forced her onto the defensive. Shortly thereafter, Dorcasina forbids Betty from partaking of "such infamous fabrications" about O'Connor, who is now under scrutiny from Dorcasina's father and other members of the village. From this point onward, Betty is inclined to keep most of her protests to herself, thus "effectually checked" by her mistress, and Dorcasina is engrossed in her relationship with O'Connor to the extent that material proof of his fraudulence bears no effect on her judgment (50). Dorcasina's detachment from the physical world around her, coupled with her swelling tendency to relegate Betty from friend-servant to utilitarian object, sets the stage for the novel's two central acts of mimesis.

After Dorcasina's father catches O'Connor in his daughter's bed-chamber and drives him out of town, Dorcasina endeavors to bring to life her fond memories of their romantic trysts in the grove. Toward this end, she approaches Betty for a favor: "Well, then, Betty, you must know I have taken a fancy to dress myself in the arbour, as I did then; and to have you dress yourself in a suit of my father's clothes, and then come to personate O'Connor." Betty does protest her mistress's request this time, but Dorcasina successfully goads her into compliance. While suiting up in the mirror, Betty "was ready to die with shame and vexa-tion, at the ridiculous figure she made" (97–98).

Betty has gone from cautionary friend-servant in the nascence of Dorcasina's flights of imagination to Lucy-like accomplice; and she suffers the consequences of this role more explicitly than does Lucy as Arabella's instrument of fantasy. After Dorcasina herself ridicules Betty for her inability to mimic O'Connor's smooth talk, the other ser-vants on the estate spot her with Dorcasina in men's clothing. Think-ing Betty a thief, they form a mob and approach her, only to find out that their thief is, inexplicably, Dorcasina's maid dressed as a man. The group of servants bursts out in raucous laughter, while Betty, "the mortified object of their mirth, sinking with shame and vexation, endeavored to conceal herself from their view, by skulking behind her mistress" (99).

Betty's forced mimesis in this case results in emotional duress at the behest of her mistress. In another instance, Betty suffers physical violence as a surrogate Dorcasina when another villain, Philander, mistakes Betty for Dorcasina and beats her. As Betty recounts the expe-rience: "I was thump'd, and cuff'd, and bounc'd, and shook, and twirl'd, and had my clothes stripp'd off, and tore to tatters, as if I had been nothing at all. Besides, what I shall not soon forget, in a grum and angry voice, that was no woman's, he call'd me old and ugly" (116). As when Sancho assumes Quixote's knightly prerogative of refusing to pay his bill at the inn, then is captured and tossed in a blanket for his transgression, Betty experiences role-playing for her mistress as a trau-matic event, even as we read such scenes, rightly, as comic instalments (1.17.135). As Sancho confusedly recounts to Quixote, "It isn't a good idea to go tempting God by taking on such a tremendous feat that you can only get out of alive by some miracle—you ought to be content with the ones that heaven worked on you when it stopped you from being tossed in a blanket, as I was, and when it brought you out safe, sound and victorious from among all those enemies that were riding with that corpse" (1.20.155).

Cathy Davidson has argued that Dorcasina "is victimized by both her own delusions and by men who calculatingly exploit those delusions."[26] Certainly Dorcasina, like her British counterpart Arabella, plays victim to an array of ill circumstances and deficient judgments. But, also like Arabella, she manages to avoid many of the material consequences of her actions. Dorcasina's socioeconomic advantage and mimetic appeal enable her to burden her servant with tasks that indulge her whims, and likewise to put her servant in harm's way in place of herself. Tenney's novel displaces onto Betty the majority of Dorcasina's romantic fallout. Gillian Brown picks up on this: "As the unwilling participant in Dorcasina's Quixotism, Betty very personally feels the difference between Dorcasina's perspective of life and the circumstances of life that they actually inhabit. Thus Tenney shows how imaginative activities, far from being merely frivolous or inconsequential, require real exertions and produce material effects. Dorcasina's pleasure proceeds at the cost of Betty's pains. . . . Betty serves as the surrogate for the sufferings to which Dorcasina could be subjected."[27]

In *Female Quixotism* Betty pays the price for Dorcasina's decisions through two kinds of mimetic struggle. In the first instance, Dorcasina and the other servants ridicule Betty because her mimetic attempt is ridiculous, and ridiculously unconvincing. Unfortunately enough, Betty is made to stand in for one of the novel's major villains; and beyond this, her attempt at mimicking O'Connor in the grove is (understandably) poor. Betty is sacrificed as Dorcasina's surrogate quite straightforwardly when she faces the brunt of the ridicule for dressing up as O'Connor, despite that the absurd idea to do so was Dorcasina's, but she is also sacrificed as O'Connor's double, as the sole remnant of the departed villain. For all of O'Connor's misdeeds—never mind Dorcasina's—it is only Betty who suffers punishment, literally, in O'Connor's name.

In the second instance, Betty again stands in for Dorcasina when she suffers physical assault at the hands of Philander. In the act of sustaining Philander's attack in place of Dorcasina, Betty forestalls any potential harm done to Dorcasina—harm that could register as a major violation of the novel's class equilibrium. As Brown suggests, "Because her mistress believes these events to be part of a familiar and cherished narrative, and because Philander carefully respects Dorcasina's actual status as an upper-class woman throughout his prank,

Dorcasina is immune to the emotions and pains that Betty suffers."[28] Betty standing in for Dorcasina while being attacked by Philander prevents the greater evil of Philander transgressing the novel's class parameters by assaulting Dorcasina. Betty, then, functions as a preventative surrogate.

Here it is important to understand that Dorcasina's exceptionalism is what brings about Betty's plight. Betty finds Dorcasina compelling— even when Betty's better judgment indicates otherwise—because Dorcasina can simultaneously bring Betty in as a confidante, enchanting her with high romance while admonishing her lack of understanding. This form of domestic exceptionalism—having it both ways when it comes to the quixote's expectations of her maid—regulates Arabella's Lucy and Dorcasina's Betty from two ends simultaneously: they are intrigued, compelled, and flattered on one end, and ordered, shamed, and ridiculed on the other.

Domestic exceptionalism raises two relatedly underexplored questions. First, how does the representation of class distinction in these novels compare with the realities of class or rank in eighteenth-century Britain and the early US? Second, how might this comparison reframe the critical conversation such that we can understand class (alongside gender) as a competing sphere of ethical concern in these novels, deserving of critical attention?

In *The Female Quixote,* Lucy's subordination is restorative: the elision of Lucy, the primary instrument of Arabella's regrettable past, allows Arabella to disavow her quixotism and marry Glanville without any remaining traces of her foible. In *Female Quixotism,* however, Betty's subordination is preventative: Betty's standing in for Dorcasina in the novel's most violent and raucous scenes forestalls any transgression of class protocol, or any infringement upon or contamination of Dorcasina's privilege of imitated, faux-aristocratic aloofness. Lucy helps to enable a relatively comical series of events, then fades into the background while Arabella's restoration furnishes the romance-like happy ending that one might expect of an eighteenth-century British quixotic narrative. Betty, by contrast, undergoes blatant assault and still appears by her mistress's side at the novel's end as the unfortunate foil for Dorcasina's socioeconomic advantage, a silent participant in Dorcasina's tragic solitude. If Lennox ties *The Female Quixote* nicely together in the mode of the British quixotic narrative, and in so doing partially compromises her critique of romantic idealism and its pitfalls, Tenney's *Female Quixotism* is a cautionary tale of the highest order, casting its quixote in its final pages as a pitiable spinster rather than a happy penitent.[29]

Davidson has described *Female Quixotism*'s disheartening conclusion as reflective of a "hard core of realism" particularly suitable for the world of the early US frontier and its readers, a realism that is perhaps distinguishable from *The Female Quixote*'s measured burlesquing and clean ending, both apropos of a British readership who were less concerned with the uncertainties of frontier life.[30] Sarah Wood concurs, noting that while the romance-reading women of British literature often inhabited comic texts raising laughter on their way toward a happy end, their US "counterparts were more frequently the tragic figures of cautionary tales, fallen women facing ridicule, ruin, and even death."[31] Missing from this dichotomy, however, is an explanation of what Lennox's and Tenney's prominent representations of servant-mistress interaction suggest about these differing British and US landscapes, and how class or class-like power dynamics in these novels tell a very different story than that of the "hard core" of the US frontier versus the British "happy ending." In other words, though reading *The Female Quixote* and *Female Quixotism* primarily through the lens of quixotic protagonist has engendered a critical affirmation of national difference in the comparative study of these novels, a reading of these novels from the perspectives of their female servants produces a counterintuitive conclusion: on account of domestic exceptionalism, both class and socioeconomic advantage are actually represented quite similarly in both texts.

Though *The Female Quixote* plausibly characterizes Arabella and her family as landed, aristocratic types, Arabella's quixotic romanticism and thorough education add elements to her social advantage over Lucy for which class or rank per se do not fully account. As I have shown, a significant component of Lucy's confusion in *The Female Quixote* is the peculiar literacy gap that renders Arabella capable of reading romances imaginatively, but Lucy incapable of "reading" Arabella's behavior as a product of overreading. Lucy respects Arabella's authority as a compelling, articulate, and impassioned reader of romance even as Lucy knows better. Curiously, Lennox emphasizes Lucy's inability to mimic adeptly or to meet Arabella's expectations that she be familiar with and conduct herself according to the conventions in Arabella's romances; however, this would seem out of step with wider eighteenth-century assumptions that romances were precisely the kind of "low" material in which morally misguided servant girls were inclined to indulge.

As Lori Newcomb illustrates, the critical study of female domestic reading habits has focused unduly on the "primal scene" of consumption in which "a lower-class woman, rapt with misdirected erotic desire, reads an indulgent text, unaware of the mocking but riveted men who have summoned her up."[32] The prospect that female domestics like Lucy would have been functionally literate and familiar with romances was, according to Newcomb, "economically possible, sociologically likely, and ideologically meaningful."[33] However, in *The Female Quixote,* it is the aristocratic Arabella, not Lucy, who occupies the "primal scene" of reading out of one's depth. Lennox's collapsing of the stereotypical servant-reader and the aristocratic quixotic-reader into mimetic doubles effectively critiques the widely represented, elitist narrative of the insolent servant girl reading rubbish, but in the service of empowering Arabella, not Lucy. If, as Newcomb argues, the scene of the servant-reader "masks elite fears that the romance of service may tell her something all too true: that service is founded on an arbitrary system of social assignment," then the "arbitrary system of social assignment" that *The Female Quixote* critiques through Arabella's fanciful reading is not Lucy's domestic servitude, but the patriarchal norms that encumber Arabella.[34] Though the historical reality of eighteenth-century Britain would suggest that a literate Lucy would have been familiar with romance reading and might have stood something to gain by the imaginative reading of romance, *The Female Quixote* rather explicitly confers the liberating potential of romance reading to Arabella, not to her servant. This reaffirms Lucy's role in the narrative as a subordinated figure, one whose potential for liberation is sacrificed in the narrative for the purpose of restoring her mistress to an acceptable degree of compliance with aristocratic norms and expectations. In this way *The Female Quixote* avoids a critique of arbitrary socioeconomic injustice or antiquated class roles while launching a critique of arbitrarily limited gender roles.

We can observe a comparable affirmation of socioeconomic norms in *Female Quixotism,* though Tenney presents perhaps a more ambivalent picture of domestic servitude in Betty. Despite Betty's outwardly American characteristics, the servant-mistress relationship in Tenney's novel suggests that, at least in terms of its portrayal of socioeconomic status, *Female Quixotism* is not as distinctly American as critics have suggested. Most prominently, Dorcasina is a faithful imitator of British aristocratic attitudes and behavior, even though such attitudes and behavior are woefully incompatible with US frontier life. Dorcasina's imitation of

aristocratic norms compels Betty, an outspoken servant character ostensibly modeled on the US domestic servant, to take on roles and characteristics that often appear as much European as American. As we would
expect from servants in the US but less so in Britain, for example, Betty
is boldly critical and sarcastic toward Dorcasina. As Laurel Thatcher
Ulrich points out, "European visitors commented frequently on the
lack of deference shown by American servants," and early US diaries
contain numerous instances of what Ulrich characterizes as maids' sarcastic responses to their mistresses.[35]

Among the servants on Dorcasina's family estate, Betty is the isolated object of ridicule, an outsider; yet beside Dorcasina, as though
part of a British household or a French romance, she is an intimate (if
unfortunate) part of her employer's domestic and amatory affairs. Tenney portrays Betty as an uneducated servant who speaks in the "low"
vernacular of the US frontier laborer and is regarded as too naïve, too
unrefined, and sometimes too insolent to understand and communicate on Dorcasina's quixotic wavelength. Yet Betty is also typically, if
unflatteringly, described in the novel as "good-hearted," "honest," and
"possessed of a tolerably good natural understanding; but very ignorant and extremely superstitious," a description that comports with
British elites' stereotype of the good-natured but readily corruptible
servant girl (8). While Betty possesses some characteristics typical of
the early US domestic servant, she is also, along with Dorcasina, a projection of British and wider European sensibilities, Americanized on
the surface in attitude and dialect but fundamentally adherent to the
servant-confidante model that Arabella acquires from French romances
and Dorcasina absorbs from British amatory fiction.

Beyond its preservation of European sensibilities in Betty's servant
role, *Female Quixotism* also preserves Dorcasina's pretensions to European-
style aristocracy. Though Dorcasina's quixotic errors do not go unpun-
ished by the end of Tenney's novel, the faux-aristocratic class position
that Dorcasina assumes remains protected, even as she renounces her
quixotism. Davidson notes that Dorcasina "almost triumphantly . . .
takes control of her life and of the final words of the text," which are
expressed in a letter that "announces she will spend the rest of her days
in assisting others less fortunate than herself, in sewing, and in reading
novels."[36] Absent from this reading is the caveat that, far from assisting
the likes of Betty, Dorcasina's charities are aimed not merely at "those
less fortunate" but also at those "who, by misfortunes, and without any

blameable misconduct of their own, have been reduced from opulent or easy circumstances to indigence" (324). In other words, Dorcasina invests charitably only in the formerly rich, a curious detail that demonstrates not only her intent to counteract any kind of US social mobility for which the opulent are "reduced . . . to indigence" but also her insistence on maintaining, after her conversion from quixotism, an aristocratic class affinity that registers as European, not American. As in *The Female Quixote*, the potential for liberation that Betty might have gained from having Dorcasina's assistance in reading novels is reserved for the socioeconomic elite.

Through the mimetic relationship between Dorcasina and Betty, which compels the latter to adopt the adopted class preferences of the former, we can see more clearly how *Female Quixotism* largely preserves a simplified European model of socioeconomic distinction, even if such a model was incommensurable with the reality (or ambiguity) of class in the early US. Betty's subjection—in which Betty stands in for her mistress in situations in which violent or uncouth behavior might otherwise rupture Dorcasina's fantasy of aristocratic living—allows for a comic critique of romantic ideals from British novels that were potentially incompatible with US frontier life, but simultaneously prevents the narrative from violating or condemning the borrowed socioeconomic elements of British amatory fiction. This sympathetic borrowing holds, even, for the class sensibilities that *Female Quixotism* borrows from *The Female Quixote*, itself a novel that also parodies aspects of British amatory fiction but avoids socioeconomic critique.

In one sense this is unsurprising, since both of these female quixote narratives, like Cervantes's original and its countless other progeny, are fundamentally based on the fraught importation and misreading of the customs of foreign times and places. In another, however, the fact that the comic (or tragic) sacrificing of servant characters carries over with such consistency in transnational rewritings of the quixote story, while other aspects of the narrative ultimately change when written for new national audiences, tells us something important about both *The Female Quixote* and *Female Quixotism*, and about quixotic narratives more generally. The preservation of socioeconomic norms though the quixote-servant relationship in quixotic narratives from Cervantes to Lennox to Tenney contradicts one of the dominant theses of quixote studies: the idea that, as Thomas Scanlan has so succinctly put it, "*Don Quixote* fails to provide ideological or some other sort of intellectual consistency to the text in which it appears."[37] Contrarily, as servant-mistress relationships in *The Female Quixote* and *Female Quixotism* demonstrate, the eighteenth-century quixotic narrative had a remarkable ability to preserve traditional class conceptions and socioeconomic power dynamics, even as it was reconfigured in its travels across time, oceans, and national borders to address or unsettle a great plurality of other ethical and political concerns.

What we learn from the success with which Tenney's *Female Quixotism* imports the class structure and concerns of Lennox's *The Female Quixote*—even as early US class systems were very different in practice—is that the exceptionalism of quixotes could also comment on and unsettle early forms of US exceptionalism. Circulated within a Revolution-era US society that saw itself as more liberated than Britain in its class structures—particularly in terms of how servants understood their roles and relationships to the families that employed them—*Female Quixotism* reached back to British literary and political models to suggest that preservation of socioeconomic rank was important for stability on the frontier. Whereas civic exceptionalist texts like *Modern Chivalry* and *The Algerine Captive* (in its opening parts set in the US) reflected a desire for civic stability, *Female Quixotism* suggests that stability of socioeconomic rank is consequential not just for Dorcasina's love life but also for the safety and civic well-being of her surrounding society.

9

Launcelot and Juridical Exceptionalism

To this point we have seen that the exceptionalism of quixotes aided writers from Swift to Tenney in interrogating exceptionalist politics at various levels, from the international order to the community to the household. In each of the case studies considered thus far, quixotes have served as engines of commentary on politics generally understood: the ideas people hold about their relationships to others, the governance systems in which they participate or fail to participate, their national identities, and the relationships between nations. Conspicuously missing from the picture of quixotic exceptionalism thus far is the relationship between quixotism and the law. Particularly as Britain and the early US both anchor conceptions of freedom and rights in exceptionalist myths of equality before the law, it is important to understand how quixotism intervened in issues of justice and juridical practice in the eighteenth century.

In particular, what separates the eponymous quixote in Tobias Smollett's *Launcelot Greaves* (1760–62) from other quixotes is his striking success within the legal system, and the extent to which Smollett vindicates Launcelot's quixotism. Launcelot certainly appears ridiculous, dressed in full armor, upon his first encounter with a group of modern Britons engaged in conversation at the tidy and comfortable Black Lion inn. However, Launcelot soon demonstrates a remarkable ability to justify his quixotic behavior, to avoid much of the martial violence typical of Don Quixote amid his travels and conflicts, and to deliver justice successfully for those he aims to assist (as well as those villains who stand in his way). Launcelot is a rare quixote who seems to get almost everything right, and who thereby challenges the framework of quixotism in particular for explaining or illuminating what looks otherwise like plain heroism.

Central to our understanding of *Launcelot Greaves* is Launcelot's relationship to justice. This includes his relative madness or sanity before the institution of the law (an institution that privileges rational argument and functions, at least theoretically, with minimal prejudice), and the ways Smollett romanticizes each of these dynamics in the novel as a critique of corruption in midcentury British legal systems. Launcelot's quixotic exceptionalism—his desire to place himself at once above and behind the law—is a function of his rather exceptional standing among quixotes as a viable romantic hero, or a thoroughly romanticized version of the quixotic mock-hero.

Mid-eighteenth-century British readers and critics began to understand *Don Quixote* (and the quixotic mode) as an increasingly romantic narrative, a trend especially relevant for the study of *Launcelot Greaves*. For Ronald Paulson, "the turn toward the side of *Don Quixote* that supports romance, imagination, and defeat at the hands of the crass world coincides with the Forty-Five, the possibility of sympathy for Scotland, its chivalric clans fallen in battle and outlawed in their own countryside."[1] Though this plausible attribution is intriguing when considered alongside a discussion of the Scottish author Smollett's heroic quixote, one need not locate the "romantic turn" in quixote criticism specifically in the Forty-Five to acknowledge its presence by the midcentury. As Anthony Close argues, though the German Romantics played perhaps the strongest role in constructing Romantic approaches to Cervantes's knight, and though the Romantic view of Don Quixote was still a "minority opinion" in early eighteenth-century Britain, it was "an increasingly weighty minority from the mid-century on." "By the beginning of the nineteenth century," Close writes, "English *Quixote* criticism began to register in an insistent way the Romantic cult of imagination, genius, passion, and sensibility as faculties opposed or superior to reason."[2] This understanding of Don Quixote registers in book 5 of Wordsworth's *The Prelude,* in which "Wordsworth's friend, while reading Cervantes' novel, muses on 'Poetry and geometric Truth' and in a dream finds himself among desert sands: 'To his great joy a Man was at his side/Upon a dromedary, mounted high / . . . / A Lance he bore, and underneath one arm/A Stone; and in the opposite hand, a Shell.' "[3]

That Launcelot's heroism is highly romanticized is solid retort to the critical accusation that Launcelot is a "pale imitation" of Quixote. While Cervantes's *Don Quixote* presents itself initially as a satire of the chivalric romance, featuring a burlesqued hero who wages war against imagined giants and drummed-up injustices, *Launcelot Greaves* features a quixote who sets out to battle real-life injustices.[4] As Paul-Gabriel Boucé observes: "The great difference between Greaves and Don Quixote is emphasized by Smollett from the very beginning of the novel. Greaves' appearance and behaviour may be eccentric, but the evils he intends to fight against are extremely real."[5] And as Oscar Mandel documents, of the different types of real-life "foes" Quixote takes on of his own volition (that is, when he is not tricked into battle by practical jokers), the vast majority are innocent and undeserving of Quixote's lance.[6] Launcelot simultaneously pays homage to the quixotic madness "so admirably displayed" in Don Quixote, as well as the "inimitable" Cervantes, and distances himself from Don Quixote by arguing, self-reflexively, for his own sanity. "I reason without prejudice," Launcelot declares, "can endure contradiction, and, as the company perceives, even bear impertinent censure without passion or resentment" (15). Smollett modifies Launcelot as a uniquely celebrated and successful quixotic hero in an effort to create, as Boucé argues, "a redresser of very real wrongs and abuses rampant about the middle of the eighteenth century."[7] Angus Easson adds, whereas Don Quixote is a man approaching fifty years of age and past his biological prime, Launcelot Greaves is "a young man, handsome, in love not with some imaginary Dulcinea, but with a girl of flesh and blood, whose supposed rejection of him has turned his wits."[8]

As we can see from the outset, then, Launcelot Greaves was constructed as a highly romanticized quixote during a period in British literary history in which the quixotic hero or heroine was becoming increasingly romanticized. By "romanticized" I mean both associated with Romantic ideals and celebrated as an exception. As the events of Smollett's novel suggest, Launcelot is indeed an especially successful quixote, lending credence to the midcentury desire to see quixotes in a favorable light.

One of the most important components of Launcelot's ability to achieve his aims as a quixote in pursuit of justice, where other quixotes fail, is, of course, his wealth. Launcelot has so much money that he can reliably use the law as a means of redressing wrongs, restoring order, and pursuing justice. While he is notably "drained of pretty large sums of money" in his various lawsuits waged on behalf of the oppressed, misjudged, or downtrodden—an indication that, though Launcelot possesses great wealth, such expenditures are not insignificant and do not draw on perpetual financial reserves—Launcelot's wealth enables one of the novel's central features, a series of effective legal proceedings (40).

In light of Smollett's portrayal of lawyers and magistrates as both central and corrupt figures in *Launcelot Greaves,* much has been made of Smollett's own run-ins with the law as an active and at times caustic literary personality in midcentury Britain. After Smollett questioned the honor, bravery, and leadership of Admiral Charles Knowles in the *Critical Review* in May 1758—in a negative review of a pamphlet Knowles released in defense of his actions in the Raid on Rochefort—Knowles successfully sued Smollett for libel, resulting in Smollett's imprisonment for three months, an experience he drew on in writing *Launcelot Greaves*.[9] What Smollett scholars term the "Knowles affair" is, however, not the first of Smollett's troubles with the law. He previously consulted lawyers over "unfortunate loans" in 1754 and 1756, including having an action brought against him for physically attacking Peter Gordon and Gordon's landlord, Edward Groom, over Gordon's unpaid debt.[10] Smollett's frustrations with what he perceived as his own ill treatment before the law were compounded by his belief that, as Alice Parker documents, "the aristocrat should have a legal status above that of the plebian." In *A Continuation of the Complete History of England* (1760), Smollett "advocates that different penalties for the same crime be imposed upon the upper and lower classes."[11]

Smollett's difficulties with the law find their way into *Launcelot Greaves,* particularly in the rendition of the extraordinarily corrupt Justice Gobble, who victimizes Launcelot before Launcelot turns the tables and avenges Gobble's ill treatment of the poor and disadvantaged.[12] Smollett's exceptionalist view of the law as simultaneously a mechanism for the noble ranks to protect the lower ranks, and a mechanism that favors the noble ranks, is reflected in Launcelot's treatment of Justice Gobble. Understandably, then, much of Launcelot's quixotic idealism is oriented toward the legal system and the roles of lawyers and magistrates in upholding justice and eschewing the sorts of institutional barriers and conflicts of interest that Swift satirizes in *Gulliver's Travels.*

If Gulliver's is a quixotism of travel, then Launcelot's could be described as a quixotism of law. When Launcelot first appears in the narrative, entering the Black Lion and engaging in conversation with a group of travelers who have already met acquaintances, Launcelot's stated impetus for donning a century-old suit of armor and pursuing a life of knight-errantry is to "honour and assert the efforts of virtue; to combat vice in all her forms, redress injuries, chastise oppression, protect the helpless and forlorn, relieve the indigent, exert my best endeavors in the cause of innocence and beauty, and dedicate my talents, such as they are, to the service of my country" (15). In other words, Launcelot has set out by means of armed knighthood to right a set of perceived wrongs that the law has failed to redress. Rather than becoming a lawyer like his compatriot Tom Clarke, Launcelot takes up the lance of vigilantism, at least ostensibly. Yet, paradoxically, Launcelot also proceeds with an idealistic belief in the potency of the law to redress the very wrongs that he would seem to want to war against extrajuridically. As Aileen Douglas writes: "*Greaves* is dominated by the discourse in which social relationships are most explicitly and confidently recorded and promulgated: the law. The novel may begin with a comic parody of legalese, but as it advances, the law becomes not only a mechanism by which elements of the plot are resolved but also a matter for serious debate."[13] Launcelot primarily avails himself not of his lance and armor, but of the law (and the socioeconomic position that grants him a facility with it and its institutions) as a means of battling injustice. His quixotic belief in the law is expressly connected with a quixotic belief in the premises of the law more generally, and of the English constitution more specifically, as institutions that can spare no injustice, and let no honest, law-abiding citizen fall by the wayside. As Douglas suggests, "despite his appearance," Launcelot's "rhetoric is that of citizenship, not chivalry. His social code is clearly that of an eighteenth-century English gentleman who believes that the law provides adequate safeguards and protection for those who live under it."[14] We can thus understand Launcelot's quixotism of law as both an idealistic belief in the power of the law to address adequately a range of social injustices (disproved by the very fact that Launcelot's intervention is frequently required to correct for legal corruption) and an idealistic belief in his ability to right wrongs wrought by the law (and its officers) when it fails to measure up to Launcelot's quixotic expectations.

As we learn early in Smollett's novel, the symptoms of Launcelot's quixotic "folly" are manifested in his generosity, his commitment to justice, and consequently his tendency to make use of his resources and intervene over and above the law on behalf of the poor and downtrodden. Scorning oppressors and going to excesses to right wrongs, Launcelot, as his attorney companion Tom Clarke intimates, "acted as the general redresser of grievances": "he involved himself in several law-suits, that drained him of pretty large sums of money. He seemed particularly incensed at the least appearance of oppression; and supported divers poor tenants against the extortion of the landlords. Nay, he has been known to travel two hundred miles as a volunteer, to offer his assistance in the cause of a person, who he heard was by chicanery and oppression wronged of a considerable estate" (40–41). On numerous occasions Smollett's quixote can be found vigorously righting wrongs by coming to the financial aid of farmers and curates, freeing the falsely imprisoned, and standing against ignorant and corrupt magistrates. Yet Launcelot's adventures differ radically from those of other quixotes because of the unquestionably favorable results they produce, as well as the verifiable soundness of the knight's rationale.

When Don Quixote frees a group of galley slaves he believes have been locked up unjustly, we find that he has only set free an ungrateful lot of criminals who swiftly hurl stones at their valiant emancipator when he demands they flee to Toboso and present themselves to Dulcinea as grateful beneficiaries of Quixote's generous heroism (1.22.184–85). Yet when Launcelot forces the corrupt Justice Gobble to retire as magistrate and let free those whom he had schemed into wrongful imprisonment, the knight indeed sets free the wrongfully imprisoned, even turning the magistrate whom he deposed into a remorseful admirer of his character (92, 98). Where Henry Fielding's austere and bookish Parson Adams struggles to connect with passersby during his travels, Launcelot draws the esteem of virtually everyone but the so-labeled misanthropic writer, Ferret. And where Hugh Henry Brackenridge's Captain Farrago finds himself continually shouted down and chased off by boisterous mobs, Launcelot manages to win favor with a mob of, among other types, stockjobbers and weavers (both frequent representatives of mob ignorance in Brackenridge's *Modern Chivalry*) with a high-minded and rationally articulated harangue (at least until he mentions the idea of "moderation," a jibe that Smollett evidently could not resist) (75). Additionally, it is Launcelot's bravery and generosity that attract his beloved Aurelia, and not without her dying mother's blessing. Smollett's knight finds his quixotism appreciated at every turn, leaving readers to question why and how such quixotic madness could be so ingratiating, or why and how such ingratiating behavior should be quixotic.

Smollett contrasts Launcelot's successful quixotism with the pseudoquixotism of Captain Crowe, who, witnessing Launcelot's success, resolves to become a knight-errant himself. Launcelot characterizes

Crowe's bumbling imitation of knight-errantry as madness but acknowl-edges a tempered madness of his own.[15] When Crowe attempts to steal Launcelot's armor, "ambitious to follow his example," and Clarke defends him as an honest man, Launcelot replies that "madness and honesty are not incompatible—indeed I feel it by experience" (59). Put-ting aside momentarily that Launcelot's madness is clearly to be differ-entiated from Crowe's, the comparison is one of a number of ways in which Smollett's novel meticulously supports the acceptability—even the virtue—of Launcelot's madness.

Remarking on Crowe, Launcelot affirms that the idea of madness can accommodate honesty. After Ferret has him imprisoned for knight-errantry (a charge for which the knight would be *legally* exculpated), Launcelot becomes "more and more persuaded that a knight-errant's profession might be exercised, even in England, to the advantage of the community," though Clarke, thinking of Crowe, persists in the view that "knight-errantry and madness [are] synonymous terms" (100). Later on, Launcelot contrives to "think himself some hero of romance mounted upon a winged steed," though "inspired with reason" and "directed by some humane inchanter, who pitied virtue in distress" (119). In each of these examples, perhaps most boldly illustrated by way of the bur-lesqued imitator Crowe, Launcelot's madness is defined circularly by the knight's own experience, effects, and esteem as a kind of heightened and humane rationality. Furthermore, however much such a definition would appear to verge on the kind of quixotic solipsism or delusion we might expect, Launcelot's actions and their results provide external validation for his own theory of "humane madness."

For example, Sycamore, Launcelot's mimetic rival in the court-ship of Aurelia, who becomes "infected" by "Sir Launcelot's extrav-agance" and challenges to "eclipse his rival even in his own lunatic sphere," finds himself initially without a challenger when Launcelot turns down his request for combat (139). Reminiscent of Captain Far-rago in *Modern Chivalry*, who refuses to duel despite that quixotes are supposed to relish a duel, Launcelot, "even in his maddest hours," "never adopted those maxims of knight-errantry which related to chal-lenges."[16] Launcelot had "always perceived the folly and wickedness of defying a man to mortal fight, because he did not like the colour of his beard, or the complexion of his mistress," believing that "chivalry was an useful institution while confined to its original purposes of protect-ing the innocent, assisting the friendless, and bringing the guilty to condign punishment: but he could not conceive how these laws should be answered by violating every suggestion of reason, and every precept of humanity" (141). By refusing to escalate the mimetic rivalry spurred by yet another imitator to the point of destruction, Launcelot displays poise and reason while adhering to his particular code of chivalry, and his particular quixotism. He shows comparable measure when he brings down the corrupt magistrate Gobble on legal grounds. He does likewise when applying to the law to shut down an unscrupulously run madhouse in which he was himself wrongfully imprisoned (a wonderful plot development for a quixote), and again by exacting upon those who deceived and tormented Aurelia "a much more easy, certain, and effectual method of revenge, by instituting a process against them, which . . . subjected them both to outlawry" (190). As Douglas argues, "The events of *Greaves,* at least in part, and the fact that various resolutions in the novel are facilitated by legal action, validate its hero's rhetoric and his faith in the law."[17]

Each time Launcelot is wronged or imprisoned, he is vindicated both by law and the esteem of others, though his imitators—the well-meaning Crowe and the villain Sycamore—are frequent objects of unredeemed scorn and humiliation. In this way, Smollett's quixote actually lies outside the conventional model for quixotes and their conventionally blighted track records. Smollett consciously demonstrates that quixotism is not flatly synonymous with madness. Though the idea of Launcelot's madness occupies center stage in the novel, Smollett's text is rather definitive about the auspiciousness of Launcelot's condition, however we characterize it. We can understand why Gulliver undergoes quixotic conversion, however unsuccessful it is in rectifying Gulliver's exceptionalist outlook, but Launcelot's conversion is perplexing.

For a quixote whose madness is already complicated by his many successful acts of heroism, and the measured and rational means by which he carries out these acts, Launcelot's quixotic conversion is a perplexing factor more than an interpretive indication or resolution. As I have suggested, what separates Launcelot from other quixotes is not his good nature and goodwill toward others, especially those he perceives to be under duress—this is, as Easson rightly acknowledges, "a highly developed Quixotic characteristic"—but his ability to perceive real injustices with accuracy, and address them not (usually) with vigilantism or violence but instead through the application of the law and of good sense.[18] Though Launcelot is certainly a comic figure at his own expense (and at the expense of quixotism more generally), Smollett's romanticized rewriting of the quixote story presents Launcelot as a far more sane and effectual character than British quixotic contemporaries like Lennox's Arabella, Fielding's Parson Adams, or Swift's Gulliver. Launcelot's relative sanity and success in quixotism—his complication of the notion of quixotism itself—raise the questions, From what, and to what, does Launcelot convert?

Further complicating Launcelot's conversion scene is that it functions in no way as a resolution to Smollett's novel, in the strictest sense, because Launcelot's conversion takes place little more than midway through the narrative. The series of events leading up to the conversion moment, and immediately following it, provide essential context for what is otherwise a very brief and subtle quixotic conversion. After having been separated from his beloved Aurelia, and operating under the false impression (conveyed by a fraudulent letter) that Aurelia did not love him back, Launcelot has a chance meeting with her and learns then that she indeed loves and esteems him and that "that fatal sentence . . . which drove [him] out an exile for ever from the paradise of [her] affection" was actually a forgery (116). Upon this meeting with Aurelia we get a brief indication that, in her presence and with the realization of her as an attainable object of desire, Launcelot begins the process of quixotic conversion, hinting at some recognition of his quixotism as a form of madness. "Cut off . . . from the possession of what my soul held most dear," explains Launcelot, "I wished for death, and was visited by distraction.—I have been abandoned by my reason—my youth is for ever blasted" (115–16).

At the same time, however, his heart begins "to palpitate with all the violence of emotion," indicating that he is also in the process of taking on a highly romanticized madness of a different sort: a violently impassioned desire for Aurelia, his lost lover returned (117). Having learned, further, that Aurelia's guardian is embroiled in a plot to portray her as a madwoman and have her locked up in an asylum, Launcelot continues to emote more drastically than he has to this point in the novel: Launcelot "bit his nether lip" and "rolled his eyes around" (118). By this point, Launcelot has not undergone quixotic conversion, but he has begun moving toward it after seeing Aurelia, and learning that her initial rejection of him—the catalyst for his quixotism—was actually a scheme hatched by her guardian, Anthony Darnel, against the two young lovers.

Launcelot's meeting with Aurelia is cut short, however, when he hears the cries of a traveler being accosted by robbers on the nearby road and dashes off to aid the victim, forebodingly leaving Aurelia behind. As Smollett writes: "The supposition of such distress operated like gunpowder on the disposition of our adventurer, who, without considering the situation of Aurelia, and indeed without seeing, or being capable to think on her, or any other subject, for the time being, ran directly to the stable, and mounting the first horse which he found saddled, issued out in the twilight, having no other weapon but his sword" (118–19). As Launcelot rides in search of the distressed traveler, incapable in the moment of thinking of Aurelia, his initial movement toward quixotic conversion begins to recede. He thinks of himself, curiously and counterintuitively, as "some hero of romance mounted upon a winged steed, inspired with reason, directed by some humane enchanter, who pitied virtue in distress" (119). Finding that the distressed traveler was none other than his squire, Timothy Crabshaw, who has been roughed up by the assailants, Launcelot summons a doctor to make sure the squire's health is in good order, finally precipitating the quixotic conversion scene. Fittingly, Launcelot has his conversion after seeing a doctor, though, in Smollett's ironic twist, the doctor's patient is not the quixote, but the Sancho.

Launcelot's actual quixotic conversion comes shortly after this interlude with Aurelia and occupies no more than a few lines of the text. In fact, as it occurs among a catalogue of quotidian concerns in the life of a quixote and endures for only a few paragraphs of the narrative, readers might easily pass over the conversion moment altogether. After seeing to Timothy Crabshaw's health and engaging in pleasant conversation with the "witty," learned, and agreeable doctor (whose first impression of Launcelot is that he is mad, though the doctor quickly changes his mind), Launcelot settles his bills, then undergoes quixotic conversion: "Next day, Crabshaw being to all appearance perfectly recovered, our adventurer reckoned with the apothecary, payed the landlord, and set out on his return for the London-road, resolving to lay aside his armour at some distance from the metropolis: for, ever since his interview with Aurelia, his fondness for chivalry had been gradually abating" (128). In this moment, we find Launcelot casting aside his traditional or superficial characteristics of quixotism—his anachronistic donning of armor, his knight-errantry, and his preoccupation with the ideals of chivalry—in a midnovel transformation of the end-of-novel quixotic conversion motif.

Having abandoned this mode of quixotism, however, Launcelot instantly reverts to a different mode of quixotic behavior, or a degree of madness that arguably outdoes his prior form of quixotism. Immediately following the narration of Launcelot's "gradually abating" fondness for chivalry, we are told that, "as the torrent of his despair had disordered the current of his sober reflection, so now, as that despair subsided, his thoughts began to flow deliberately in their antient channel. All day long he regaled his imagination with plans of connubial happiness, formed on the possession of the incomparable Aurelia" (129). Here Launcelot's prior quixotism—the result of having thought himself spurned by Aurelia—begins to return as his imagination begins to work once more on thoughts of Aurelia. With Aurelia now firmly in his sights, Launcelot rides calmly toward London, fantasizing about "connubial happiness." In the immediate paragraph following his conversion, Launcelot reverts to his original mode of quixotism. As he approaches a mob of "men and women, variously armed with flails, pitch-forks, poles, and muskets" cornering a lance-wielding figure on horseback, Launcelot, "not so totally abandoned by the spirit of chivalry," takes off to rescue the cornered knight: "Without staying to put on his helmet, he ordered Crabshaw to follow him in the charge against those plebians: then couching his lance, and giving Bronzomarte the spur, he began his career with such impetuosity as overturned all that happened to be in his way; and intimidated the rabble to such a degree, that they retired before him like a flock of sheep" (129). The experience of discovering that the knight he rescued from the mob was none other than Captain Crowe, his ineffectual imitator, urges Launcelot yet more intensely back into quixotism.

As we can see, a sign of Launcelot's sustained madness through what appears at first like a conversion moment is his inability to resist certain stimuli without reacting violently, either with martial violence otherwise uncharacteristic of him or with violent emotions. Launcelot reacts chivalrously when he beholds someone in distress, and he experiences drastic changes of mood and outlook each time Aurelia departs from or enters into his immediate considerations. For Boucé, Smollett's description of Launcelot's impetuousness—that hearing the cries of distress "operated like gunpowder" on Launcelot's state of mind—"stresses Launcelot's blind obedience to this impulse which promptly suspends all his rational faculties" (118–19).[19]

If we understand quixotism merely in the mimetic sense of Launcelot behaving like a chivalric knight-errant, however, then we miss the fact that Launcelot remains quixotic, even in the interlude during which he casts off his armor in pursuit of Aurelia. As Boucé argues: "The irony of Launcelot's decision to abandon armour and chivalry becomes immediately obvious. He renounces one form of madness only to plunge straightaway into another, to wit sweet daydreams of the happiness he will enjoy with Aurelia."[20]

With respect to Launcelot's quixotism, we can observe a progression leading up to and through his conversion moment. Though Launcelot acknowledges that having been jilted by Aurelia is what led him to be "abandoned by [his] reason," his actions in the beginning of the novel, after having been turned "mad" by this jilting, are for the most part measured, benevolent, and rational (116). Despite the fact that he goes about on horseback and in one-hundred-year-old armor, the particularity of Launcelot's quixotism is, as I have suggested, that he believes that "madness and honesty are not incompatible" and behaves as such, practicing a largely successful brand of quixotism that, as Easson and others have pointed out, provides the reader with "little direct experience of an insane Launcelot" (59).[21] Launcelot's mode of quixotic exceptionalism—which allows him to function simultaneously as a skeptic toward and successful manipulator of the law in his pursuit of justice—is, like that of Parson Adams or Updike Underhill, that of the honest madman, or the visionary revisionist.

Once the possibility of realizing his passion for Aurelia is renewed upon their chance meeting about halfway through the novel, the measured quixote begins to act with more emotion and impetuousness than he had previously. He quits Aurelia suddenly when he hears cries of distress, irrationally leaving Aurelia vulnerable to the kidnapping (which, in conjunction with the attack on Crabshaw, was all by design to divert Launcelot). Then, having returned to find that she had been kidnapped, Launcelot is bizarrely content. He is "on a candid scrutiny of his own heart . . . much less unhappy than he had been before his interview with Aurelia; for, instead of being as formerly tormented with the pangs of despairing love, which had actually unsettled his understanding, he was now happily convinced that he had inspired the tender breast of Aurelia with mutual affection" (125). Pleased with having been relieved of the "pangs of despairing love," even though Aurelia has just been kidnapped, Launcelot gains satisfaction from the plot twist that turns his pursuit of Aurelia into a more traditional romance narrative: his beloved has been kidnapped, and it is now her knight's duty to rescue her. In the very moment in which Launcelot appears to retire his interest in chivalry, he embarks on a classically chivalric mission, emboldened by the promise of Aurelia, continuing in this revised quixotic mode in a manner more mad and impetuous than before.

What this ultimately amounts to is that Smollett's heavily ironized quixotic conversion scene depicts the shedding of the overt trappings of quixotism (conversion) alongside a stark intensification of Launcelot's madness and impetuous behavior. Though Launcelot notably resolves to take his time on his way into London in pursuit of Aurelia, thinking it more prudent to "wait with patience, until the law should supersede the authority of her guardian," he does so, tellingly, so as not to "hazard the interest of his passion" (129). Smollett's language here is loaded: Launcelot aims carefully not just to "hazard" Aurelia, who is "the interest of his passion," but also not to hazard the interest of his passion itself, which has begun to alter his entire quixotic approach.

Launcelot's degree of madness is a function of his relationship with Aurelia, and the prospects of that relationship, while his quixotism of law remains a separate factor and is sustained even as the objects of his immediate idealism shift. Whether his present concerns are primarily upholding the law, rescuing the endangered, aiding the poor and downtrodden, or pursuing Aurelia as a love interest, Launcelot proceeds quixotically. His exceptionalist perspective on the role and application of the law cause him to esteem the law as an institution and a corrective mechanism while at the same time fighting to address its shortcomings. His impulsive need to rescue imperiled travelers and stand up for the poor is fueled by a more traditional quixotic idealism, a belief in the basic laws of chivalry. And his pursuit of Aurelia fills him with so much passion and emotional and sensory overload that it diffuses his otherwise logical and prudent apprehension of the world around him, drawing him into a similarly traditional quixotic world of abducted ladies in distress and the heroic knights who come to their rescue. The qualitative change in Launcelot's brief, midnovel conversion moment, then, is not from quixotism to sanity—a "cured" quixote—but from Launcelot's characteristic version of measured and effective quixotism to an impetuous quixotism focused on Aurelia, his Dulcinea, and more closely resembling earlier interpretations of quixotism as chivalric madness. It is important to emphasize that even this conversion moment is fleeting, such that Launcelot is launched back into his prior form of measured, legalistic quixotism just as impetuously as he was moved, briefly, to abandon it.

There remains one final element of Launcelot's quixotism worth mentioning. Though Smollett gives a clear nod to the tradition of quixotic conversion in Launcelot's midnovel conversion moment, placing what is typically an end-of-novel confession rather subtly amid the midnovel height of action, Smollett's closing chapter also hints less explicitly at quixotic conversion. After Launcelot rescues Aurelia, finding the "leisure to unravel the conspiracy which had been executed against his person," he chooses rather coolly to avenge the conspiracy by way of the law rather than hunting the conspirators down on horseback to vanquish them with a violent attack, as Don Quixote might have done (189). Boucé reads this aspect of the final chapter as an indication that, by painting Launcelot as a figure of measure by the novel's end, "Smollett confirms that Launcelot is definitely cured." However, it is also clear that a quixotic belief in the power of the law, which proves a precarious position, has been a significant part of Launcelot's default quixotism all along, a quixotism of law that remains with him through the novel's end. Though *Launcelot Greaves* comes together in the end in a tidy manner similar to the ending of *Joseph Andrews,* Launcelot never actually experiences an end-of-novel conversion. That is, Launcelot, like Fielding's Parson Adams, never actually has his quixotic expectations shattered, let alone seriously challenged. Instead, he has his quixotism logically and empirically affirmed by his considerable successes.

What this suggests about quixotic conversion in *Launcelot Greaves,* foremost, is that Smollett's novel, despite being typically read by both his contemporaries and ours as a somewhat slavish imitation of *Don Quixote,* is actually, like *Gulliver's Travels,* a prime example of the eighteenth-century British departure from the hard-and-fast traditions of the quixotic narrative in its strictest, most imitative sense. Just as in *Gulliver's Travels* we can observe the emergence of quixotic behavior in Gulliver that is not superficially or allusively tied with Cervantes's *Don Quixote,* we can see in *Launcelot Greaves* an inverse narrative strategy: Launcelot appears ostensibly and unmistakably, both to Ferret and to critics, "a modern Don Quixote," yet his quixotism is a radical departure from quixotism in the referential sense, the superficial aspects of Don Quixote's appearance, attire, and antiquated mannerisms (15). Smollett rewrites the quixote story, providing readers with all of the salient trappings of quixotism, but twisting the effect of quixotism such that it becomes the basis not of folly, but of the successful pursuit of justice.

10

Knickerbocker and Reactionary Exceptionalism

Like *Launcelot Greaves,* Washington Irving's *A History of New York* (1809) is guided by the question of whether the legal system works as advertised. Among the central political concerns of US elites at the turn of the nineteenth century was whether the recent legacy of the Constitution had laid sufficient groundwork for the US to flourish in the new century. Washington Irving conceived of a quixote in Diedrich Knickerbocker who would rewrite the nationalist history of the US as an homage not to landmark eighteenth-century moments like the Declaration of Independence or the drafting of the Constitution, but to the halcyon days of liberal Dutch settlement well before the establishment of the US state. In this sense *A History of New York* takes a critique of US legalism as a basis for proffering a reactionary quixotism, one that reaches back before the glorified founding of the US state to a putatively simpler and nobler time.

Knickerbocker, the fictional historian of Irving's *A History of New York,* made his first public appearance in the October 26, 1809, edition of the *New-York Evening Post.* In an elaborate hoax, Irving introduced Knickerbocker in a series of letters to the *Post* under the persona of a landlord who claims that a mysterious "elderly gentleman, dressed in an old black coat and cocked hat" and "not entirely in his right mind," had disappeared from his lodgings without settling his bill. But the gentleman did leave behind a "curious" manuscript. In Irving's following letter to the *Post,* again under the landlord persona, the landlord claims that if Knickerbocker does not return to pay his bill, he will endeavor to recover the balance by publishing Knickerbocker's abandoned manuscript.[1] Thus unfolded Irving's ingenious plot, which created, in the vernacular of viral marketing, a buzz surrounding the publication of *A*

History of New York, a mock-historical narrative Irving penned in the persona of the quixotic historian, Knickerbocker.[2]

Fittingly, in light of Irving's public hoax in the *Post,* we get to Knickerbocker's narration in *A History of New York* by way of an "account of the Author" by "the public's humble servant," Seth Handaside, a landlord who houses Knickerbocker before Knickerbocker mysteriously absconds without paying for his room and board, leaving behind instead a manuscript, "History of New York." What follows is Knickerbocker's "most excellent and faithful" history, as published by Handaside, in which Knickerbocker assumes the narrative mantle of quixotic historian.[3] The history chronicles the earliest seventeenth-century Dutch settlements in the Manhattan area, what Knickerbocker terms the "Dutch Dynasty," from the generally placid reign of its first governor, Wouter Van Twiller (Wouter the Doubter), through the embattled tenure of its second governor, Wilhelmus (William) Kieft (William the Testy), to the final era of Dutch reign, that of the heroic Peter Stuyvesant (Peter the Headstrong, Peter the Great), leading up to the British takeover that made Dutch New Amsterdam into British New York.

Though *A History of New York* includes plenty of Quixote allusions and a second quixotic hero, Peter Stuyvesant, with a Sancho-like sidekick in the trumpeter Antony Van Corlear, it is Knickerbocker's quixotism that drives *History*'s critique of American exceptionalism and Jeffersonian legalism. Foremost, Knickerbocker proceeds with a basic form of quixotic exceptionalism in his approach to the act of writing history. Knickerbocker likens "the writer of a history" to "an adventurous knight, who having undertaken a perilous enterprise, by way of establishing his fame, feels bound in honour and chivalry, to turn back for no difficulty nor hardship, and never to shrink or quail whatever enemy he may encounter" (412). In this way Knickerbocker succinctly describes his reactionary quixotism, a propensity to find greatness in the past even as history itself casts doubt on the notion that it was better then than now. As quixotic historian, Knickerbocker holds an idealistic view of his role in "rescu[ing] from oblivion the memory of former incidents, and . . . render[ing] a just tribute of renown to the many great and wonderful transactions of our Dutch progenitors." In so doing he romanticizes the idle, law-averse rule of Wouter Van Twiller as a golden age in which no legal intervention was necessary to keep the peace (377).

In a manner similar to that of Parson Adams and Captain Farrago, Knickerbocker positions himself above, or as exception to, other historians whose truth claims must withstand the scrutiny of historiography that Knickerbocker applies to other histories but not to his own. Apart from recurring claims that his is a true history, unerring in its devotion to fact by virtue of Knickerbocker's skill and alacrity for the task, he also believes himself a wholly objective historian. Distinguishing himself from booksellers and literary writers, Knickerbocker writes:

> To let my readers into a great literary secret, your experienced writers, who wish to instil peculiar tenets, either in religion, politics or morals, do often resort to this expedient—illustrating their favourite doctrines by pleasing fictions on established facts—and so mingling historic truth, and subtle speculation together, that the unwary million never perceive the medley; but, running with open mouth, after an interesting story, are often made to swallow the most heterodox opinions, ridiculous theories, and abominable heresies. . . . I will proceed with my history, without claiming any of the privileges above recited. (511–12)

Irving is self-aware in writing Knickerbocker, allowing Knickerbocker to put forth a number of theories that stretch the limits of logic, draw comically overdetermined connections between historical events, and arrive at spurious conclusions. Yet Knickerbocker, in his criticisms of various authors before him, remains oblivious to the fact that he partakes of precisely the underhanded narrative strategies that he rails against. This understanding—or misunderstanding—is the result of Knickerbocker's quixotic idealism about the truth-seeking and truth-affirming potential of historians and historical writing. Knickerbocker's frequent reliance upon classical texts, bookish demonstration of erudition and classical learning, and grandiose approach to his history (starting with chapters on "a Description of the World, from the best Authorities," "Cosmogony," and "peopling America" before getting to the subject of New York's Dutch roots) give rise to a historical narrative comically unaware of its place within broader historiography, denying as such the concept of historiography itself. Knickerbocker hails from a line of ancestors named for a bookish characteristic: as he tells us, his family name is derived from "*Knicker* to nod, and *Boeken* books; plainly meaning that [his ancestors] were great nodders or dozers over books" (631). He fashions himself a historian above history, arising from a lineage of tenacious readers, writing with greater purpose and gravity than the common historian, bookseller, or fiction writer.

Like Parson Adams and Captain Farrago, Knickerbocker possesses nostalgia for the past, a generally backward-oriented outlook, which characterizes his reactionary quixotism. And like Arabella and Dorcasina, Knickerbocker's nostalgia is for a foreign culture. The progression of his history of the Dutch settlers of the New York region takes something of an eschatological path, tracing events from the "golden reign" of the "renowned" Wouter Van Twiller and his "unparalleled virtues" as governor in book 3, to the "fearful" wrath of William the Testy that begins the decline of the Dutch dynasty in book 4, to the heroic struggles of Peter Stuyvesant that lead to the ultimate end of New Amsterdam, and the transition into British-ruled New York in books 5–7 (461–63, 525).

Throughout this progression, people of other nations enter the history and begin to compete more aggressively with the Dutch for land and resources, until the very end of the glorious reign of Wouter Van Twiller. Knickerbocker attributes the decline of Dutch New Amsterdam largely to the policies of William the Testy, which Irving aligns in his satirical way with the progressive policies of the Jeffersonian Democratic-Republicans. Such "progress" during William's governorship—the formation of rancorous political parties, an emphasis placed on education, and the elevation of legislation and the law as virtues in and of themselves—stands in contrast to Wouter Van Twiller's "golden" tenure, in which, "in his council [Van Twiller] presided with great state and solemnity," sitting in a "huge chair of solid oak hewn in the celebrated forest of the Hague," smoking a "magnificent pipe" (465). When Jeffrey Insko calls Irving "a casualty of chronology," arguing that Irving "would seem to be a victim of the very historical processes his historian alter-ego Diedrich Knickerbocker attempts to forestall," he implicitly acknowledges the backward-orientation of Knickerbocker, for whom the present seems never so good as the past.[4] "Luckless Diedrich!" Knickerbocker writes, "born in a degenerate age" (454). Knickerbocker calls our attention to his power to frame narratives for posterity. So when Knickerbocker quotes "unhappy William Kieft!" from the apocryphal "Stuyvesant manuscript," a source Knickerbocker may well have invented, readers get not just a second perspective that aligns with Knickerbocker's, but a perspective colored and rewritten by Knickerbocker himself (550).[5] Knickerbocker's desire to recount the past, and to laud the values of the past in his recounting, is part of his nostalgic or reactionary quixotism, enabled by the fact that, as quixote, he is also author and historian.

In addition to romanticizing his task as a historian and his objects of study, Knickerbocker takes a chivalrous approach to writing history. Like Don Quixote, who seeks fame bestowed upon him by appreciative monarchs, Knickerbocker conceives of historians as "the sovereign censors who decide upon the renown or infamy of . . . fellow mortals." "We are the public almoners of fame," writes Knickerbocker, "dealing out her favours according to our judgment or caprice—we are the benefactors of kings—we are the guardians of truth—we are the scourgers of guilt—we are the instructors of the world—we are, in short, what we are not!" (662). Highlighting the disparity between the power he believes those of his noble profession rightfully exercise and the lack of recognition historians receive, as he sees it, compared to "the lofty patrician or lordly Burgomaster," who "stalk contemptuously by the little, plodding, dusty historian," Knickerbocker puts forth an image of the historian as a simultaneously humble and exalted chivalric knight, an exception to the norms of both scrutiny and praise (662).

Knickerbocker's chivalric style is also evident in the way he addresses his readers, in his antiquated pronouncements and exceedingly formal and courteous language. Akin to how Gulliver speaks to the Lilliputian court, Knickerbocker addresses his readers directly and with plodding formality: "But let not my readers think I am indulging in vain glorious boasting, from the consciousness of my own power and importance," he writes (662). Elsewhere, he apologizes: "I am extremely sorry, that I have not the advantages of Livy, Thucydides, Plutarch, and others of my predecessors" (620). He addresses the reader as "most venerable and courteous" and troubles himself not to "fatigue [his] reader with . . . dull matters of fact, but that [his] duty as a faithful historian, requires that [he] should be particular" (607, 451). Knickerbocker adheres to a chivalric code in his writing as Don Quixote does in his speech and actions. Daniel Williams calls Knickerbocker's sense of authorship "heroic," commenting that authors of Knickerbocker's kind are "ever protective of their readers, guarding them from confused erudition and muddled description." "Both courteous and chivalrous," Williams writes, "Knickerbocker himself paused throughout his narration to caution his readers before plunging them into thick passages."[6] This chivalric breed of authorship reflects Knickerbocker's quixotic outlook, framing him as a quixote whose chivalric code calls on him to lead readers through a narrative adventure, supporting readers through times of presumed distress as the fantastic and outright nonsensical turns of his history unwind.

As we can see then, Knickerbocker's quixotic idealism develops not merely as a romantic view of history and the potency and importance of the historian but also as a literary idealism about the potency of the written word, the structured narrative, the authorial voice, and the cumulative pitfalls and ambiguities of the written text. In other words, Knickerbocker turns the quixotic fallacy on its head: while Don Quixote (like most of his literary offspring) is bewitched by reading romances— or an idealized source-text—and engrossed in the written word to the extent that he takes the exception from fiction as the everyday norm, Knickerbocker is so thoroughly aware of the potency of text that he misleads himself into thinking that *writing* and narration should be handled as though they were producing physical effects on reality in real time.

For Don Quixote, the text is reality, but for Knickerbocker, the text—and thus the author—makes reality. For this reason, Knickerbocker takes his quixotic understanding of the potency of writing a step further, inflating his authorial importance to the extent that, by the end of *History*, Knickerbocker describes himself as fighting alongside his valiant Dutch hero Peter Stuyvesant. As Stuyvesant prepares to ward off a Swedish invasion, Knickerbocker writes: "Trust the fate of our favourite Stuyvesant to me—for by the rood, come what will, I'll stick by Hard-koppig Piet to the last; I'll make him drive about these lossels vile as did the renowned Launcelot of the lake, a herd of recreant Cornish Knights—and if he does fall, let me never draw my pen to fight another battle, in behalf of a brave man, if I don't make these lubberly Swedes pay for it!" (645).

Though Knickerbocker's history is charged with Irving's satirical swipes and ample nods to quixotism and is certainly not written as a thoroughly "serious" history (Irving did write scholarly biographies of George Washington and Christopher Columbus), it does contain a great deal of accurate historical information and scrupulous historical scholarship. In fact, including in *History* a great deal of legitimate historical material was a significant part of Irving's strategy in critiquing through Knickerbocker the prevailing, heavily nationalist historiographical approaches of prominent, early US historians like Jeremy Belknap and Benjamin Trumbull. As Jeffrey Insko writes, "At the time of its publication, *A History of New York* was the best (in fact, the only) account of the early Dutch reign of New York that had yet been published and could thus—and was intended to—take its place" among the work of these "serious" historians.[7]

The historiographical concerns of *A History of New York* function both to "deflate the high moral import of nationalist historiography," as Insko suggests, and to introduce a layered structure and series of clichés, imitated from historians of Irving's time, aimed at challenging the romantic and legalistic tradition of the US "Founding Fathers."[8] From the beginning of his history, Knickerbocker continually alludes to the conventional language of historians justifying their histories. He makes frequent reference to his as "this most accurate of histories"; he makes ample references to classical texts and scholarship; and he draws attention to evidence from historical records or documents, or from "authority still more ancient, and still more deserving of credit, because it is sanctioned by the countenance of our venerated dutch ancestors . . . founded on certain letters still extant" (424, 445).

In these ways Knickerbocker mounts a critique not just of early US historians and historiography, but of what Irving saw as the patrician Democratic-Republicanism of Thomas Jefferson's presidential tenure more specifically, and the founding project of the US more generally. Though Irving is known to have been a Federalist, and to have taken a number of seemingly pro-Federalist stances in *History*, the narrative's ambiguities and contradictions render it a more general burlesque of US legalism, politics, and culture than a coherent political allegory.[9] In this vein, Robert Ferguson identifies *A History of New York* as "the first American book to question the civic vision of the Founding Fathers," Diedrich Knickerbocker being "the natural enemy of . . . rational, legal spokesmen in early American literature."[10]

By taking the law and its practitioners as objects of satire, *History* operates in a way similar to Smollett's *Launcelot Greaves*, reflecting the tendency of both Irving and Smollett to write their own legal concerns into quixotic narratives. Only for Irving, *History* is a unique instance of portraying the quixote as a writer, and the process of writing as a quixotic endeavor, the creation of a quixotic narrative whose turns and adventures are literary in more ways than one.

Having studied and practiced law for ten years before writing *History*, Irving had plenty of reason, in his circumstances, to bring his views on the law and the legal profession to bear on Knickerbocker's quixotism. He initially admired the profession, "admired Cicero, dreamed of success as a heroic citizen before the bar, and made the customary resolution 'to sacrifice *all* to the law.'" Nonetheless, as Irving's notebooks and letters suggest, he soon became jaded in his pursuit of a legal career, applying himself to the study of law with minimal interest and motivation, eventually lamenting that "wrangling drying unmerciful profession" and its "ponderous fathers."[11]

When in 1808 Irving pronounced his love to Matilda Hoffman, the youngest daughter of "Irving's employer and one of the leading lawyers in New York," his employer, Josiah Ogden Hoffman, offered to grant Irving his daughter's hand in marriage, but with the caveat that Irving establish himself more securely as a legal professional. After Irving started writing *A History of New York* on the side—and in a divided state of mind about his professional and personal ambitions—Matilda Hoffman died abruptly of consumption in April 1809, leaving Irving in despair but simultaneously resolving his conflict of interest. Irving then "abruptly 'abandoned all thoughts of the law' and turned for solace to his writing."[12]

As with Smollett and his series of midcentury legal troubles that manifest themselves in caricatures of lawyers and magistrates in *Launcelot Greaves,* Irving's experience with and understanding of the law are evident throughout *History.* Ferguson understands Irving's rejection of the law in Knickerbocker's history as a transformation of Irving's "private alternative to professional ambition" into "a writer's formal act of rebellion," claiming that "Irving's emotional rejection of law—fictionally portrayed through the collapse of New Amsterdam—supplies a dramatic unity and thematic coherence that set *A History of New York* apart from his other imaginative works."[13] This claim finds support in Knickerbocker's innumerable references to the law (or laws) as harmful and inefficient when conceived in abundance, or seemingly reproduced haphazardly and for their own sake.

In contrast to Knickerbocker's characterization of the placid reign of Wouter Van Twiller, in which the Dutch settlers spend so much time eating, smoking, and lazing around that the law need not apply, the ruinous reign of the Thomas Jefferson stand-in, Wilhelmus (William) Kieft, or William the Testy, is one of legal and legislative hyperactivity. As Knickerbocker writes, William the Testy "conceived that the true policy of a legislator was to multiply laws, and thus secure the property, the persons and the morals of the people, by surrounding them with men traps and spring guns, and besetting even the sweet sequestered walls of private life, with quick-set hedges, so that a man could scarcely turn, without the risk of encountering some of these pestiferous protectors" (539–40). Irving goes further to compare William's hyperlegalistic approach to governance, and his propensity to be "continually dipping into books, without ever studying to the bottom of any subject," to Sancho Panza's would-be rule over the fictional island of Barataria in *Don Quixote,* positioning William as something of a quixote wannabe who too frequently resembles a bumbling sidekick instead:

> There is a certain description of active legislators, who by shrewd management, contrive always to have a hundred irons on the anvil, every one of which must be immediately attended to; who consequently are ever full of temporary shifts and expedients, patching up the public welfare and cobbling the national affairs, so as to make nine holes where they mend one—stopping chinks and flaws with whatever comes first to hand. . . . Of this class of statesmen was William the Testy—and had he only been blessed with powers equal to his zeal, or his zeal had been disciplined by a little discretion, there is very little doubt but he would have made the greatest governor of his size on record—the renowned governor of Barataria alone excepted. (535)

The positioning of William the Testy in these terms is part of Knickerbocker's ability to question "the whole legal vision of America upon which Jeffersonianism is based. [Knickerbocker] argues that legal administration favors the rich and contentious over the ignorant poor and that it quickly becomes an instrument of oppression."[14] In the process of writing this argument into his history, Knickerbocker, like Launcelot Greaves, fixates on the law as the primary mechanism of social and political change, whether the law is portrayed as a barrier to productive change (as for Knickerbocker) or a compromised avenue for it (as for Launcelot Greaves).

In light of Knickerbocker's quixotism and the explicitly legal inflection of Irving's satire in *History,* it is necessary to trace the interplay between quixotism and the law through each of the distinct periods of governorship recounted in Knickerbocker's history—those of Wouter Van Twiller, William the Testy, and Peter Stuyvesant—to illuminate the strands of quixotic exceptionalism operating in the text. Before examining the reign of Wouter Van Twiller in book 3, however, the first two books of Irving's narrative merit some attention, as they trace the development of Knickerbocker's quixotism.

Book 1, described by Knickerbocker as "being, like all introductions to American histories, very learned, sagacious, and nothing at all to the purpose," functions primarily as a parody of nationalist histories and grandiloquent historical claims, positioning the narrative as a mock-history, or, in Knickerbocker's understanding, a history to end all histories on the subject (383). It is, for Knickerbocker, "an improvement in history, which [he claims] the merit of having invented" (404). Book 1 also introduces some of Knickerbocker's quixotic tendencies, positioning him as a combatant against the "fiery dragons and bloody giants" of historical writing (412).

Knickerbocker's quixotism continues in book 2, which tells of the Dutch settlers' contact moment with the "new" land, staging the founding moments of the Dutch dynasty in mythical terms. Following from Irving's attack on nationalist historians in book 1, book 2 parallels the mythologizing of national histories and founding moments of the early US with ample allusions to classical myth placed alongside its glorified description of the "fine Saturday morning, when jocund Phoebus, having his face newly washed, by gentle dews and spring time showers, looked from the glorious windows of the east, with a more than usually shining countenance," when Henry Hudson sets off from Holland "to seek a north-west passage to China" (427). In his vindication of the accuracy of Hudson's initial discovery of the region, Knickerbocker continues to reason quixotically, affirming his romantic view of Hudson's discovery despite material evidence to the contrary: "Though all the proofs in the world were introduced on the other side, I would set them at naught as undeserving of my attention" (430). Exceptionalism is manifested here as the recognition of counterevidence and the simultaneous and open refusal to bend to it.

Knickerbocker adds to the mythical and romanticized origins of the Dutch settlement by introducing in book 2 the quaint settlement of Communipaw and the "honest dutch burghers" who occupy it, providing his readers with a primordial picture of Dutch settlement against which we can contrast the increasing complexity of its progression from the first of its governors to the last. Knickerbocker reinforces thereby in his first two books the eschatological bent of his history, and the notion that the mythical simplicity of the "golden" earlier years becomes adulterated by "progress" and increasing legal and governmental complexity (438).

Beginning with the reign of Wouter Van Twiller in book 3, Knickerbocker's narrative takes a polemical turn. As Charlton Laird remarks, "The treatment is more expansive, more personal, less rambling" in book 3.[15] Knickerbocker appears less distant and more invested in creating a favorable portrait of Van Twiller, yet his quixotic romanticizing of the past, introduced in books 1 and 2, persists. At times Irving's irony in writing Knickerbocker comes through in Knickerbocker's sentimental apologia for the past, such that it overpowers Knickerbocker's romanticism. When, for example, Knickerbocker muses about the "further particulars of the Golden Age," noting that "these were the honest days, in which every woman staid at home, read the bible and wore pockets," we get the distinct sense that Irving's ironic authorial voice is making an appearance through the voice of Knickerbocker (438). Nonetheless, book 3 is full of slightly more believable moments of Knickerbocker's quixotic (and law-averse) outlook, moments in which Knickerbocker appears zealous in his judgments. Knickerbocker praises Van Twiller for having so "tranquil and benevolent" a reign that it contained no "single instance of any offender being brought to punishment," which Knickerbocker judges as "a most indubitable sign of a merciful governor" rather than an unambitious and ineffectual one (466). Knickerbocker lauds Van Twiller's "legal acumen" in the very first (and last) case over which the esteemed governor presides, in which Van Twiller rules on a grievance of fraudulent refusal to settle an account by counting the leaves in each party's account books, weighing them in his hands, and pronouncing the accounts perfectly "balanced" thereby (466–67). Thereafter, "not a single law suit took place throughout the whole of his administration," a mark, for Knickerbocker, of Van Twiller's great success as governor (467).

In numerous examples of this sort, Knickerbocker characterizes Van Twiller's reign not just by Van Twiller's passivity and refusal to engage in the legalistic policies and practices that will become hallmarks of the early US republic but also by his ability to avoid legal and legislative solutions to the grievances of individuals in the community. Among these avoided practices, even, is the selection of government officials under the guise of choosing leaders for their erudition, experience, and intellectual credentials, or even for their popularity, such that their sovereignty is derived from democratic processes. Van Twiller is clearly different from US elected officials, "those worthy gentlemen, who are whimsically denominated governors, in this enlightened republic—a set of unhappy victims of popularity." Knickerbocker writes with fondness that "the dutch governors enjoyed that uncontrolled authority vested in all commanders of distant colonies and territories" (468). Similarly, the burgomasters "were generally chosen by weight—and not only the weight of the body, but likewise the weight of the head" (the rationale behind this is that "the body is in some measure an image of the mind," and that a board of rotund magistrates will "think, but very little" and be "less likely to differ and wrangle about favourite opinions—and as they generally transact business upon a hearty dinner, they are naturally disposed to be lenient and indulgent in the administration of their duties") (469–71). Additionally, from his descriptions of the admirable qualities of "good housewives" and the constant, relaxed ways of the patriarchal family of "those happy days" under Van Twiller, Knickerbocker conveys a sense that, beyond the political affairs of the Golden Age, traditional values are preferable to any gestures toward a disruptive progress (478–79).

Van Twiller's Golden Age is, then, the comically romanticized historical background against which Knickerbocker sets the subsequent decline of the Dutch dynasty in *History*. Much like Updike Underhill's romanticizing of and apologies for the principles and tendencies of his ancestor Captain John Underhill (whom Updike tells us is liberalized while living among the Dutch) in *The Algerine Captive,* Knickerbocker's romance novels are "true histories" of the Golden Age of early, prerepublican settlement in North America.

Toward the end of book 3 and Van Twiller's reign, we already glimpse the movement of Irving's satirical focus toward issues within his contemporary republic during the Jefferson presidency (1801–9), despite the fact that Irving's critical attention to Jeffersonianism is more pronounced and extensive in book 4. Chapter 6 of book 3 gives an account of "the ingenious people of Connecticut and thereabouts," whose rights-based and legalistic discourse Knickerbocker criticizes before tackling the same tendencies in William the Testy in book 4. While Tyler's Updike Underhill makes exceptionalist apologies in *The Algerine Captive* for the illiberal treatment of his ancestor, which he describes as "those few dark spots of zeal, which clouded [the] rising sun" of the early settlers' liberal discourse, Knickerbocker tempers his apologetic tendencies for "the zeal of these good people" of Connecticut "to maintain their rights and privileges unimpaired," claiming that this zeal "did for a while betray them into errors, which it is easier to pardon than defend" (Tyler 18–19; Irving 494–95). Updike's ancestor is cast out of New England because of religious intolerance, the very subject of Knickerbocker's grievances against the people of Connecticut in chapter 6. And, like Royall Tyler, Irving, through Knickerbocker, takes past illiberal behavior as a point of departure for critiquing his contemporary republic:

> Where then is the difference in principle between our measures and those you are so ready to condemn among the people I am treating of? There is none; the difference is merely circumstantial.—Thus we *denounce,* instead of banishing—We *libel* instead of scourging—we *turn out of office* instead of hanging—and where they burnt an offender in propria personae—we either tar and feather or *burn him in effigy*—this political persecution being, some how or other, the grand palladium of our liberties, and an incontrovertible proof that this is *a free country!* (496)

The use of the legalese "in propria personae" as a pun—in the legal sense, to mean appearing on one's own behalf without an attorney present, and in the literal sense (in the context of this passage), to be burned "in one's own person," or to have one's body burned—provides commentary on both the illiberal practice of burnings at the stake in the absence of a legitimate trial (and legitimate legal representation) for the accused and the ways in which a more sophisticated, rights-based legal framework in the early republic was nonetheless ineffectual when it came to protecting one's body from less severe but comparably archaic punishments like tarring and feathering. The legalistic critique is wholly present in book 3, leading into the decline of the Van Twiller governorship and the trials of the following reign of William the Testy.

As I have suggested, the book 4 governorship of William the Testy is the primary site of legal and republican critique in *History,* or is at least the section on which critics have focused most intently in discussions of Knickerbocker's satirical turn. Laird notes that in book 4, "the satire becomes dominant and loses some of its genial impersonality," attentive to the recognizable and much-discussed pillorying of Thomas Jefferson in the personage of William the Testy.[16] Book 4 is also a curious section of the narrative in light of Knickerbocker's description of the villain William the Testy in quixotic terms.

The central strategy of Knickerbocker's criticism of William's reign is to present William as, as the first chapter heading of book 4 suggests, one who "may learn so much as to render himself good for nothing" (511). While writing William as the scapegoat for the decline of the Dutch dynasty and the transition away from the antiquated values of the Golden Age of Van Twiller, Knickerbocker unconsciously mocks the standards of pompous erudition, along with the quixotic investment in book-learning, that he himself possesses. As Knickerbocker writes, William makes a "gallant inroad into the dead languages"; and what he "chiefly valued himself on, was his knowledge of metaphysics, in which, having once upon a time ventured too deeply, he came well nigh to being smothered in a slough of unintelligible learning . . . from the effects of which he never perfectly recovered" (514). In these ways William is not just a satirized stand-in for Jefferson, but a vehicle for portraying the Jeffersonian emphasis on classical learning as a quixotic characteristic.

Knickerbocker's quixotism emerges as a critique not only of Jeffersonian legalism but of American exceptionalism more broadly. Knickerbocker's task in his writerly quest is to give an account of an underacknowledged history while critiquing an especially legalistic Democratic-Republicanism (especially in its Jeffersonian form), "demolish[ing]" along the way "the intellectual foundations for a progressive interpretation of American culture."[17] In looking "to a golden age of simplicity and virtue in much the way as Blackstone or a whig historian regards Anglo-Saxon England with its pure legacy of immemorial common law," Knickerbocker lambastes not just a history of American exceptionalism but also the ongoing exceptionalist attitudes produced by the rhetoric of the "Founding Fathers," "in which opponents were either fools, unpatriotic knaves, or traitors." For this reason—the limited leniency for critique as radical as *History* allowed by the political climate in Irving's early US—Irving turns to "the saving mask of comic humor" to render his satire more effective.[18] This recognition that a turn to comic humor would be more politically viable makes the quixotic narrative mode a fitting vehicle for Irving's (and Knickerbocker's) critical interventions.

Toward these ends, Knickerbocker's quixotism becomes more literal toward the end of the narrative, as he endows the *other* hero of the text, Peter Stuyvesant, with chivalric qualities that mirror those with which he endows himself as historian. Knickerbocker describes Stuyvesant, with his trumpet-bearing sidekick Antony Van Corlear in tow, as a "Cavalier" engaged in "knight-errantry," brave, and chivalrous, proceeding into battle alongside Knickerbocker, his historian-protector, who "can just step in, and with one dash of my pen, give . . . a hearty thwack over the sconce" (644). In these passages, Knickerbocker's riff on the pen-sword conceit draws its comic value from the fact that Knickerbocker does not understand this relationship as a metonymic one.

While Knickerbocker writes as though he possesses the power to alter history with the stroke of a pen as one could with a swipe of the sword, he also recurrently posits his history as, as I have suggested, unwaveringly true—a singular, true history—which is not susceptible to the scrutiny that historiography brings to bear on historical account. In Knickerbocker we see a combination of three beliefs in particular—the belief in the absolute truth of his historical account (the removed, ahistorical quixote), the belief in the author's pastoral duty to the reader (the practice of authorial chivalry), and the belief in the absolute potency of the act of historical writing (the inverted quixotic fallacy)—that produce an inversion of the reading quixote, a writing quixote who, antilegalism notwithstanding, appears all too similar in temperament to Brackenridge's Captain Farrago and the early US legislative elite. Whereas Don Quixote believes in the absolute potency of reading and in the absolute truth of the books he consumes, Knickerbocker believes he can rewrite history. Both kinds of beliefs underlie the quixotic conflation of narrative and physical reality. Only Knickerbocker writes himself so thoroughly into his historical narrative that historiography proves no viable means of extraction.

We should thus broaden the critical focus on satirizing Thomas Jefferson in book 4 to understand William the Testy as a quixotic idealist with his head buried too deeply in books for him to govern properly.[19] William is, like Quixote, a combative figure, taking rhetoric and the law as instruments of battle. William wages a type of warfare against the encroaching Yankees by "the art of fighting by proclamation." When he employs the method of "defeating the Yankees by proclamation," constructing a proclamation "perfect in all its parts, well constructed, well written, well sealed and well published," in the hope that "the Yankees should stand in awe of it," they instead "treated it with the most absolute contempt" (519). William's bookish idealism proves ridiculous in the face of the Yankees' continued encroachment upon the Fort Goed Hoop; yet this exposure of such a tactic as absurd only emphasizes the quixotic absurdity of Knickerbocker's eventual authorial strategy in book 6 of fighting alongside the valiant Peter Stuyvesant with the historian's pen. Likewise, when William attempts to protect his city by erecting "a great windmill on one of the bastions," the quixotic historian Knickerbocker explains in a critical tone the quixotic martial policies of William the Testy (527). As I mentioned previously, William battles domestic difficulties with a legalistic approach, presiding over

the introduction and expansion of "petty courts," the building of a gal-
lows, and the proliferation of lawyers and "bum-bailiffs" (539–40). On
this point, Knickerbocker resumes his disdainful attitude toward the
law, separating himself once again from the quixotism of William the
Testy with an ironic blow:

> I would not here, for the whole world, be thought to insinuate any
> thing derogatory to the profession of the law, or to its dignified
> members. Well am I aware, that we have in this ancient city an
> innumerable host of worthy gentlemen, who have embraced that
> honourable order, not for the sordid love of filthy lucre, or the
> selfish cravings of renown, but through no other motives under
> heaven, but a fervent zeal for the correct administration of justice,
> and a generous and disinterested devotion to the interests of their
> fellow citizens! (541)

Knickerbocker goes on to lament the overabundance of lawsuits and
the "herds of pettifogging lawyers that infest" the courts during the
reign of William the Testy, further distancing this progression from the
Golden Age of Van Twiller (542).

Book 4 is, then, an opportunity for Irving to mirror Knickerbocker's
quixotism in the quixotic William the Testy, lending a characteristic
double edge, or a critique of quixotism, to Knickerbocker's critique of
his contemporary republicanism and its legal and philosophical foundations. More importantly, however, recognizing the quixotic qualities
of William the Testy provides an essential perspective for understanding Knickerbocker's quixotic exceptionalism. Knickerbocker positions
himself not merely above history as a writer of history but also, in the
process of writing, excuses himself from (or simply fails to acknowledge) the similarities between himself and his objects of critique. While
Knickerbocker mocks William for his pedantic and shortsighted focus
on classical learning and philosophy, Knickerbocker makes constant
references to classical mythology in his glorification of his Dutch ancestors. While Knickerbocker criticizes William's tactic of waging war
with words, he repeats—and literalizes—the very same strategy with
Peter Stuyvesant in book 6. Only when it comes to the law does Knickerbocker's critique of William become more scathingly satirical than
quixotically naïve and exceptionalist.

If book 4's account of the reign of William the Testy permits Knickerbocker to portray quixotism in a negative light, the chronicles of

Peter Stuyvesant, the third and final ruler of the Dutch dynasty, present in books 5–7 a quixote in Stuyvesant who looks more like quixotic hero in the mold of Launcelot Greaves. Stuyvesant's first measure as governor is to dismiss William the Testy's free-talking and cantankerous council members because they "have acquired the unreasonable habit of thinking and speaking for themselves during the preceding reign," reversing the republican trend of William the Testy (569). As a governor, the headstrong Stuyvesant takes a no-nonsense approach comparable to that of Van Twiller. What mainly separates Stuyvesant from his predecessors, however, is his penchant for battle. In writing the reign of Peter Stuyvesant, Knickerbocker's positioning of himself as a quixote becomes more forceful and direct. Rather than writing about the lesser skirmishes between Stuyvesant and his Connecticut adversaries, Knickerbocker, "like that mirror of chivalry, Don Quixote . . . [leaves] these petty contests for some future Sancho Panza of an historian," reserving for Stuyvesant his "prowess and [his] pen for achievements of a higher dignity" (579).

Alongside Knickerbocker, Stuyvesant, who "perhaps had never heard of a Knight Errant," is "a hero of chivalry struck off by the hand of nature at a single heat" (581). He proceeds as though he had "studied for years, in the library of Don Quixote himself" (582). As Knickerbocker and Stuyvesant prepare for "the most horrible battle ever recorded in poetry or prose; with the admirable exploits of Peter the Headstrong," Knickerbocker collapses the narrative strains of the two quixotic figures, writing himself directly into his history (648). "My pen has long itched for a battle—siege after siege have I carried on, without blows or bloodshed," writes Knickerbocker, before joining Stuyvesant in the battle against the Swedes, delivering writerly blows with his pen as a knight-errant does with his sword or his lance (644). With shades of Sterne's narrative approach of commingling the writing of action and the action itself in *Tristram Shandy*, and Fielding's account of Parson Adams's mock-heroics in *Joseph Andrews*, Irving's quixotic narrator, unlike Smollett's more measured Launcelot Greaves, engages in battle with the alacrity of the original Don Quixote.

Despite his prowess in battle, however, the republican-style political culture created under William the Testy becomes the catalyst for Stuyvesant's downfall, and the eventual surrendering of the Dutch dynasty to the British. While Stuyvesant is away in battle, William's political factions become increasingly involved in the political affairs of the settlement, invoking again the patriotic discourse of republicanism (670–71). Under siege from all angles, with Stuyvesant overextended from constant battles, New Amsterdam turns again to the high-minded form of governance of William the Testy's reign, fortifying itself with "resolutions," vacuous displays of patriotism, histrionics, and mob rule (692–95). As the dynasty reaches its "destined end" by way of the British takeover of New Amsterdam and a treaty that renames it New York, it is neither Stuyvesant's mode of quixotism nor of chivalry that marks the end of the dynasty and Knickerbocker's history (as Knickerbocker tells it), but a lack thereof: republican-style politics reemerge to the extent that instead of fighting their enemies in the manner of Stuyvesant, the Dutch settlers resort to ineffectual resolutions (720). As Ferguson notes, "Peter Stuyvesant . . . completes the fall of the Dutch civilization by negotiating legalistic, hence ineffectual, treaties with his neighbors."[20]

In its close, then, Knickerbocker's narrative takes its final jabs at Jeffersonianism. Unlike book 4, however, *History*'s final chapters construe quixotism not as the bookish, legalistic mode of William the Testy, but as the heroic, chivalric, militant mode of Peter Stuyvesant. Alongside this shift, Knickerbocker alters his own quixotic language, referring to himself more explicitly as a chivalric knight, though not without maintaining his bookish, classical references and exceptionalist approach to the writing of history.

Knickerbocker's history winds through each Dutch governor with different narrative inflections. Van Twiller's tenure represents a reactionary Golden Age of inactivity for which Knickerbocker is nostalgic; William's tenure introduces an obsession with legal and legislative solutions to problems that Knickerbocker does not acknowledge would have existed under William's predecessor, drawing Knickerbocker's narrative ire; and Stuyvesant's tenure represents the chivalric final period of the Dutch dynasty struggling to fend off foreign assailants, a period that Knickerbocker treats with writerly zeal. Moving through each of these sections of his history, Knickerbocker's quixotic exceptionalism allows him, as I have suggested, to claim the ultimate validity of what he writes without maintaining ideological consistency or historiographical evenhandedness in his treatment of each of the governors. Reading Knickerbocker as a quixote who employs exceptionalist thinking in his history to uphold an a priori nostalgia for the values of the past, which is also Irving's way of self-consciously mimicking the nationalist exceptionalisms of his contemporary US historians and politicians, one must allow that Knickerbocker is not as self-aware in his historical project as Irving is in his. Or at least, that even if Knickerbocker's history is Knickerbocker's parody, and Knickerbocker is self-aware, he nonetheless exhibits markedly quixotic qualities along with ironic moments of self-awareness like those Don Quixote's interlocutors occasionally witness.

Although Knickerbocker's quixotism is apparent independent of his intentionality or degree of awareness as a fictional narrator of history, the virtually impossible question over the extent to which Knickerbocker is in on his jokes (or Irving's) has preoccupied and confounded readers and critics alike. William Hedges best expresses this conundrum when he questions: "Is he the earnest antiquarian he claims to be or is he idiot or madman? Is he a deliberate falsifier of the past or an ingenious ironist—or is he somehow all of these? Whatever the peculiar persona is, it seems that the reader is continually thrown off balance by wanting or trying to believe him even when what he is saying is absurd."[21]

More recently, Jeffrey Scraba has contended that Knickerbocker's production of a "cultural memory" of New York, in light of challenges to the Dutch history of New York from foreign peoples (and historians), is indeed self-aware. Scraba argues that Irving is not only writing commentary on nationalist historiography in *A History of New York* but that Knickerbocker's narrative is to be read as self-conscious irony as well, or as a kind of quixotic historiography that is nonetheless self-conscious in its use of quixotic motifs.[22]

While the question of whether Knickerbocker's historical account is self-aware has been ongoing in studies of *History*—and whether we can assume a closing of ironic distance between Irving and Knickerbocker—Knickerbocker's quixotism would seem not to allow enough self-awareness to render Knickerbocker more Cervantic than quixotic in his authorship. As Hedges argues in this vein, citing Knickerbocker's tone in his preface "To the Public" and its contradictory elements of seeming genuineness (acknowledgments to the New-York Historical Society) and blatant literary tomfoolery ("all you small fry of literature, be cautious how you insult my new launched vessel . . . lest in a moment of mingled sportiveness and scorn, I sweep you up in a scoop net, and roast half a hundred of you for my breakfast") (378–81):

> While he sounds quite mad, his paradoxical rant makes a weird sense. Yet at almost the same time I am conscious of a secondary reaction, namely that the passage ["To the Public"] mocks the

pride of historians in claiming for themselves the right to award personages "the meed of immortality." So there is confusion: If Knickerbocker is at this point sincere but deluded, he cannot be aware of the satire that Irving is voicing through him. Yet maybe he is aware, maybe he is not mad but very cunning; maybe the irony is not dramatic but, for the persona himself, intentional.[23]

As we can see, Hedges hedges against his initial impression because, given that Knickerbocker is not just a narrative persona but an authorial one, one can never be sure whether his intentionality is the same as or separated from Irving's. In this sense the question of Knickerbocker's self-awareness as a narrator and an author writing a narrative within a narrative is a nonquestion.

If we read Knickerbocker as a quixote himself (and not as a quixotic author, or as Cervantic), as Scraba does, then, as I have suggested, attributing to him such self-awareness of quixotic folly would not overshadow or disqualify his quixotic behavior. As we have seen in Captain Farrago and Launcelot Greaves, a quixote is certainly capable of certain degrees of self-awareness. We must recognize, however, that simply because Knickerbocker is an author in Irving's narrative does not mean he is, by that very fact itself, an omniscient narrator more so than a quixotic character of Irving's.

As Scraba rightly points out, however, regardless of Knickerbocker's level of self-awareness, much of Knickerbocker's mission is to assign a coherent cultural identity to a city that, as Knickerbocker's own history illustrates, actually had a tumultuous past full of changing and conflicting cultural identities. By reclaiming the history of New Amsterdam from the city we now call New York, as Scraba contends, Knickerbocker "challenges the emerging argument, first developed by eighteenth-century historians, and later wholeheartedly embraced by nationalist historians, that the idea of America grew from the Puritan desire for religious freedom."[24] This is to suggest that the near-constant New England Puritan encroachments upon New Amsterdam, depicted in Knickerbocker's history, reflect Knickerbocker's concern that his New Amsterdam, and his early US, could potentially take on an identity not his own (not just a different ethnic or cultural identity but a legalistic, republican identity as well). From this type of anxiety over colonial Swedish and legalistic New England foes in nearby settlements and, perhaps more importantly, over history's role in assigning identities that are eventually folded into cultural memories of place, stems Knickerbocker's quixotic need to document as the only "true history" of New York that of himself and his Dutch ancestors.

This is precisely how mythmaking works. The legends of New Amsterdam's three redoubtable governors, the renderings of the Dutch settlers as an often wretched (but ultimately victimized) lot, the villainy of the New Englanders and the Swedes, and, of course, the heroism of Knickerbocker himself, historian extraordinaire, discoverer of Truth, all emanate from Knickerbocker's exceptionalist production of myth. Though the Dutch Dynasty ultimately falls to the British at the end of the history, a walk around present-day New York City, with its abundance of cafés, restaurants, and bars named "Knickerbocker," to say nothing of the city's professional basketball team, the Knicks, makes clear that Knickerbocker has in fact been quite a successful manufacturer of a particular New York identity.

Essential to this mythical construction of identity is Knickerbocker's quixotism. By making Knickerbocker a quixote, Irving invokes a literary tradition marked by ironic remove or authorial distance, humor, burlesque, and, above all, exceptionalism. Instantly, then, as Knickerbocker's quixotic mien recalls a long intertextual history of untrustworthy narrators and overdetermined readings, the reader of Knickerbocker's history can identify his history of New York as the writings of a quixote. Knickerbocker's numerous comic delusions compound this recognition, from his gratuitously implausible assertions that his is an objectively true history, and the first of its kind, to his shrewd interjection of himself into the historical narrative. As a quixote prone to conflations of myth and reality—exception and example—Knickerbocker is well positioned to write an unselfconscious history—a mythical history—that itself becomes his iconic text—his chivalric romance—circularly driving his quixotic delusion with each stroke of the pen. By making Knickerbocker a quixote whose quixotism is characterized by the construction of myth—the primacy of an idealized Dutch–New Amsterdam cultural identity long since suffused with the historical pluralism of New York—Irving, not Knickerbocker, emerges as Cervantic historiographer.

11

Marauder and Radical Exceptionalism

While Knickerbocker's exceptionalism is reactionary, allowing him to place his account of New York's history above others in the service of celebrating Van Twiller's "golden" reign, Charles Lucas's *The Infernal Quixote* (1801) portrays quixotism as a radical form of exceptionalism. Lucas's quixote, James Marauder, possesses talents and advantages akin to those of Smollett's Launcelot Greaves, though Marauder's idealism is not one of justice under law and for the benefit of the wider community, but one of an unrelenting self-regard that leads to anarchism and libertinism.

The Infernal Quixote typically appears as a footnote rather than a focus in studies of British quixotism and of the anti-Jacobin novel, though it represents a watershed moment for quixotic exceptionalism.[1] To this point I have discussed the exceptionalist tendencies of quixotes as means of intervening in politics at the social, national, and international levels, contending that exceptionalism is a unifying characteristic of quixotes, even as it takes different objects, and even as it results in different political orientations. *The Infernal Quixote* marshals exceptionalism in this way as well, but it also places quixotic exceptionalism directly in conversation with its contemporary political theory, particularly William Godwin's *Political Justice* (1793).

As Susan Staves notes, Marauder is a "more extreme example of . . . the ideological quixote," a vehicle through which Lucas could convey the extent to which he "obviously loathed the very idea of the French revolution."[2] Not only is Lucas straightforward in his loathing of any hint of British sympathy for the French Revolution, but he also included in *The Infernal Quixote* footnotes to passages in Godwin's *Political Justice* that Marauder was meant to expose as dangerous and destructive. In this way *The Infernal Quixote* portrays quixotic exceptionalism as a precondition of radical political theory.

When *Political Justice* first appeared in 1793, it made Godwin something of a celebrity political philosopher. The primacy of reason and rationality underpinned the foundational texts of Enlightenment political philosophy, like Locke's *Two Treatises of Government* (1689), Rousseau's *The Social Contract* (1762), and Burke's *Reflections on the Revolution in France* (1790), all of which made the rational case for stable government despite the fact that government meant giving up certain natural liberties. *Political Justice,* on the other hand, was the first book of political philosophy in the British tradition to make the rational case for anarchism. Godwin did so by offering a compelling critique of Lockean, rights-based individualism, rendering an argument for anarchism from an otherwise unlikely repudiation of individual rights as a driving force of civil society. That is, Godwin rejects the notion of individual rights, claiming rights are "superseded and rendered null by the superior claims of justice." At the same time, however, he elevates "independence of the individual" to a higher status than individual rights, drawing an important distinction between a sense of political justice based in the liberal individual-rights tradition and one based in the liberal individualist tradition of independence from government.[3] For Godwin, independence is not about rights but rather the freedom to develop moral frameworks. As such, *Political Justice* was received as an exception to the dominant strands of eighteenth-century political philosophy.

Godwin, too, was treated as an exception in more ways than one, since his rapid ascent to the stratosphere of political philosophy was met shortly after with a rapid descent into controversy and infamy. He was celebrated as having surpassed the likes of Paine, Locke, Rousseau, and Burke with his new book. *Political Justice* sold for three guineas, ten times more than Burke's *Reflections,* so that when the threatening prospect of the book's radicalism initially came up, William Pitt the Younger is said to have argued against suppressing it on grounds that the book was too expensive to reach a broad enough audience to cause any real problems.[4] William Hazlitt described Godwin in 1793 as "blazed as a sun in the firmament of reputation; no one was more talked of, more looked up to, more sought after." By Hazlitt's account, Wordsworth is said to have told a young student to "throw aside your books of chemistry, and read Godwin."[5] Not surprisingly, then, Wordsworth was an admirer of Godwin, as were Coleridge and Percy Shelley; and Godwin was thought to have been particularly influential upon the young.[6]

But when the French Revolution turned toward the Terror, vindi-cating Burke's much cheaper book and calling Godwin's arguments in *Political Justice* into question, Godwin was made an exception in another way, as a scapegoat for British radicalism in the face of the Terror in France. Wordsworth and Coleridge disavowed Godwin's philosophy amid Pitt's efforts to suppress English radicalism before it might foment into a British version of the most horrifying elements of the French Revolution. As Isaac Kramnick notes, Godwin was singled out for par-ticularly harsh condemnation in the years of the British loyalist back-lash during and immediately after the Reign of Terror. Godwin was a common target in anti-Jacobin pamphlets, associated with atheism and sin and mocked in the press when he and Mary Wollstonecraft—both of whom were open critics of the institution of marriage—decided to wed when Wollstonecraft became pregnant.[7] It is this image of Godwin—as a godless radical, hypocrite, and fomenter of Jacobin malfeasance—to which Lucas responds in *The Infernal Quixote*.

But is this a fair portrait of Godwin? To understand how quixo-tism works in *The Infernal Quixote,* we need to understand what ideas from *Political Justice* Lucas was interested in engaging and undermining. Despite its portrayal in Lucas's novel, *Political Justice* itself warned of the dangers of revolution and of mob mentality and was certainly more nuanced on the issue of marriage than Godwin's detractors gave him credit for. Given that Lucas associates Marauder with both the French Revolution and the Irish Rebellion of 1798, the first of Lucas's read-ings of *Political Justice* that demands attention is the idea that *Political Justice* advocates revolution.

It would be difficult to make a convincing argument that Godwin was a revolutionary and that *Political Justice* advocated revolution, partic-ularly of the kind that transpired in France in 1793–94. Godwin notes in his preface to *Political Justice* that, having read Swift's political writings and the "Latin historians," he was convinced twelve years before writing *Political Justice* that "monarchy was a species of government essentially corrupt." He also credits Rousseau for providing "additional stimulus" and ultimately acknowledges the French Revolution for "the determi-nation of mind which gave birth to [*Political Justice*]" (5). But while the French Revolution was an inspiration for what Godwin called "the desirableness of a government in the utmost degree simple," the French Revolution itself was not a model for achieving the ideal society God-win envisioned in *Political Justice*.

Godwin's central argument is indeed radical, relative to the Enlightenment liberal tradition from which he deviated, but the means by which Godwin envisioned social progress were far from radical or revolutionary. By "government in the utmost degree simple," Godwin meant stripping down the assumptions of social contract to a society in which justice was a consequence not of government, but of reasoned, sincere, moral cultivation of just social relations among individuals. Godwin posited three kinds of authority: the authority of reason, by which, as reasoned persons, we have authority over ourselves; the authority of the esteemed other, by which estimable people influence others who rightly look up to those deserving of esteem; and, finally, the authority of government.[8] For the desirable progression to take place from what Godwin understood as unjust and irrational governmental authority to anarchical society run by the authority of reason and of estimable social models, societies needed to cultivate the preconditions of sincerity, justice, and duty to self and others.

What this amounts to in Godwin's political theory is not bloody revolution but its opposite. Godwin calls for a gradual transition away from reliance on government, a vision of reform whose pace and wariness of abrupt change are much closer to Burke's cautions in *Reflections on the Revolution in France* than to Jacobinism. As Godwin writes, describing this vision:

> Government cannot proceed but upon confidence, as confidence on the other hand cannot exist without ignorance. The true supporters of government are the weak and uninformed, and not the wise. In proportion as weakness and ignorance shall diminish, the basis of government will also decay. This however is an event which ought not to be contemplated with alarm. A catastrophe of this description would be the true euthanasia of government. If the annihilation of blind confidence and implicit opinion can at any time be effected, there will necessarily succeed in their place an unforced concurrence of all in promoting the general welfare. (181–82)

What Godwin calls the "decay" of government—not a radical uprising through immediate political action—is the goal of *Political Justice,* and too abrupt a change would be a serious barrier to the outcomes that most interested Godwin.

We have further evidence that Godwin did not advocate abrupt, radical change. When Godwin became ensnared in the conflict between Pitt's government and the London Corresponding Society, a group seeking suffrage and parliamentary reform, largely inspired by *Political Justice,* Godwin sided against the reformers agitating in his name. The Pitt government took the relatively modest London Corresponding Society to trial for treason in 1794.[9] In a pamphlet Godwin published anonymously, *Considerations on Lord Grenville's and Mr. Pitt's Bills Concerning Treasonable and Seditious Practices and Unlawful Assemblies* (1795), Godwin claims the London Corresponding Society is a threat to social order, its activism premature and impetuous. Quoting Pope—"fools rush in, where angels fear to tread"—Godwin urges recognition of the delicate and volatile nature of "the machine of human society."[10] In the end, Godwin, the supposed radical, not only defended his vision in *Political Justice* from English Jacobin groups like the London Corresponding Society but in so doing aligned himself with the Pitt government's illiberal "Grenville and Pitt Bills," the Treason Act and the Seditious Meetings Act, both of 1795. These are not the actions of a radical revolutionary.

While Godwin's ideas in *Political Justice* constituted a radical departure from the rights-based, contractarian center of Enlightenment political philosophy, Godwin was nevertheless far from radical in the Jacobin sense. "If conviction of the understanding be the compass . . . we shall have many reforms, but no revolutions," writes Godwin; "revolutions are the produce of passion, not of sober and tranquil reason" (186). And perhaps more tellingly, in relation to the reactionary quixotism of Diedrich Knickerbocker, and the radical quixotism of Marauder, Godwin was suspicious of both extreme reactionary politics ("friends of antiquity") and extreme futurism ("friends of innovation"), both of which he deemed "enemies" of "the great cause of humanity" (196).

Beyond general associations of *Political Justice* with Jacobinism, Lucas also focuses in *The Infernal Quixote* on Godwin's views on marriage and on women's rights and education. A central conflict in *The Infernal Quixote*—Marauder's reckless seduction and ruination of Emily Bellaire—makes pointed references to *Political Justice* and its potential to lead virtuous young women like Emily into ruin. While *Political Justice* is perhaps less attentive to the institution of marriage than is Mary Wollstonecraft's *Vindication of the Rights of Woman* (1792) (to which Lucas also reacts), Godwin does devote an appendix to "Co-operation, Cohabitation and Marriage."

As the title of the appendix suggests, Godwin's views on marriage are an extension of his views on cooperation. Godwin reasons from the rhetorical question, "Can there be a good reason for men's eating together, except that they are prompted to it by the impulse of their own minds?" (675). Here he recognizes the importance of social interactions, conversations, and various forms of cooperation for what he calls "moral independence," the ongoing critique that each person in a society levels upon another for the purpose of progressive moral improvement. However, he argues that any otherwise avoidable cooperation—any supererogatory cooperation—should be avoided (674, 679). Cooperation is for Godwin an evil because it demands the interruption of one's own best thoughts and desires as they might lead to "progressive improvement," and thus the sacrificing of time and attention one might otherwise spend pursuing one's own best inclinations and intellections: "The ideas, associations and circumstances of each man are properly his own; and it is a pernicious system that would lead us to require all men, however different their circumstances, to act by a precise general rule. Add to this that, by the doctrine of progressive improvement, we shall always be erroneous, though we shall every day become less erroneous" (678).

It follows from this viewpoint that cohabitation only intensifies the conundrum cooperation introduces, the conflict between humans as social beings who must not withdraw from society, lest they risk interrupting progressive improvement, and humans as reflective beings whose personal time and individual needs are of utmost value. Godwin expresses this conundrum in terms of "the limits of individuality": "Every man that receives an impression from any external object has the currents of his own thoughts modified by force; and yet, without external impressions, we should be nothing. Every man that reads the composition of another suffers the succession of his ideas to be, in a considerable degree, under the direction of his author" (680). As we will see when we come to Marauder's quixotism and seduction strategies in *The Infernal Quixote*, Godwin's recognition that reading necessarily interrupts our thoughts by force is important for thinking about how quixotes read. But the risk of cohabitation that concerns Godwin here is that living in continual proximity with another imposes the likelihood of supererogatory cooperation at every turn. Those who cohabitate risk losing the ability to think and judge for themselves without interruption (681).

Not only are thoughts interrupted, such that cohabitation can "melt our opinions into a common mould," but cohabiting parties face the additional prospect of growing into hostile and unhappy relations with one another (681). "To oblige them to act and to live together," writes Godwin, "is to subject them to some inevitable portion of thwarting, bickering and unhappiness. This cannot be otherwise, so long as men shall continue to vary their habits, their preferences, and their views" (681). Cohabitation, then, is a recipe for both the diminution of the independent, free-thinking self, and the close-quarters struggle over inevitable differences of habit and thought between parties, and the fluctuation of those differences over time.

It is important to understand that when Godwin critiques marriage in *Political Justice,* his critique arises from general principles as opposed to an attempt to specifically target the institution of marriage for radical reform. Godwin's concerns about cooperation and cohabitation precede and inform his concerns about marriage. Living together produces an overfamiliarity between cohabitating parties "where intercourse is too unremitted," such that the politeness one might practice in disagreement or conflict with a stranger can give way to "surliness and invective" between husband and wife or intimate friends (682). Nevertheless, we can understand why Lucas was alarmed by the critique of marriage in *Political Justice,* given the extent to which Godwin critiqued marriage as injurious not simply to the married, but to European societies at large.

Godwin's opposition to marriage is rooted in practical as well as principled observations. Especially relevant to the impact of quixotism on the young and idealistic, Godwin's contention that marriage is "for a thoughtless and romantic youth of each sex to come together, to see each other, for a few times and under circumstances full of delusion, and then to vow eternal attachment" turns the conservative concern about promiscuity on its head. "In almost every instance," observes Godwin, "[romantic youth who marry] find themselves deceived" (682). Marriage is for Godwin too final a proposition, and too much like a monopoly in which exclusive rights of possession over women is the operative motive, what Godwin calls "the most odious selfishness" (682). Such a monopoly creates the preconditions for bickering of the sort any general cohabitation arrangement fosters, as well as for abuse and possessiveness.

In light of this critique, Godwin anticipates responses like the ones Lucas levels in *The Infernal Quixote,* responses centered on the potential of a society to devolve into promiscuity and crass, unstructured, and socially destructive forms of relations between women and men. To address such expectations of "brutal lust and depravity" overtaking European societies, Godwin challenges the assumption that promiscuous relations would be the default human desire in a marriage-free society: "It is a question of some moment whether the intercourse of the sexes, in a reasonable state of society, would be promiscuous, or whether each man would select for himself a partner to whom he will adhere as long as that adherence shall continue to be the choice of both parties. Probability seems to be greatly in favor of the latter" (683). Godwin draws this conclusion based on the rationale that parties who have initiated some form of selection—who saw something of merit in one another from the start— are not likely to forget the merits they saw "when the interview is over" (683). In other words, "friendship . . . may be expected to come in aid of the sexual intercourse, to refine its grossness, and increase its delight" (683). While these arguments for how amorous relationships develop are marshaled in favor of marriage, reasons Godwin, they should apply just as well to relationships out of wedlock.

Godwin points out a number of arguments typically made in favor of marriage that should apply just as well to nonmarital relationships. Inconstancy, for example, is a form of promiscuity; but it only becomes magnified as a grave problem when practiced "in a clandestine manner," as in marriage (684). Raising and educating children well is in the interest of society at large when understood as a benefit of marriage, but the burdens of childcare and education may "be amicably and willingly participated by others" in the event the mother's "share of the burden" is rendered unequal (684). Since marriage is for Godwin a barrier to a more "public" system of educating young people, it inhibits not only healthier and more just courtship and friendship practices but the health of society more broadly (685).

Given the quantity and focus of Lucas's direct references to Godwin's views on government and marriage in *The Infernal Quixote*, we might expect that Marauder's quixotism is a consequence of having read *Political Justice* as avidly as Don Quixote reads chivalric romances, though Marauder's reading habits are only part of his quixotism. Marauder does read the likes of Godwin, Rousseau, and Voltaire, all representatives of Francophone or Francophile radicalism in the novel, but Lucas constructs an image of Marauder from a young age that illustrates how Marauder was always predisposed to forms of political philosophy that Lucas regarded as fundamentally empty and self-serving.

Toward the middle of volume 2 of *The Infernal Quixote*, Lucas schematizes a collection of "modern" and "modernized" philosophies he

deems a threat to order and morality, including "Epicureans," "Illuminati," "Libertinians," "Naturals," "Reasoners," and "Nothingers."[11] For
Lucas, Godwin is a Nothinger, one who abides by the maxim "there is
nothing but what [Nothingers] know—Of course it follows, that they
know everything" (2.289, 285). As Lucas writes, "every Jacobin is of the
sect" (2.291). But most tellingly, Marauder is no mere acolyte of Godwin, but a subscriber to all of these malignant philosophies (2.295).

As I mentioned, however, Marauder was not simply "turned," in quixotic fashion, by any one philosopher or even by any number of them.
Lucas gives us an account of how Marauder was raised and how he came
to regard himself the way he does, and Marauder's upbringing is the root
of his quixotism. I have suggested that while quixotes need not be rich—
as Launcelot Greaves and Marauder both are—they must possess enough
socioeconomic privilege to access and cultivate the high-minded mentality that enables a powerful literary imagination. Lucas opens *The Infernal
Quixote* by contrasting the births of his hero and villain, Wilson Wilson
and Marauder, with the precise effect of demonstrating how Marauder is
raised with an air of superiority—to believe boundlessly in his superiority
at every turn—whereas Wilson is raised with humility. Wilson, the son of
a carpenter, and Marauder, of noble birth, are born on the same day in
the same town, mere moments apart. Whereas Wilson's life demonstrates
how "the seeds of virtue and religion . . . so sedulously planted in his
mind, were now producing their true fruits," Marauder's tutelage leads
him down a path of infamy that he, whom Lucas describes as naturally
"of a dark complexion," appears destined to tread (1.81; 3.26). Nevertheless, Marauder develops a quixotic exceptionalist outlook in perhaps the
purest form we have yet seen (1.15).

When I suggest that Marauder's quixotism is pure quixotic exceptionalism, I mean that his quixotism is not merely defined by his exceptionalist outlook but also perpetually focused on the idea of his own
exceptionality. Parson Adams proceeds with an exceptionalist outlook in attempting to address the injustices in the eighteenth-century
English countryside, and Arabella evinces her exceptionalism in proceeding with a reality that her servants struggle to access; but unlike
Marauder, neither of these quixotes seeks self-aggrandizement for its
own sake. Marauder's is a quixotism of self-possession and self-regard,
and for an important reason. Considering that Godwin's chief remedy
in *Political Justice* for innovating beyond unjust and irrational government is the cultivation of a morally independent self—a self beholden to
the noblest form of authority, the authority of reason one exercises over

oneself—Lucas's critique relies on portraying Marauder's quixotism as a magnified and exalted version of Godwinian individualism. Even in his extreme self-regard Marauder pursues a form of justice, which Lucas associates with Godwin's notion of political justice.

Lucas tells us that Marauder's education from youth differed dramatically from Wilson's education, as the former was conducted "with far greater *éclat*" (Lucas peppers his narration with French words throughout, either as backhanded compliments or overt insults) (1.38). When Wilson and Marauder first meet as children, in a fight over a contest on which Marauder has wagered, we are told Marauder "considered himself an adept at the broadsword; and confident of his strength," and spoke of Wilson as "the carpenter's indolent son," implying Wilson fails to earn equivalence with the position Marauder was born into (1.46, 48). Volume 1 of the novel is filled with intimations about how Marauder views himself as exceptional. Described with dogged frequency as "haughty" or possessing "*hauteur,*" Marauder "saw himself in the first situation in the kingdom, and in every other person, but the Majesty, fancies he beheld an inferior" (1.52). Similarly, Marauder fancied himself a philosopher from a young age and always disdained modesty: " 'What is modesty?' he would say. 'It is a consciousness of some defect or weakness. Is it not proverbial that a villain cannot look you in the face, and why are men ashamed or shy, but under the idea that the people they are addressing, are their betters—or that the actions they are performing, are not altogether right?' " (1.69–70).

Marauder's disdain for modesty is rooted not merely in arrogance but in the belief that one who is behaving with modesty must be doing something morally and epistemologically wrong. Recalling Godwin, Marauder's exceptionalism challenges what Lucas views as a dangerously exceptionalist element of Godwin's political philosophy, the logic by which moral independence or "free-thinking" might create a self-assuredness detached from reality, or from a conflicting, shared morality outside the individual's belief system. As Lucas informs us, "Unlike those young men of fortune who have a conductor or leader, commonly called a tutor, to attend them, [Marauder] in every case acted and judged for himself" (1.84). Further, of the nature of Marauder's tutelage, "his tutors had not led his mind to what *they* thought was proper, but had improved it in those points in which he thought proper to be instructed" (1.164). In Marauder's belief in his own exceptionality—his quixotism of self-regard—we see a narrow interpretation of the guiding ideology of *Political Justice,* that of reason's sovereignty over the individual as the prime sovereign relationship in an ideal society.

We can summarize Marauder's quixotism, then, as a quixotism of self-regard, inculcated by and through the fact that "from [Marauder's] youth every thing had been subservient to him. His haughty, ambitious soul could ever brook restraint from any one" (1.164). This extraordinary self-regard conditions Marauder to believe unflinchingly in his own exceptionality, which Lucas emphasizes repeatedly throughout the novel. Lucas links Marauder's exceptional qualities and abilities to his quixotism of self-regard. At one point Lucas describes Marauder as "ever quicksighted," an expression of his ability to quickly discern the best angles for prevailing upon others but also a play on words that sounds like "quixoted" in the English pronunciation (2.213).[12] As the stakes of Marauder's scheming and deception build and become more pronounced as the novel progresses, Marauder's most intense outbursts of "violent" "agitation of . . . mind" are occasioned almost always by blows to his formidable pride (4.19). And when Marauder is defeated while posing as his alter ego, "M'Ginnis," in the Irish Rebellion, we are told "the natural pride and turbulence of Marauder's temper was heightened by his late disappointment" (3.34).

Further, Marauder refuses to serve as an acolyte to any one philosophy or political party, as "his watchful prudence had thus prevented his enslaving himself to a party, before he had the power or full means to be a principal" (1.213). And perhaps more tellingly of his exceptionalist attitude, recalling Lucas's assignation of Marauder to "*all*" of the radical "modern" and "modernized" philosophies, Marauder does not actually subscribe to them all but is, as Lucas writes, "*Above them all*" (2.295). In this sense Marauder is the quixotic exceptionalist par excellence, his quixotism rooted in a fantastic idealism about his own worth and capabilities and directed exclusively at aggrandizing its only object, himself, as a superior to everyone else.

Having constructed this foundation of quixotism, Lucas moves to demonstrate that such a quixotism of self-regard leads one naturally and logically to embrace the radical tenets of Jacobinism. Because Lucas's contention is that Godwin's political philosophy is a form of "Nothingism" and that Jacobinism is buoyed more by evil and waywardness than any coherent or tangible political philosophy, Lucas must be clever in his rendering of Marauder's quixotism. That is, if Marauder were simply an avid reader of Godwin, Wollstonecraft, and Rousseau—a traditional quixote turned by a particular kind of book—then Lucas would be conceding that Jacobinism has some substance that might be attractive to men of considerable ability, like Godwin and Marauder (much of the fear and concern *The Infernal Quixote* works to generate is related to the seductive power of radicalism over impressionable young women like Emily Bellaire). If, on the other hand, Marauder's quixotism were only generally fanatical, without connection to the ideas Lucas deems responsible for the French Revolution and the Terror of 1793–94, the critique would miss its mark. Instead, Lucas ingeniously writes Marauder's quixotism as a quixotism of self-regard that aligns with a reductio ad absurdum of the guiding logic of *Political Justice,* tacitly picking up on the exceptionalist tradition in quixotic narratives and positing a kind of Godwinian exceptionalism as a precondition for Jacobin politics.

Perhaps no object of quixotic exceptionalism is better looked after in Lucas's novel than the virtue and sensibilities of young women, who stand in the novel in metonymic relation to the evils of the French Revolution writ large. That Marauder's exceptionalism enables him to prevail upon Emily and gravely endanger Emily's younger sister, Fanny, speaks to the strength of the link Lucas perceives between libertinism, "free-thinking" women, and the breakdown of social order necessary to bring about the Reign of Terror in France. For this reason it is important to observe the relationship between Marauder's quixotic exceptionalism and the central plot that drives both Marauder's iniquity and Wilson's heroism in the novel, Marauder's interest in seducing Emily.

Responding to some of the fears and concerns—over what and how women read—that animate the female quixote novels of Lennox and Tenney, Lucas re-creates quixotic reading scenes of the sort that imperil Arabella and Dorcasina. Just as Arabella reads French romances, and Dorcasina reads British romances whose endings are too tidy to accurately represent the challenges of the US frontier, Marauder's hauteur develops through tours in France and Italy. Outsider values that do not align with the customs, values, and challenges of the "home" society come from books in the case of female quixotes, prevented by eighteenth-century gender norms from traveling freely as their male counterparts do; but Marauder absorbs French influence firsthand. Marauder "surpassed every European nation in their own characteristics" (1.87). Having returned from France prepared to initiate his designs to vigorously pursue Emily, Marauder relies on a mixture of his self-assuredness and exceptionalism and his familiarity with the writings of Godwin,

Wollstonecraft, Rousseau, Diderot, and Voltaire. The rival Wilson vies for Emily's affection as well, but the fact that his humility, propriety, and moral steadfastness are no match for Marauder's haughty charm highlights the novel's paternalistic concerns about women's judgment.

Lucas introduces Emily as so prepossessing, "so perfectly fascinating," that Marauder "could not behold her with indifference," a buildup to the pivotal moment in which Marauder successfully convinces Emily of the value of Godwin's and Wollstonecraft's ideas on marriage and women's rights (1.91). The humble Wilson, whose social rank is below Emily's, is equally taken by Emily's appearance and manner but resolves, rather than to conquer Emily, to "conquer his fruitless, his presumptuous love" (1.96). Wilson fires a warning shot for readers when he informs Emily that he suspects Marauder is harboring passions for Emily without disclosing them to her in earnest, worrying rightly that Emily might fall for Marauder's deceptive courtship tactics (1.118).

Yet it turns out to be Wilson's traditionalism—his premature invocation of marriage—that scares Emily off into the arms of Marauder, suggesting a critique of Emily's tutelage as much as Marauder's. As Lucas writes: "Wilson, with increasing ardour, proceeded.—But will my lovely girl promise me her favour, will she sanction my love, will she consent to my wishes, and kindly permit me to speak to her guardians, to say I have her approbation to address them, to hasten—" (1.120). Emily, taken aback, cuts him off: "Oh dear me! what a hurry the good man is in! Indeed I can promise nothing. You know we are both children in the eyes of the law" (1.120). Whereas the novel represents Wilson as its moral center who demonstrates solicitation of "consent," "sanction," "permission," and "approbation" to propose—not even to Emily (given her age), but to her guardians to answer for Emily first—Emily's refusal represents her first step down a dangerous path. Even as her actions are themselves both prudent and moral—Emily tells Wilson to "'wait patiently' . . . laying her hand familiarly on his"—her refusal to move too quickly in the direction of marriage echoes Godwin's own cautionary words in *Political Justice* about "thoughtless and romantic youth of each sex [who] come together . . . under circumstances full of delusion" (Lucas 1.120; Godwin 682).

Emily's judgment, even when prudent, is always on slippery ground, priming her for Marauder's philosophical intervention. Unlike the cautious but sincere Emily, Marauder is every bit the exceptionalist as a beau, as assured of his amatory success each step of the way as of the failure of his competition. When his pressuring leaves Emily both intrigued and speechless, Marauder interprets her look as "in his own favour" (1.125). Lucas tells us that, whereas Wilson doubts his suitability for Emily, Marauder believes Emily is superior to Wilson but inferior to himself, a function of his quixotism of self-regard (1.132). Convinced of his superiority and the superiority of his own philosophy, Marauder assumes the role of tutor to instruct Emily in philosophical principles that will flatter her and mold her in his favor.[13] And when Marauder does at last prevail upon Emily, Lucas attributes it to "flattery . . . levelled . . . at a weak fortification," for which "Vanity commanded in chief, and Folly was Prime-Minister" (1.148). Marauder repeats this self-assured predation with Emily's sister, Fanny, exclaiming, "I know what women are!" and "how easily are women taken!" in signals of both his self-assurance and the emptiness of his ostensible concern for women's education and autonomy (4.185, 230).

In Lucas's reconfiguration of the female quixote reading scene, Marauder "br[ings] many books" to Emily, having marked particular passages for her attention, sometimes venturing to "pointedly" read passages aloud to her. "What do you think of this lady's notions?" he asks after introducing Wollstonecraft's *Vindication of the Rights of Woman*. "I think she is very favourable to *our* sex," Emily replies (1.135). She questions the values of the people of France, stating "they were the most polite and gallant nation in the world," but when they "killed their king," they became "no better than savages"; then Marauder minimizes and apologizes for regicide (1.168). Marauder continues by lavishing upon Emily compliments about her intellect, invoking "such a string of female names, that even Emily began to fancy herself half a Grecian" (1.136). Then Marauder introduces Emily to Rousseau and French novels, which Emily delights in and annotates in the margins, indicating her attentiveness and approbation (1.174).

Similar to the politics of the female quixote narrative, in which women discover a set of newly empowering values and ideas through readings of culturally or temporally foreign texts, Marauder tempts Emily with his reading material. Unlike the female quixote narrative, however, the fact that liberal ideas are coming from Marauder poisons the exercise, turning the liberation potential of the female quixote reading scene into a predatory scenario in which the operant quixotism belongs to Marauder, not Emily, who becomes a victim of it through no power of her own. Marauder carefully manipulates her with texts that foreground women's independence, like *Vindication* and, presumably, Rousseau's *Julie* (1761), which features an illicit sexual relationship between Julie and her tutor.[14]

When it comes to marriage, Marauder deftly takes the opposite approach to Wilson, invoking Godwin's argument that long-term cohabitation is likely to lead to bickering and unhappiness. Rather than asking Emily, with Wilson's avidity, to consent to the opposite of the marital arrangement Wilson proposes—that is, to consent to an intimate relationship without matrimony—Marauder insinuates the possibility of the relationship he wants without avowing his own desire. Quoting *Political Justice* verbatim on the ills of cohabitation, Marauder "laughed at its author"; and quoting Godwin again on the selfishness of making an exclusive and permanent claim on a partner in marriage, Marauder quips that he is "the most selfish man breathing!" (1.153–54). In refusing to come on too strong, as Wilson did previously, Marauder disavows his Godwinian principles as a means of advancing them.

Here again Marauder's quixotism, which enables him to proceed with total confidence in his schemes and to be continually reinforced by his successes, sets up Lucas's critique of Godwin. That Emily falls for Marauder and eventually elopes with him against her younger sister's better judgment is a consequence of her "young and inexperienced mind" and the fact that "her guardian and his wife were weak, silly, fashionable people." This is "more a consequence" than her beauty and charm, such that Lucas presents young women like Emily as never really having much agency to resist the self-assured and beguiling courtship of men like Marauder (1.154). The issue is not simply that Godwin or Wollstonecraft might directly poison the sensibilities of young women but that they might imperil young women by way of the savvy and unscrupulous men who use such ideas to prevail upon women. Once again, though Godwin's expressed concerns in *Political Justice* about marriage as a destructive force are geared primarily toward the ways marriage actually encourages clandestine inconstancy and the monopolization of women's bodies and attention, Marauder's quixotism represents an interpretation of Godwin as an enabler of destructive self-regard that leads to predatory behavior.

Marauder's predatory behavior extends as well to Emily's sister, Fanny, whom Marauder lures to and holds captive in his isolated, private house, threatening to "exert the rights of conqueror" unless Fanny yields consent (4.241). Having abandoned Emily after compelling her to elope with him, and after having pursued other women as well behind Emily's back, Marauder's endless desire for self-gratification functions as a critique of libertinism, linking libertinism to his quixotism of self-regard, which is itself an adulterated version of Godwinian moral independence. A less salient and underacknowledged critique of Godwin in Lucas's novel goes beyond libertinism and Jacobinism and focuses on the heart of *Political Justice,* the idea of moral independence. For this reason, quixotism—and particularly the exceptionalist quality of quixotes—becomes for Lucas an essential vehicle for critique.

We can observe Lucas's most powerful critique in *The Infernal Quixote* only by understanding Marauder's quixotism, particularly his quixotic conversion. The novel ends with Wilson getting wind of Marauder's scheme to capture Fanny and discovering where Marauder has taken her. Just as Marauder is about to take Fanny by force, Wilson arrives to stop him. The two battle, resulting in Marauder taking a fall that leaves him severely injured and dazed. Wilson and his army hold Marauder in custody while he receives medical treatment. Awakening from a fever-induced swoon, Marauder appears to be experiencing a traditional quixotic conversion. He initially "spoke but little" upon awaking after his fever broke, and the next day "the amendment on Marauder was truly astonishing. He spoke rationally, even professed a readiness to set off immediately towards Ireland" to be held accountable for his role as M'Ginnis in the Rebellion. And he refuses to see "that infamous villain, Imphell," his trusted attorney and agent in a number of devious schemes (4.349–50).

The climax of the novel comes soon after when Marauder, with "no appearance of insanity returning," is being escorted to Ireland and decides suddenly to break free of the group and begin running "alone and free . . . with maddening fury . . . desperately through the most arduous places" (4.354–55). What appears at first like an escape attempt becomes something else altogether: "One moment he paused. Recollection shot across his mind. A guilty pang smote him; and, with incredible speed, he flew across the plain. . . . The soul of Marauder staggered. The figure stopped. Every deadly fiend of guilt, depravity, and madness urged Marauder forward. He was about to force his way against it when lo! another form sprung forward, in which his appalled heart recognized the features of Wilson" (4.356–57). That Wilson has conquered Marauder, dealing him a rare setback that punctures his quixotism, is significant here. But we also learn that for the first time

Marauder feels guilt, which throws him headlong into emotional and existential disarray. Wilson is the impetus for Marauder's conversion, but the conversion is in this moment not yet complete, particularly as Marauder is about to break back into his quixotism of self-regard before he sees Wilson, that sudden reminder of his limitations, standing in his path. "Every form but this, Marauder could have opposed," Lucas tells us. "Against every other he had been successful; here he had been again and again subdued and humbled" (4.357).

The most remarkable turn in Marauder's conversion comes in the next moment, when, in response to seeing Wilson in his path, Marauder "guided only by fear . . . flew—no matter where": "Each Fury aided the speed of Marauder—Despair goaded him forward to the edge of the yawning precipice that overhangs the town;—just tottering on the brink, one look he threw behind him—he saw—and leaped, with his utmost exertion, into the deadly abyss. . . . Wilson . . . first learned of the frenzied virulence with which disappointed guilt had smote the soul of Marauder" (4.358–59).

In the end, Marauder, confronted with his fallibility and failure in the form of Wilson, is urged to take his own life by "despair" and "disappointed guilt," feelings of which Marauder had been virtually incapable prior to his final and fateful confrontation with Wilson. The exceptionalist quixote, "whose birth, fortune and expectations made him *equal* with the first characters in the *Kingdom*," but "whose pride, conceit, and ambition lifted him *above* them all," would sooner throw himself off a cliff than face the prospect that he is not exceptional after all (4.361).

For this reason Lucas's ending is remarkably important for the study of quixotism, because it acknowledges the logical limits of the politics of exceptionalism. Because Marauder's quixotism is pure exceptionalism, to the extent that his self-regard perpetuates a program of endless self-gratification and self-reinforcement, the cure becomes the total annihilation of self. Marauder's suicide becomes the dark scene of quixotic conversion, and so Marauder becomes quixotism's ultimate cautionary figure. By the same stroke, this is also Lucas's most compelling critique of Godwin's *Political Justice*. That is, if we are concerned about the potential of Godwin's rational anarchism to produce solipsistic or morally intransigent individuals, on account of Godwin's focus on the evils of cooperation and government, then we might fear a quixotic Godwinian. Marauder is just such a figure, so enamored of his own philosophies and abilities that he is incapable of apprehending the destruction they cause, not even the destruction of his own life in that searing moment when Marauder realizes he is not and was never equipped to process and to live through the death of his exceptionalism.

As I have suggested, *The Infernal Quixote* has important implications for our understanding of quixotism as eighteenth-century political theory, an eighteenth-century theory of exceptionalism. *The Infernal Quixote*'s direct engagement with *Political Justice*—a major work of eighteenth-century political theory—brings quixotic exceptionalism full circle. In his rendering of Don Quixote as a justice-oriented character who proceeds in the dress and with the ethos of Spanish imperialism, Cervantes opened the door for authors to re-create quixotes as exceptionalists in various forms. In Marauder, Lucas gives us a character whose quixotism is pure exceptionalism and whose exceptionalism is in the service of expressly critiquing Godwin's theory of sovereignty long before scholars like Carl Schmitt, Giorgio Agamben, and Paul Kahn began to theorize the relationship between exceptionalism and sovereignty. In this sense *The Infernal Quixote* shows us that the concept of quixotic exceptionalism was developed enough in the minds of eighteenth-century novelists that, by the rise and fallout of the French Revolution at the turn of the nineteenth century, the quixote motif was both logical and potent as a means of engaging issues of political theory.

In the following coda I will bring some of the case studies we have covered in this book back into perspective to elaborate on this idea that exceptionalism was a discernable motif in quixotic narratives by the time Lucas portrayed quixotic exceptionalism in *The Infernal Quixote*. But I also conclude the argument of this book by touching on a few of the ways quixotic exceptionalism is relevant beyond even political theory, relevant to yet more fundamental questions about how we know what we know. As Marauder hunches over his wounded coconspirator, Fahaney, before departing for Ireland to join the Rebellion, he "was careful to whisper a few *data* in Fahaney's ear" (3.16). Further, and very characteristic of quixotes, Marauder believed "in reality every thing was subservient to his interest" (3.21). Exceptionalism impacts how quixotes see the world, share their impressions, and interpret their realities. And because of this, exceptionalism illustrates the important ways quixotism and epistemology become mutually relevant.

CODA

Quixotism, Phenomenology, Epistemology

The impetus for this study was the recognition that prior studies of quixotism have been unable to find intellectual consistency among so many quixotic figures in fiction of the long eighteenth century and beyond. Consequently, the concept of the quixotic has reached—in literary studies, as in the broader world of politics—a critical mass of meaning, resulting too often in confusion rather than clarification. This is an exigent problem, because Don Quixote is among the most widely influential characters in literary history. Because quixotes can be different genders, different ranks, and of different political persuasions, nationalities, and professions, quixotism would seem incapable of describing much more than a loose association with *Don Quixote.* The temptation has been to conclude therefore that quixotism is simply an allusive phenomenon, not capable of offering any conceptual coherence where applied (even though the term "quixotic" is indeed frequently applied). As I have argued, however, quixotism is a coherent disposition common to quixotes of vastly differing politics and demographics in the seventeenth, eighteenth, and early nineteenth centuries, and that disposition is fundamentally a form of exceptionalism. Quixotic exceptionalism explains the prevalence and influence of quixotic characters in eighteenth-century literatures in English in particular, and it helps explain a range of eighteenth-century social, legal, and political conflicts.

Quixotic exceptionalism is the logic that enables one to continually subordinate competing evidence and concerns to the quixotic worldview, on the grounds that whatever it is that animates quixotism—belief in a higher form of justice, of morality, or of self-actualization—shapes and takes precedent over everything else. Quixotes rely on exceptionalism to maintain their quixotism, even after supposed conversions from quixotism (at least, the kind that do not result in the quixote's death, as in Marauder's case). Further, as we can observe in the quixotes presented in this study, the bookishness of quixotes that enables quixotism's high-minded attitude equips quixotes to carry out exceptionalist practices, whether in denying the flaws in one's own nationalism, as Gulliver does, or in denying a lesser, more stifling reality, as Arabella does. Understanding that quixotes are exceptionalists allows us to understand both how they function and why they were such popular choices for novelistic political interventions.

Crucial to understanding quixotic exceptionalism is understanding that exceptionalism is not simply a function of difference or aberration. Cervantes's Quixote is not merely an exception because of his madness, a character unlike others around him. Quixote believes he is a modern incarnation of a set of past values that he holds sacred, and he proceeds as though others should make accommodations for this belief, or else face the lance. Gulliver, too, considers himself not merely different from those he meets along his travels, but representative, in some sense, of ways of life he believes superior. Whether as an Englishman in Brobdingnag or a Houyhnhnm-convert among fellow English Yahoos upon his final return, Gulliver thinks himself responsible for upholding what he takes to be the superior values that he has left behind (or that have left him behind). For Gulliver, the naïve and isolated King of Brobdingnag cannot possibly have the breadth of insight and understanding of interconnected Britain and Europe, though later in the narrative Gulliver laments that his English family and friends cannot possibly know the exemplary qualities of the Utopian Houyhnhnms from the isolated, faraway land of England. Gulliver's exceptionalism takes its ultimate form when, as a consequence of his quixotism, he manages to identify with a different species from his own, and from that of his family.

In the early US, too, quixotic exceptionalism played a significant role in policing and reforming notions of American exceptionalism. In *The Algerine Captive,* for example, Updike Underhill's quixotism helped illustrate the contradictions of American exceptionalism while simultaneously differentiating between English and US notions of freedom and opportunity. Updike admires Benjamin Franklin's ability to adjust to uncertain circumstances and to learn from misjudgments (in a way Updike so often fails to do); but he ridicules a group of Londoners for boasting of their "glorious freedom" despite "hereditary senators" and other clear forms of injustice (86). Given *Don Quixote*'s role in satirizing the bellicose attitudes and nationalisms of the Spanish Empire in its bygone zenith, eighteenth- and early nineteenth-century writers found an enticing and effective character model in Quixote, taking him up to interrogate national exceptionalisms.

We can see in each of the quixotes in this study varying strands of exceptionalism, many of which overlap and form something of a mosaic impression of quixotic exceptionalism, the result of idealism, mimetic appeal, and a high-minded literary sensibility that fosters imagination. Each of the instances of quixotic exceptionalism covered in this book has roots in Cervantes's *Don Quixote,* though each has moved in some way beyond *Don Quixote* as well. Whether by reconfiguring Quixote as an international traveler or a stationary dreamer, an aspiring politician, a preacher, a writer, a savior, or a radical libertine, quixotic roots anchor a form of exceptionalism but also nourish the branching off of this mind-set into different directions and toward different ends. When we look at the branches of this quixotic tree we see a sprawling and multitudinous network that appears too vast and multiform to understand as coherent. But when we consider the roots beneath the surface, the unifying frame-work of the exceptionalism of quixotes becomes apparent. Even in our contemporary, journalistic renderings of people and actions as "quix-otic," we can glimpse the exceptionalist roots of quixotism. A "quixotic" governmental decision frequently involves a paternalistic turn away from the will of the populace, a claim to visionary exceptionalism like that of Captain Farrago. A "quixotic" political campaign is an effort against the odds, an exceptionalist belief in one's destiny over reason, like Gulliver's continual testing of his fortune overseas in strange and dangerous lands. Whether understood as acts or instances of resilient heroism or woeful imprudence, quixotic efforts entail a belief in some form of exceptional-ism, or a willingness to proceed according to a separate set of rules that follow from a sense of moral superiority.

Exceptionalism is both a root of quixotism and, when quixotes inspire mimesis, a product of it, stemming from the behavior of Cer-vantes's Don Quixote and present in the subsequent proliferation of quixotic narratives. Returning to our point of departure—the heuris-tic list of quixotic characteristics with which I began—we can see after reading a series of quixotic narratives how quixotic characteristics fuel exceptionalism. The first characteristic, that the quixote is an imagina-tive idealist, rather than a trickster or delinquent, enables quixotes to adopt grand purposes that become powerful drivers of the quixotic imagination. In this sense, quixotes can envision an ideal for which no set of rules or laws, save those according to which the quixote lives and operates, can deter the pursuit of the ideal. Even with her inheritance at stake, Arabella will not suffer Glanville refusing to read her romances for himself, nor will Updike hear the Mollah's talk of religious conversion, even if it means his deliverance from slavery.

The second characteristic, that the quixote is of the noble or educated ranks, means that quixotes are heavily invested in a bookish, literary high-mindedness that makes them ideal candidates for testing the limits of fictionality. Quixotes are privileged and educated enough not merely to read avidly and adeptly, but to place extraordinarily high value both on what they read (whether books of chivalry, travel, history, philosophy, or religion) and on a literary understanding of the world itself. Parson Adams and Updike Underhill, the only quixotes in this study not of some kind of noble socioeconomic background, become fixated nonetheless on a kind of belletristic and moral high-mindedness and enter into the discourse of the ruling elites by way of their superior educations. Like Gulliver, their privileging of industriousness and self-regulation within their worldviews creates grounds for their exceptionalism, enabling them to construct standards for themselves that supplant those of the surrounding people and societies they deem inadequate. Socioeconomic advantage and its attendant literary high-mindedness provide grounds for quixotes to imagine themselves as exceptions.

Thirdly, in their capacity to produce exceptions, quixotes empower their exceptionalism. When Launcelot Greaves demonstrates his sanity to Ferret, denying that he is merely an imitator of Don Quixote, while continuing to don armor and ride on horseback throughout the countryside addressing legal grievances, he sets himself up as an exception to the assumed rule that all quixotes are mad. Winning thereafter the esteem of those he aids, including his beloved Aurelia, Launcelot proceeds with his own mode of quixotic madness, reinforcing his understanding that he is an exceptional quixote rather than a Don Quixote imposter. Dorcasina empowers her exceptionalism similarly by ordering Betty to dress as and impersonate O'Connor, producing an alternate reality that, however burlesque, sustains Dorcasina's fantasy and perpetuates her quixotic worldview.

Finally, that quixotes are themselves mimetic and also inspire mimesis drives their exceptionalism. Quixotes continue to believe as they do because they act according to their ideals, thinking themselves modern incarnations of the heroes and heroines of an idealized world. This tendency not only positions quixotes as anachronisms and aberrations but also generates the exceptionalist understanding that, as with Parson Adams, Captain Farrago, and Diedrich Knickerbocker, the quixote's mimicking or representation of an idealized past both justifies and is justified by the quixotic claim to superior values. By imitating idealized models, quixotes make exceptions of themselves as citizens of or participants in a wider social order. By inspiring others, as Arabella and Dorcasina do, to participate in quixotic fantasy and adhere to quixotic modes of conduct, quixotes reinforce their exceptionalist positioning of themselves *above* the social order, soliciting feedback in the process that often empirically confirms their quixotic expectations.

This is precisely how exceptionalism functions as an engine of quixote reproduction, and how exceptionalism explains the vast proliferation of quixotic narratives during the long eighteenth century. By its nature, exceptionalism demands continual reinforcement of the terms of exception, at least until an audience or a surrounding society has acquiesced to the exceptionalist's worldview (and even then, as with national exceptionalism, it demands routine maintenance). This means, in a fairly straightforward way, the market for exceptionalist politics and political figures is almost always thriving. Even as seventeenth-century British readers became acquainted with Don Quixote at the translation stage, it had already become clear that Quixote was originally placed within a lineage of reproduction, as if designed to be rewritten and reconfigured on an ongoing basis. Because Cervantes's Quixote was an exceptionalist in an early modern Spanish society that tried desperately to rein him back to reality, he could become an exceptionalist anywhere and for any cause while maintaining the character blueprint Cervantes sketched out: idealistic, educated, capable of inspiring imitation in others, an adept exceptionalist. Further, because Quixote was an exceptionalist, his story invited authors to do what the Priest and the Barber do to Quixote: to intervene, perhaps to imitate in jest or in an effort to make sense of Quixote.

As I have argued, the period during which quixotes ran amok in literatures in English, from the early seventeenth to the early nineteenth century, also produced heavy demand for exceptionalist politics, particularly national exceptionalism. The quips about the French we see in *Joseph Andrews, The Female Quixote,* and *Launcelot Greaves* are still around by the turn of the nineteenth century and the publication of *The Infernal Quixote*. Anti-French sentiment in British literature of the period is certainly widespread and widely observed, but the point here is that quixotism became a way not only of aligning Francophile tendencies with poor character, libertinism, effeteness, moral laxity, epicureanism, traitorousness, or other well-trodden stereotypes but also of staking out the boundaries of English exceptionalism and lambasting those who stepped outside those boundaries. For Fielding and Lucas, for example, quixotes step outside of Englishness in very different ways, but in so doing they highlight the boundaries each author was setting for what Englishness was and should be. Quixotic exceptionalism in this sense helped police national exceptionalism in some cases (*The Infernal Quixote*) and reform it in others (*Joseph Andrews, Gulliver's Travels*).

There remains one final strand of quixotic exceptionalism's implications worth considering in this study—and worth attention in future study—and that has to do with the relationship between exceptionalism, epistemology, and phenomenology. I opened this book with the claim that Quixote is not simply mad, but actually quite logical. As we have seen, the basis of this claim is that exceptionalism produces for quixotes a self-sealing logic. When quixotes act on their idealism, their exceptionalism shields them to some extent from counterevidence for their belief system, enabling them to proceed where others turn back and correct course. Two giants of Spanish philosophy, Miguel de Unamuno and José Ortega y Gasset, both recognized this phenomenological account of quixotism, which is fundamentally driven by Quixote's experience, his motivation to pursue his objects undeterred.[1] A significant consequence of this emboldening function of quixotic exceptionalism is that others begin to respond to quixotes by imitating quixotism, hoping to communicate on the quixote's register. Both Glanville and Sir George, for example, begin to adhere to Arabella's expectations even as they understand Arabella's behavior is aberrant and potentially dangerous. As they make a show of themselves acting favorably in terms of Arabella's expectations, Arabella perceives a scenario in which reality further confirms her expectations. In this way quixotism is logical, because what quixotes empirically witness is often commensurate with the expectations created by the quixotic worldview.

Given that quixotism can be both logical and wrong, and given that exceptionalism is what enables this dynamic in quixotes and their

interlocutors, a phenomenological account of quixotism poses important epistemological challenges.[2] This is particularly the case because so
much of quixotism in eighteenth-century fiction is signaled by direct
failures of empiricism, as with Arabella, Dorcasina, and Gulliver, in particular. These quixotes, like Cervantes's original, see what everyone else
sees but derive radically different impressions about what is happening.
If quixotic exceptionalism can change the interpretation without challenging the terms of empirical observation, what, then, are the effects of
exceptionalism on epistemology?

This is of course a larger question for another book, but it reflects the
stakes of this study of quixotic exceptionalism. The role of exceptionalist politics in nineteenth-century Britain and the US was, in a word,
transformative, reshaping not just how people lived but how they perceived the world around them. While this study goes only so far in its
conclusion as to gesture toward the possibilities of studying the politics
of quixotism further as a study of quixotic epistemology, we already
know that exceptionalist politics and quixotic behavior have been inte-
gral to expansions of British and US imperialism, just as they were to
Spanish imperialism in the centuries before *Don Quixote* was published.
As Britain extended its empire in South Asia and Africa, and the US
sought its Manifest Destiny across the North American continent, the
specter of Don Quixote, once again, rattled his lance.

ACKNOWLEDGMENTS

This book is a product of so many opportunities for which I'm eternally grateful. If literary studies is a party, I arrived late and confused, and Ghislaine McDayter, who patiently fielded my questions about graduate study in English, was kind enough to let me through the door with my bachelor's degree in political science. Newly arrived and inclined still toward political philosophy, I found welcome conversation partners in different corners of the room—Harold Schweizer on aesthetics and the history of criticism, and the late Mike Payne on critical theory. As everyone who knew Mike can attest, he was the most generous teacher and friend, a model of kindness and scrupulous mentorship whose legacy I strive to honor every day in my own work with students.

It was ultimately Greg Clingham and his illuminating course on law and literature that drew me to Enlightenment and eighteenth-century studies in a crucial moment. I decided to scrap my law school applications and pursue the quixotic adventure that has landed me here, writing acknowledgments for this book. That adventure has been no less peripatetic than Quixote's, originating in an obscure part of Spain—or central Pennsylvania—that the narrator of this story might have chosen not to remember, were it not for the good people and exceptional departmental support at Bucknell. At Dartmouth thereafter I had first-rate guidance working with the astonishingly incisive Donald Pease on a master's thesis that brought together my interests in the eighteenth-century Atlantic world and the larger heuristic question of how we organize knowledge in literary studies.

With the generous support of Dartmouth's James B. Reynolds Scholarship for Foreign Study and Linacre College, Oxford's Mary Blaschko Scholarship, I had the opportunity to trace Quixote's transatlantic journey in reverse, enrolling in the doctoral program at Oxford, where this book started to take form. I'd have been fortunate to get one of the most lucid and attentive supervisors among the Oxford English faculty, but instead I got two of them. Ros Ballaster and Christine Gerrard are still among the sharpest and most careful readers I've ever worked with. They helped me refine a project that always risked outgrowing its own breeches, and taught me so much about the eighteenth century along the way. In numerous presentations on early versions of this material in Oxford, at least one self-satisfied person in the audience would say, "But aren't you just tilting at windmills?" Ros and Christine helped me distinguish between windmills and giants in this project. At Oxford—Linacre College in particular—I had interlocutors across disciplines who challenged my assumptions and helped sharpen my thinking: a chemist; some mathematical modelers; some neuroscientists and biologists; and Paul Slack, FBA, former Principal of Linacre College, and eminent early modern social historian who in retirement is still publishing work that shapes my understanding of seventeenth- and eighteenth-century Britain. To my knowledge there is no better crucible for cross-disciplinary intellectual exchange than the Linacre College Common Room.

I'm grateful, too, to many scholars in eighteenth-century studies and beyond who read versions of this book, parts and whole. Eve Tavor Bannet read and offered essential feedback on versions of the manuscript well after she fulfilled her duty as external examiner for my doctoral work. The late Susan Manning kindly advised me from afar on transatlantic elements of the project and helped me think through my conception of character. My colleagues at Georgetown, Kathryn Temple, Dennis Todd, and Patrick O'Malley lent me not only their time and expertise but also their encouragement and professional support (Dennis, recently retired, also lent me a chunk of his library, which I hope to pass along to another scholar someday). When I presented framing and introductory material on quixotism and political theory at the Clark Seminar at UCLA, Helen Deutsch helped me make difficult decisions about the role of political theory in the book. Jason Pearl has been a friend and a reliable voice of reason in my moments of self-doubt. Cliff Siskin and Bill Warner have helped me link my work on quixotism to the next phase of my scholarship.

From the moment Cedric Bryant called to offer me the job at Colby College, I gained a whole department of brilliant and supportive colleagues who have helped me see this book to completion. Elizabeth Sagaser, Laurie Osborne, Mary Ellis Gibson, and Megan Cook have read or heard portions of this book, as well as written letters on my behalf for grants that were indispensable for the archival work this book required. I'm grateful for the generous grant and fellowship support of the Chawton House Library, the William Andrews Clark Memorial Library and the Center for 17th- and 18th-Century Studies at UCLA, the Andrew W. Mellon Foundation and the Huntington Library, as well as Georgetown University and Colby College for grant support. All of these funding bodies and libraries—and their tremendously knowledgeable and helpful staff of archivists, librarians, and others—made this book possible.

I'm also grateful to the journals *Comparative American Studies* (Taylor & Francis); *Connotations* (and Professor Matthias Bauer, editor); and *The Eighteenth Century: Theory and Interpretation* (University of Pennsylvania Press) for granting me permission to republish parts of my previously published work. This includes work in chapters 5 (*Connotations*), 6 (*Comparative American Studies*), and 8 (*ECTI*). Thanks go to Cambridge University Library as well for permission to publish images in chapter 3 from their rare books collections.

I acknowledge, too, that at the University of Virginia Press, Angie Hogan has built such an exceptional list of authors—many of us first-time authors—that it's truly humbling to be part of this group. Angie assembled a deeply insightful and careful group of readers for my manuscript, whose input—simultaneously challenging and encouraging—has made this book the very best possible version of itself. I could not have asked for better reader reports, nor could I have asked for a better and more attentive editorial, marketing, and production team than the UVA Press group.

Finally, I wish to thank my brilliant and caring partner, the neuroscientist April Nhi Le, source of my strength and purpose, and my endlessly supportive family, parents Donna and Ray Hanlon, and brother, Sean. My work is a product of more love and support than a person could possibly deserve, and whatever benefits I take from this work, I take them knowing that too many deserving scholars have not had the support and the opportunities I've enjoyed thus far in my life and career. For this reason I reserve my last acknowledgment for those living and working in precarity, whose labor props up a system that acknowledges too few voices. No scholarship is possible without you.

NOTES

Introduction

1. Miguel de Cervantes, *Don Quixote,* trans. John Rutherford (London: Penguin, 2003), 1.10.81. All subsequent references to Cervantes's *Don Quixote* are to this edition and are cited in the text by part, chapter, and page number.

2. Jorge Luis Borges, *Ficciones,* ed. and trans. Anthony Kerrigan (New York: Grove, 1994), 48–49.

3. In Wendy Motooka's *The Age of Reasons: Quixotism, Sentimentalism, and Political Economy in Eighteenth- Century Britain* (New York: Routledge, 1998), Motooka describes Quixote as "an embodiment of radical political difference," defining "quixotism" as "epistemological problems that become political problems, or political problems that turn out to have their basis in epistemological divisions" (4). This is the most incisive characterization of quixotism we have. In this book I argue, however, that quixotism is not simply political difference nor a failure of the senses, but an outlook arising from exceptionalism, not simply misprision or epistemological difference.

4. Sarah F. Wood, *Quixotic Fictions of the USA, 1792–1815* (New York: Oxford University Press, 2005), vi. Fielding's review appears in the *Covent-Garden Journal,* vol. 1, ed. Gerard Edward Jensen [New Haven, 1915], 279–82, 279. Another study that takes a primarily taxonomic approach to quixotism is J. A. G. Ardila, *The Cervantean Heritage: Reception and Influence of Cervantes in Britain* (Oxford: Legenda, 2009).

5. Cathy Davidson, *Revolution and the Word: The Rise of the Novel in America* (New York: Oxford University Press, 2004), 151–211.

6. Thomas Scanlan, "Review of *Quixotic Fictions of the USA, 1792–1815,*" *Early American Literature* 43 (2008): 237.

7. John Skinner, "*Don Quixote* in 18th-Century England: A Study in Reader Response," *Cervantes: Bulletin of the Cervantes Society of America* 7 (1987): 45. As Skinner notes, eighteenth-century readers tended to focus "more readily on the actual character of Don Quixote."

8. Vladimir Nabokov, *Lectures on "Don Quixote,"* ed. Fredson Bowers (New York: Harcourt, 1983), 27–28.

9. Roberto González Echevarría, *Cervantes' "Don Quixote": A Casebook* (New York: Oxford University Press, 2005), 4.

10. Schmitt has been an influential political theorist whose work cannot be ignored for the purpose of this study. I acknowledge, however, that he was sympathetic to and involved in Nazi authoritarianism, a legacy to be reckoned with and most certainly not celebrated.

11. Charlotte Lennox, *The Female Quixote,* ed. Margaret Dalziel (1752; New York: Oxford, 1998), 311. All subsequent references are to this edition and appear parenthetically in the text.

1. QUIXOTIC EXCEPTIONALISM

1. Schmitt's definition of the sovereign appears in *Political Theology* (Chicago: University of Chicago Press, 1985), 5. For a history of American exceptionalism, see the work of Jack Green, especially in *The Intellectual Construction of America: Exceptionalism and Identity from 1492–1800* (Chapel Hill: University of North Carolina Press, 1993).

2. Giorgio Agamben, *Homo Sacer: Sovereign Power and Bare Life,* trans. Daniel Heller-Roazen (Stanford: Stanford University Press, 1998), 72–73.

3. Paul Kahn, *Political Theology: Four New Chapters on the Concept of Sovereignty* (New York: Columbia University Press, 2011), 9, 125.

4. Joseph Nye, *Soft Power: The Means to Success in World Politics* (New York: Public Affairs, 2004), 5–6.

5. Kahn, *Political Theology,* 8–9.

6. Donald Pease, "Re-Thinking 'American Studies after US Exceptionalism,'" *American Literary History* 21 (2009): 19–20.

7. Jack P. Greene, *The Intellectual Construction of America: Exceptionalism and Identity from 1492 to 1800* (Chapel Hill: University of North Carolina Press, 1993), 4–5.

8. Octavio Paz, *Convergences: Essays on Art and Literature,* trans. Helen Lane (San Diego: Harcourt Brace Jovanovich, 1987), 132.

9. Agamben, *Homo Sacer,* 22.

10. See, for example, James Chace, "Quixotic America," *World Policy Journal* 20 (2003): 7–15. George Washington and Thomas Jefferson famously kept and enjoyed copies of *Don Quixote* in the late eighteenth century.

11. Gallagher, "The Rise of Fictionality," in *The Novel,* vol. 1: *History, Geography, and Culture,* ed. Franco Moretti, 336–63 (Princeton: Princeton University Press, 2006), 338.

12. Gallagher, "The Rise of Fictionality," 339.

13. Gallagher, "The Rise of Fictionality," 340.

14. Motooka, *The Age of Reasons,* 2.

15. Gallagher, "The Rise of Fictionality," 347.

16. As Dalziel tells us in her explanatory notes, people even suspected that Samuel Johnson wrote this portion of Lennox's novel for her. John Mitford, editor of the *Gentleman's Magazine* (August 1843), was the first to float this notion (414).

17. Sarah Kareem, *Eighteenth-Century Fiction and the Reinvention of Wonder* (New York: Oxford University Press, 2014), 21.

18. Diana de Armas Wilson, *Cervantes, The Novel, and the New World* (New York: Oxford University Press, 2001), 20.

19. Wilson, *Cervantes, The Novel, and the New World,* 22–23.

20. Clarence Haring, *The Spanish Empire in America* (Oxford: Oxford University Press, 1947), 27–28.

21. Fernand Braudel, *Civilization and Capitalism, 15th–18th Century,* vol. 3 (London: Collins, 1984), 352.

22. Brinley Thomas, *The Industrial Revolution and the Atlantic Economy* (London: Routledge, 1993), 37.

23. Thomas, *The Industrial Revolution and the Atlantic Economy,* 41.

24. Michael Gilmore, "Eighteenth-Century Oppositional Ideology and Hugh Henry Brackenridge's *Modern Chivalry,*" *Early American Literature* 13 (1978): 184.

25. Stephen Shapiro, *The Culture and Commerce of the Early American Novel: Reading the Atlantic World-System* (State College: Pennsylvania State University Press, 2008), 1.

26. Gilmore, "Eighteenth-Century Oppositional Ideology," 183–84.

2. Anatomy of Quixotism

1. Susan Manning, *Poetics of Character* (Cambridge: Cambridge University Press, 2013), xii.

2. Manning, *Poetics of Character,* xiii.

3. Alexander Parker, *Literature and the Delinquent: The Picaresque Novel in Spain and Europe 1599–1753* (Edinburgh: Edinburgh University Press, 1967), 19.

4. Erich Auerbach, *Mimesis: The Representation of Reality in Western Literature* (Princeton: Princeton University Press, 2003), 338.

5. Roberto González Echevarría, *Cervantes' "Don Quixote"* (New Haven: Yale University Press, 2015), 218.

6. Nabokov, *Lectures,* 27–28.

7. Tobias Smollett, translator's note to *The History and Adventures of the Renowned Don Quixote,* by Miguel de Cervantes, trans. Smollett (London, 1755), xxi. As the pages of Smollett's prefatory material to his 1755 translation are unnumbered, I have counted them from the beginning and assigned them numbers for citation purposes.

8. Tobias Smollett, *The Life and Adventures of Sir Launcelot Greaves,* ed. Robert Folkenflik and Barbara Laning-Fitzpatrick (1760–62; Athens: University of Georgia Press, 2002), 62. All subsequent references are to this edition and appear parenthetically in the text.

9. Edmund Gayton, *Pleasant Notes upon Don Quixot* (London, 1654), i.

3. Character and Front Matters

1. Franco Moretti, *Atlas of the European Novel: 1800–1900* (London: Verso, 1999), 171–72.

2. Barbara Fuchs, *The Poetics of Piracy: Emulating Spain in English Literature* (Philadelphia: University of Pennsylvania Press, 2013), 1.

3. Mary Helen McMurran, *The Spread of Novels: Translation and Prose Fiction in the Eighteenth Century* (Princeton: Princeton University Press, 2009), 2.

4. Miguel de Cervantes, *The History of the Valorous and Wittie Knight-Errant, Don Quixote of La Mancha,* trans. Thomas Shelton (London, 1612), 3.

5. Shelton, dedication to *Don Quixote,* by Cervantes, trans. Shelton (1612).

6. Thomas Shelton, dedication to *The History of the Valorous and Wittie Knight-Errant, Don Quixote of La Mancha,* by Miguel de Cervantes, trans. Shelton (London, 1620).

7. Shelton, dedication to *Don Quixote,* by Cervantes, trans. Shelton (1612).

8. Shelton, dedication to *Don Quixote,* by Cervantes, trans. Shelton (1612).

9. John Phillips, Dialogue, in *The History of the Most Renowned Don Quixote of La Mancha,* by Miguel de Cervantes, trans. Phillips (London, 1687), i. The pages of Phillips's opening epistle to the reader are unnumbered, so I have counted them from the beginning and assigned them numbers for the purposes of citation.

10. Phillips, Dialogue, in *Don Quixote,* by Cervantes, trans. Phillips, i–ii.

11. Phillips, Dialogue, in *Don Quixote,* by Cervantes, trans. Phillips, ii.

12. The translator's name was Charles Jervas, but because of a printer's error, the surname appeared as "Jarvis." Consequently, the text is frequently referred to as the "Jarvis translation."

13. Miguel de Cervantes, *The History of the Renowned Don Quixote de la Mancha,* trans. Peter Motteaux (London, 1700).

14. Charles Jarvis, translator's preface to *The Life and Exploits of the Ingenious Gentleman Don Quixote de la Mancha,* by Miguel de Cervantes, trans. Jarvis (London, 1742), iv.

15. Julie Candler Hayes, "Eighteenth-Century English Translations of *Don Quixote,*" in *The Cervantean Heritage: Reception and Influence of Cervantes in Britain,* ed. J. A. G. Ardila (Oxford: Legenda, 2009), 66.

16. Miguel de Cervantes, *The Life and Notable Adventures of That Renown'd Knight, Don Quixote de la Mancha, Merrily Translated into Hudibrastick Verse,* trans. Edward Ward (London, 1711–12).

17. Jarvis, dedication to John Lord Carteret in *Don Quixote,* by Cervantes, trans. Jarvis, v.

18. Jarvis, dedication to John Lord Carteret in *Don Quixote,* by Cervantes, trans. Jarvis, iv.

19. Jarvis, translator's preface, *Don Quixote,* by Cervantes, trans. Jarvis, vi–vii.

20. Jarvis, translator's preface, *Don Quixote,* by Cervantes, trans. Jarvis, xxii.

21. Smollett, translator's note, in *Don Quixote,* by Cervantes, trans. Smollett.

22. David Brewer, *The Afterlife of Character, 1726–1825* (State College: University of Pennsylvania Press, 2005), 17. Brewer calls the "social canon" "that unwritten list of texts kept alive in the hearts and minds of myriad individual readers from generation to generation."

4. RELATIONAL QUIXOTISM

1. Manning, *Poetics of Character,* xii–xiii.

2. Manning, *Poetics of Character,* 13–14.

3. Jed Rasula, "When the Exception Is the Rule: *Don Quixote* as Incitement to Literature," *Comparative Literature* 51, no. 2 (1999): 146.

4. Brewer, *The Afterlife of Character,* 22.

5. I draw this term in part from Brewer's discussion of character ontology as a consequence of character reproduction in *The Afterlife of Character, 1726-1825,* 10. Brewer also uses "sociability" to describe how prominent characters engender common feeling and sociable practices among a community of readers who know of and become invested in the lives of such characters (14).

6. James Boswell, *Life of Samuel Johnson,* ed. Pat Rogers (1791; New York: Oxford University Press, 2008), 36.

7. Jorge Luis Borges, *Professor Borges: A Course on English Literature,* trans. Katherine Silver, ed. Martín Arias and Martin Hardis (New York: New Directions, 2013), 95.

8. Qtd. in Gallagher, "The Rise of Fictionality," 350.

9. Brewer, *The Afterlife of Character,* 3.

10. Gallagher, "The Rise of Fictionality," 355.

11. Deidre Lynch, *The Economy of Character: Novels, Market Culture, and the Business of Inner Meaning* (Chicago: University of Chicago Press, 1998), 35.

12. Brewer, *The Afterlife of Character,* 17.

13. Lynch, *The Economy of Character* 6.

14. Brewer, *The Afterlife of Character,* 14.

15. Lynch, *The Economy of Character,* 76, 57.

16. Lynch, *The Economy of Character,* 47–48.

17. Lynch, *The Economy of Character,* 47–48.

18. Henry Fielding, *Don Quixote in England* (London, 1734), 14.

19. Hayes, "Eighteenth-Century English Translations of *Don Quixote,*" 69–71.

20. Lynch, *The Economy of Character,* 6.

21. Gallagher, "The Rise of Fictionality," 355–56.

22. Brewer, *The Afterlife of Character,* 6–7.

23. Brewer, *The Afterlife of Character,* 110.

24. In "The Rise of Fictionality," Gallagher quotes Peter McCormick's argument that "fictional characters are surprisingly exhaustible as objects of knowledge since, unlike material objects, they lack the infinity of ever-receding perceptual horizons and, unlike self-conscious entities, they lack the inexorable privacy of ever-changing varieties of mental states" (358). Brewer considers Falstaff "inexhaustible" in *Afterlife* (86).

25. Brewer, *The Afterlife of Character,* 83.

26. Brewer, *The Afterlife of Character,* 78.

27. Brewer, *The Afterlife of Character,* 24.

5. Gulliver and English Exceptionalism

1. Wood, *Quixotic Fictions of the USA,* 7–8.

2. Jeanne K. Welcher and George E. Bush Jr., *Gulliveriana,* vol. 1 (Gainesville, FL: Scholars Facsimiles and Reprints, 1970), vii, v.

3. Jeanne K. Welcher, *Gulliveriana VIII: An Annotated List of Gulliveriana, 1721–1800* (Delmar, NY: Scholars Facsimiles and Reprints, 1988), 51.

4. Brown, "The Quixotic Fallacy," 260.

5. Evidence that Swift began a translation of *Don Quixote,* and probably contributed to a preface for it, appears in an essay by A. C. Elias, "Swift's *Don Quixote,* Dunkin's *Virgil Travesty,* and Other New Intelligence: John Lyon's 'Materials for a Life of Dr. Swift,' 1765," *Swift Studies* 13 (1998): 27–104.

6. Paulson's inclusion of Amhurst's comparison between *Gulliver's Travels* and *Don Quixote* appears in *Don Quixote in England: The Aesthetics of Laughter* (Baltimore:

Johns Hopkins University Press, 1998) as an aside in Paulson's discussion of Hogarth's Oppositionalist political prints. Curiously, then, Paulson's brief discussion of the Gulliver-Quixote comparison appears in the context of a wider discussion of art and fiction as political tools, rather than as a discussion of Gulliver's quixotism (136).

7. Studies like J. A. Downie's "The Political Significance of *Gulliver's Travels*," in *Swift and His Contexts*, ed. John Irwin Fischer, Hermann Josef Real, and James D. Woolley (New York: AMS, 1989): 1–18, and David Bywaters's "*Gulliver's Travels* and the Mode of Political Parallel during Walpole's Administration," *ELH* 54 (1987): 717–40, were part of a late twentieth-century focus on *Gulliver's Travels* as political allegory. More contemporary work in this lineage includes David Womersley's "Dean Swift Hears a Sermon: Robert Howard's Ash Wednesday Sermon of 1725 and *Gulliver's Travels*," *Review of English Studies* 60 (2009): 744–62; and Deborah Armintor's "The Sexual Politics of Microscopy in Brobdingnag," *SEL* 47 (2007): 619–40.

8. Christine Rees, *Utopian Imagination and Eighteenth-Century Fiction* (New York: Longman, 1996), 123.

9. Jonathan Swift, *Gulliver's Travels,* ed. Claude Rawson and Ian Higgins (1726; Oxford: Oxford University Press, 2005), 15. All subsequent references are to this edition and appear parenthetically in the text.

10. Frank Boyle, *Swift as Nemesis: Modernity and Its Satirist* (Stanford: Stanford University Press, 2000), 29.

11. Here Gulliver hints at what will become his fate after joining and being exiled by the Houyhnhnms, forever altering his orientation toward humankind.

12. Though travel is a quixotic ideal in itself for Gulliver, the broader ideal that Gulliver quixotically seeks is described concisely by David Fishelov, "Parody, Satire, and Sympathy in *Don Quixote* and *Gulliver's Travels*," *Connotations* 12 (2002–3), as a quest for utopia, one of the primary objects of Swift's satire, illustrated in part 4 in the Country of the Houyhnhnms. For Fishelov, part 4 "is mocking the genre of utopia, especially some of its underlying optimistic ideological assumptions concerning human nature" (130). Fishelov goes on to compare with "sympathetic satire" in *Don Quixote* the dynamic in *Gulliver's Travels* that allows for a sympathetic portrayal of the Houyhnhnms' utopia alongside the satirical current running through this portrayal (131). This analysis stops short, however, of tracing the connection between the predispositions of mind and behavioral modes of the quixotic, illustrated in *Don Quixote*, and comparable qualities in Gulliver, which enable the same kind of quixotic duality in Swift's narrative that is present in *Don Quixote*: the quixote is at once a madman who does material wrong and a well-meaning, sympathetic character capable of drawing attention to the flaws of the people and societies around him.

13. Michael McKeon, "Parables of the Younger Son: Swift and the Containment of Desire," in *Jonathan Swift: A Collection of Critical Essays*, ed. Claude Rawson, 197–215 (Upper Saddle River, NJ: Prentice Hall, 1995), 199.

14. McKeon, "Parables of the Younger Son," 200. McKeon calls Gulliver an "obsequious sycophant who seems always in the act of 'prostrating' himself."

15. Neil Chudgar, "Swift's Gentleness," *ELH* 78 (2011): 139.

6. Underhill and American Exceptionalism

1. Royall Tyler, *The Algerine Captive*, ed. Caleb Crain (1797; New York: Modern Library, 2002), 18–19. All subsequent references are to this edition and appear parenthetically in the text.

2. María Antonia Garcés, *Cervantes in Algiers: A Captive's Tale* (Nashville: Vanderbilt University Press, 2005), 1.

3. Wood, *Quixotic Fictions*, 107–8.

4. Davidson, *Revolution and the Word*, 300.

5. Davidson, *Revolution and the Word*, 300.

6. Bruce Burgett, "Every Document of Civilization Is a Document of Barbary? Nationalism, Cosmopolitanism, and Spaces Between: A Response to Nancy Armstrong and Leonard Tennenhouse," *American Literary History* 20 (2008): 689.

7. Davidson, *Revolution and the Word*, 300.

8. Wood, *Quixotic Fictions*, 109.

9. John Engell, "Narrative Irony and National Character in Royall Tyler's *The Algerine Captive*," *Studies in American Fiction* 17 (1989): 28.

10. Edward Larkin, "Nation and Empire in the Early US," *American Literary History* 22 (2010): 514.

11. Davidson, *Revolution and the Word*, 289.

12. Wood, *Quixotic Fictions*, 137.

13. Larry Dennis, "Legitimizing the Novel: Royall Tyler's *The Algerine Captive*," *Early American Literature* 9 (1974): 77, 79.

14. Davidson, *Revolution and the Word*, 302–3.

15. Wood, *Quixotic Fictions*, 123.

16. Joseph Schopp, "Liberty's Sons and Daughters: Susanna Haswell Rowson's and Royall Tyler's *Algerine Captives*," in *Early American Re-Explored: New Readings in Colonial, Early National, and Antebellum Culture*, ed. Klaus H. Schmidt and Fritz Fleischmann (New York: Peter Lang, 2002), 302.

17. Shapiro, *The Culture and Commerce of the Early American Novel*, 8–9.

18. Engell, "Narrative Irony and National Character," 31.

19. Edward Watts, *Writing and Postcolonialism in the Early Republic* (Charlottesville: University of Virginia Press, 1998), 92.

20. Shapiro, *The Culture and Commerce of the Early American Novel*, 5.

21. Gesa Mackenthun, "The Transoceanic Emergence of American 'Postcolonial' Identities," in *A Companion to the Literatures of Early America*, ed. Susan Castillo and Ivy Schweitzer (Malden: Blackwell, 2005), 342.

22. Nancy Armstrong and Leonard Tennenhouse, "The Problem of Population and the Form of the American Novel," *American Literary History* 20, no. 4 (2008): 667–85.

23. Mackenthun, "The Transoceanic Emergence of American 'Postcolonial' Identities," 341–42.

200 NOTES TO PAGES 80-97

24. Eve Tavor Bannet, "Quixotes, Imitations, and Transatlantic Genres," *Eighteenth-Century Studies* 40, no. 4 (2007): 553.

25. Armstrong and Tennenhouse, "The Problem of Population," 668.

26. Armstrong and Tennenhouse, "The Problem of Population," 672.

7. ADAMS, FARRAGO, AND CIVIC EXCEPTIONALISM

1. Michel Foucault, *Madness and Civilization: A History of Sanity in the Age of Reason*, trans. Richard Howard (London: Routledge, 1989), 220.

2. Foucault, *Madness and Civilization*, 200. By "Great Confinement," Foucault refers to a seventeenth-century phenomenon, primarily in Paris, in which a significant portion of the population of the poor, unemployed, and criminal were institutionally confined. The English workhouse movement, however, practiced similar methods of concentrating the poor and indigent in areas of confinement.

3. Foucault, *Madness and Civilization*, 202, 213.

4. Foucault, *Madness and Civilization*, 215.

5. Christopher Parkes, "*Joseph Andrews* and the Control of the Poor," *Studies in the Novel* 39 (2007): 17.

6. Henry Fielding, *Joseph Andrews*, ed. Douglas Brooks-Davies and Thomas Keymer (1742; Oxford: Oxford University Press, 1999), 44, 207. All subsequent references are to this edition and are cited parenthetically in the text.

7. Walter Reed, *An Exemplary History of the Novel: The Quixotic versus the Picaresque* (Chicago: University of Chicago Press, 1981), 126.

8. Martin Battestin, *The Moral Basis of Fielding's Art* (Middletown, CT: Wesleyan University Press, 1959), 113.

9. Judith Frank, *Common Ground: Eighteenth-Century English Satiric Fiction and the Poor* (Stanford: Stanford University Press, 1997), 3.

10. Parkes, "*Joseph Andrews* and Control of the Poor," 18.

11. Gilmore, "Eighteenth-Century Oppositional Ideology," 182.

12. Christine Gerrard, *The Patriot Opposition to Walpole: Politics, Poetry, and National Myth, 1725-1742* (Oxford: Clarendon, 1994), 175.

13. Gerrard, *The Patriot Opposition to Walpole*, 176.

14. Gerrard, *The Patriot Opposition to Walpole*, 181.

15. Battestin, *The Moral Basis of Fielding's Art*, 26.

16. Mandel, "The Function of the Norm in *Don Quixote*, *Modern Philology* 55 (1958): 154.

17. Mandel, "The Function of the Norm," 154.

18. See, for comparison, Ruth Mack, "Quixotic Ethnography: Charlotte Lennox and the Dilemma of Cultural Observation," *Novel: A Forum on Fiction* 38 (2005): 193-213.

19. Mack, "Quixotic Ethnography," 193.

20. See, for example, John Trumbull's "An Elegy on the Times" (1774), a retort to Oliver Goldsmith's unflattering portrayal of America in "The Deserted Village" (1770).

21. Gilmore, "Eighteenth-Century Oppositional Ideology," 186-87.

22. Bannet, "Quixotes, Imitations, and Transatlantic Genres," 554.

23. Joseph Harkey, " "The *Don Quixote* of the Frontier: Brackenridge's *Modern Chivalry*," *Early American Literature* 8 (1973): 194.

24. Hugh Henry Brackenridge, *Modern Chivalry*, ed. Claude M. Newlin (1792–1815; New York: American Book Co., 1937), 257. All subsequent references are to this edition and appear parenthetically in the text. Cathy Davidson calls Teague Farrago's "Id" in *Revolution and the Word*, 260.

25. Wendy Martin, "On the Road with the Philosopher and the Profiteer: A Study of Hugh Henry Brackenridge's *Modern Chivalry*," *Eighteenth Century Studies* 4 (1971): 249.

26. Brackenridge, *Modern Chivalry*, 270.

27. Bannet, "Quixotes, Imitations, and Transatlantic Genres," 559.

28. Stephen Adams, "Philip Freneau's Summa of American Exceptionalism: 'The Rising Glory of America' without Brackenridge," *Texas Studies in Literature and Language* 55 (2013): 391.

29. Michael Warner, *Letters of the Republic: Publication and the Public Sphere in Eighteenth-Century America* (Cambridge: Harvard University Press, 1990), 1–2.

30. Davidson, *Revolution and the Word*, 260.

8. Arabella, Dorcasina, and Domestic Exceptionalism

1. Jan Fergus, *Provincial Readers in Eighteenth-Century England* (New York: Oxford University Press, 2007), 238.

2. Michael McKeon, *The Secret History of Domesticity* (Baltimore: Johns Hopkins University Press, 2005), 73.

3. McKeon, *The Secret History of Domesticity*, 73.

4. McKeon, *The Secret History of Domesticity*, 74. McKeon notes that two major critiques of Habermas's understanding of the public sphere include questions about women's access and the access of "commoners" and "plebeians."

5. Critics have responded in abundance to the gender-subversive qualities of *The Female Quixote* and *Female Quixotism* for good reason. The gesture of changing the gender of Cervantes's quixote was both radical and clever, allowing Lennox and Tenney to critique not just certain kinds of romantic idealism but also the sexist view, expressed by Henry Fielding in his 1752 review of *The Female Quixote* in the *Covent-Garden Journal* (no. 24, March 24, 1752), that romantic idealism was itself a particularly "feminine" quality (see *The Covent-Garden Journal*, vol. 1, ed. Gerard Edward Jensen [New Haven, 1915], 279). Eve Tavor Bannet argues of Lennox's heroine in *The Female Quixote* that "in making Arabella a Dulcinea, Lennox transformed the latter from a figure who was, in her way, as much a passive occasion for masculine heroics as [Fielding's] Fanny, into a controlling agent" (Bannet, "Quixotes, Imitations, and Transatlantic Genres," 562). Likewise, Patricia Meyer Spacks has contended that Arabella is someone who, with "no opportunities for action and with little companionship imagines, on the basis of her reading of romance, a world in which she can claim enormous significance" (Spacks, "The Subtle Sophistry of Desire: Dr. Johnson and *The Female Quixote*," *Modern Philology* 85 [1998]: 535). Cathy Davidson gives us a similar reading of *Female Quixotism*, arguing that it provides a feminist counterbalance to

both picaresque texts featuring male protagonists and the titular conventions of various "female" texts in the eighteenth and early nineteenth centuries (Davidson, *Revolution and the Word*, 279). Sarah F. Wood has described American quixotes as marginal but subversive, as "alone and on edge," and as "counter-cultural figures who most frequently inhabit the geographical and ideological margins of American society" (Wood, *Quixotic Fictions of the USA*, 125). This list of readings is not exhaustive, but representative of the critical focus on female quixotes as subversive and liberated figures.

6. This scenario is perhaps best described by what Elisabeth Schüssler Fiorenza terms "kyriarchy," an interconnected social system in which one who might be oppressed or subjugated in one context (a woman within a patriarchy) could also be advantaged within another (a woman of wealth) (see Fiorenza, "Introduction: Exploring the Intersections of Race, Gender, Status, and Ethnicity in Early Christian Studies," in *Prejudice and Christian Beginnings: Investigating Race, Gender, and Ethnicity in Early Christian Studies,* ed. Laura Nasrallah and Elisabeth Schüssler Fiorenza [Minneapolis: University of Minnesota Press, 2009], 1–23).

7. Fiorenza, "Introduction: Exploring the Intersections," 131.

8. Straub, *Domestic Affairs,* 4.

9. G. E. Mingay, *English Landed Society in the Eighteenth Century* (London: Routledge, 1963), 270.

10. Ronald Schultz, "A Class Society? The Nature of Inequality in Early America," in *Inequality in Early America,* ed. Carla Gardina Pestana and Sharon V. Salinger (Hanover, NH: University Press of New England, 1999), 212, 216.

11. Schultz, "A Class Society?, 211–14.

12. Christopher L. Tomlins, *Law, Labor, and Ideology in the Early American Republic* (New York: Cambridge University Press, 1993), 238.

13. Tomlins, *Law, Labor, and Ideology,* 253–54.

14. Jon Elster, *Alexis de Tocqueville: The First Social Scientist* (New York: Cambridge University Press, 2009), 126.

15. Elster, *Alexis de Tocqueville,* 127.

16. Thomas Schmid, "'My Authority': Hyper-Mimesis and the Discourse of Hysteria in *The Female Quixote,*" *Rocky Mountain Review of Language and Literature* 51, no. 1 (1997): 21.

17. Bannet, "Quixotes, Imitations, and Transatlantic Genres," 562.

18. Alliston, "Female Quixotism and the Novel," 264–65.

19. Daniel Defoe, *The Behaviour of Servants in England Inquired Into* (London, n.d.), 17, cited in Straub, *Domestic Affairs,* 7.

20. Straub, *Domestic Affairs,* 4. See also Bruce Robbins, *The Servant's Hand: English Fiction from Below* (New York: Columbia University Press, 1986) for further discussion of the complex relationship between servants and their employer-families.

21. Brown, "The Quixotic Fallacy," 251.

22. *Quando caput dolet, caetara membra dolent,* or, "when the head aches, other members will also ache." This is Don Quixote's analogy for explaining to Sancho Panza why, as knight-errant (head) and servant (body), when one is inflicted with suffering, they suffer mutually.

23. After Arabella recognizes her quixotic error, Glanville is "recovered to the free Use of all her noble Powers of Reason" (382).

24. Tabitha Gilman Tenney, *Female Quixotism,* ed. Jean Nienkamp and Andrea Collins (1801; New York: Oxford, 1992), 8. All subsequent references are to this edition and appear parenthetically in the text.

25. Betty is "preferred ... to the double capacity of servant and confidante" (8).

26. Davidson, *Revolution and the Word,* 275.

27. Brown, "The Quixotic Fallacy," 264.

28. Brown, "The Quixotic Fallacy," 263–64.

29. Davidson, *Revolution and the Word,* 279.

30. Davidson, *Revolution and the Word,* 279.

31. Wood, *Quixotic Fictions of the USA,* 168.

32. Lori Newcomb, *Reading Popular Romance in Early Modern England* (New York: Columbia University Press, 2001), 209.

33. Newcomb, *Reading Popular Romance,* 217.

34. Newcomb, *Reading Popular Romance,* 217.

35. Laurel Thatcher Ulrich, "Martha Ballard and Her Girls: Women's Work in Eighteenth-Century Maine," in *Work and Labor in Early America,* ed. Stephen Innes (Chapel Hill: University of North Carolina Press, 1988), 102. Ulrich's account is from records from women's household labor in Maine.4

36. Davidson, *Revolution and the Word,* 278.

37. Scanlan, Review of *Quixotic Fictions of the USA,* 237.

9. Launcelot and Juridical Exceptionalism

1. Paulson, *Don Quixote in England,* 184.

2. Anthony Close, *The Romantic Approach to "Don Quixote"* (Cambridge: Cambridge University Press, 1978), 43.

3. Angus Easson, "Don Pickwick: Dickens and the Transformations of Cervantes," in *Re-Reading Victorian Fiction,* ed. Alice Jenkins and Juliet John (London: Palgrave, 2002), 175.

4. Certainly Don Quixote also battles real injustices under false pretenses, as, for example, with the bound apprentice boy being whipped by his employer in part 1, chapter 4.

5. Paul-Gabriel Boucé, *The Novels of Tobias Smollett* (London: Longman, 1976), 93.

6. Mandel, "The Function of the Norm," 161–62.

7. Boucé, *The Novels of Tobias Smollett,* 146.

8. Easson, "Don Pickwick," 178.

9. Robert Folkenflik, introduction to *Launcelot Greaves,* by Tobias Smollett (1760; Athens: University of Georgia Press, 2014), xviii.

10. Boucé, *The Novels of Tobias Smollett,* 20. See also Alice Parker, "Tobias Smollett and the Law," *Studies in Philology* 39 (1942): 547.

11. Parker, "Tobias Smollett and the Law," 556.

12. Boucé, *The Novels of Tobias Smollett,* 59.

13. Aileen Douglas, *Uneasy Sensations: Smollett and the Body* (Chicago: University of Chicago Press, 1995), 117.

14. Douglas, *Uneasy Sensations,* 119.

15. Launcelot believes that Captain Crowe is mad, while Launcelot's squire Timothy Crabshaw insists that his knight, too, is mad. Completing the circle, Launcelot accuses Crabshaw of being mad for "serv[ing] and follow[ing] a lunatic" (62).

16. Brackenridge, *Modern Chivalry,* 412.

17. Douglas, *Uneasy Sensations,* 121.

18. Easson, "Don Pickwick," 185.

19. Boucé, *The Novels of Tobias Smollett,* 186.

20. Boucé, *The Novels of Tobias Smollett,* 186–87.

21. Easson, "Don Pickwick," 179.

10. KNICKERBOCKER AND REACTIONARY EXCEPTIONALISM

1. Christopher Benfey, "The Mysterious Mythmaker of New York," review of *Knickerbocker: The Myth behind New York,* by Elizabeth L. Bradley. *New York Review of Books,* April 29, 2010, http://www.nybooks.com/articles/2010/04/29 /the-mysterious-mythmaker-of-new-york/. Benfey's review includes the quoted excerpt from Irving's published letters to the *Post.*

2. Irving published *A History of New York* under Knickerbocker's name.

3. Washington Irving, *A History of New York,* in *History, Tales, and Sketches,* ed. James Tuttleton (New York: Library of America, 1983), 376. All subsequent references are to this edition and appear parenthetically in the text.

4. Jeffrey Insko, "Diedrich Knickerbocker, Regular-Bred Historian," *Early American Literature* 43 (2008): 605.

5. Insko, "Diedrich Knickerbocker," 605.

6. Daniel Williams, "Authoring the Author: Heroes and Greeks," *Early American Literature* 30 (1995): 264.

7. Insko, "Diedrich Knickerbocker," 609–10.

8. Insko, "Diedrich Knickerbocker," 610.

9. William Hedges, "The Knickerbocker History as Knickerbocker's 'History,'" in *The Old and New World Romanticism of Washington Irving,* ed. Stanley Brodwin (New York: Greenwood, 1986), 158.

10. Robert Ferguson, "'Hunting down the Nation': Irving's *A History of New York,*" *Nineteenth-Century Fiction* 36 (1981): 30.

11. Ferguson, "Hunting down the Nation," 23–24.

12. Ferguson, "Hunting down the Nation," 25.

13. Ferguson, "Hunting down the Nation," 26.

14. Ferguson, "Hunting down the Nation," 29.

15. Charlton Laird, "Tragedy and Irony in Knickerbocker's *History,*" *American Literature* 12 (1940): 168.

16. Laird, "Tragedy and Irony in Knickerbocker's *History,*" 168.

17. Ferguson, "Hunting down the Nation," 32.

18. Ferguson, "Hunting down the Nation," 32, 36.

19. See Stanley T. Williams and Tremaine McDowell, introduction to *A History of New York,* ed. Williams and Tremaine McDowell (New York: Harcourt, 1927), xliv–li; and David Durant, "Aeolism in Knickerbocker's *A History of New*

York," *American Literature* 41 (1970): 493. Williams and McDowell observe this critical focus in the introduction to their 1927 edition of *A History of New York*. David Durant understood by 1970 that the critical interest in satirizing Jefferson in book 4 had become so entrenched that it obstructed other viable readings of book 4. In many cases this focus persists today.

20. Ferguson, "Hunting down the Nation," 28.

21. William Hedges, introduction to *The Old and New World Romanticism of Washington Irving,* ed. Stanley Brodwin (New York: Greenwood, 1986), 8.

22. Jeffrey Scraba, "Quixotic History and Cultural Memory: Knickerbocker's *History of New York,*" *Early American Studies* 7 (2009): 389.

23. Hedges, "The Knickerbocker History as Knickerbocker's 'History,'" 154.

24. Scraba, "Quixotic History and Cultural Memory," 409.

11. MARAUDER AND RADICAL EXCEPTIONALISM

1. Essays in which *The Infernal Quixote* merits reference but not extensive discussion include Claire Grogan, "The Politics of Seduction in British Fictions of the 1790s: The Female Reader and *Julie, ou la Novelle Heloise,*" *Eighteenth-Century Fiction* 11 (1999): 459–76; John Mee's review essay "Anti-Jacobin Novels: Representation and Revolution," *Huntington Library Quarterly* 69 (2006): 649–53; Jonathan Den Hartog, "Transatlantic Anti-Jacobinism: Reaction and Religion," *Early American Studies* 11 (2013): 133–45; and Michael Taylor, "British Conservatism, the Illuminati, and the Conspiracy Theory of the French Revolution, 1797–1802," *Eighteenth-Century Studies* 47 (2014): 293–312.

2. Susan Staves, "Don Quixote in Eighteenth-Century England," *Comparative Literature* 24 (1972): 200.

3. William Godwin, *Political Justice,* ed. Isaac Kramnick (London: Penguin, 2015), 131, 480. All subsequent citations are to this edition, which is based on Godwin's final, 1798 revision, and appear parenthetically in the text. I cite the 1798 revision in light of the publication of *The Infernal Quixote* in 1801, and thus with the objective of comparing with Lucas's novel Godwin's most recent revision of *Political Justice.*

4. Isaac Kramnick, introduction to Godwin, *Political Justice,* xi–xvi.

5. William Hazlitt, *Spirit of the Age* (London: Everyman, 1964), 202.

6. Kramnick, introduction to Godwin, *Political Justice,* xvi.

7. Kramnick, introduction to Godwin, *Political Justice,* xvi–xvii.

8. Kramnick, introduction to Godwin, *Political Justice,* xxiii.

9. Kramnick, introduction to Godwin, *Political Justice,* xl–xli.

10. William Godwin, *Considerations on Lord Grenville's and Mr. Pitt's Bills Concerning Treasonable and Seditious Practices and Unlawful Assemblies* (London, 1795), 4–5.

11. Charles Lucas, *The Infernal Quixote* (London, 1801), vol. 2, 225. All subsequent references are to this edition and appear parenthetically in the text; references are to volume and page number.

12. The *OED* indicates that "quick-sighted" was typically hyphenated from the seventeenth century onward, which makes it curious that Lucas rendered it into one word, perhaps for the sake of punning. Smollett also used "quick-sighted," perhaps also as a pun, in his 1755 translation of *Don Quixote*: "The boys,

who are quick-sighted as lynxes" (*OED Online,* s.v. "quick-sighted, adj," www.oed
.com/view/Entry/156455?redirectedFrom=quicksighted).

13. Later, in volume 3, we learn that Marauder "ever felt himself elevated
when he reviewed his *own philosophy,*" a testament to his exceptionalist attitude
and the assuredness with which he broached the subjects of Godwin and Wollstonecraft's views with Emily (3.103).

14. Claire Grogan argues that "no one novel appears to epitomize the genre
[of female-reader-centered seduction novels] so well as Jean-Jacques Rousseau's
Julie" in "The Politics of Seduction in British Fiction of the 1790s," 460.

Coda

1. See John T. Graham, *The Social Thought of Ortega y Gasset* (Columbia: Uni-
versity of Missouri Press, 2001), 346; and Miguel de Unamuno, "The Life of
Don Quixote and Sancho," in *Selected Works of Miguel de Unamuno,* vol. 3, trans.
Anthony Kerrigan (Princeton: Princeton University Press, 1967): 3–326.

2. Both Motooka's *Age of Reasons* and Scott Paul Gordon's *The Practice of Quixotism* offer extensive explorations of quixotism's implications for empiricism.

BIBLIOGRAPHY

Adams, Stephen. "Philip Freneau's Summa of American Exceptionalism: 'The Rising Glory of America' without Brackenridge." *Texas Studies in Literature and Language* 55, no. 4 (2013): 390–405

Agamben, Giorgio. *Homo Sacer: Sovereign Power and Bare Life.* Translated by Daniel Heller- Roazen. Stanford: Stanford University Press, 1998.

Alliston, April. "Female Quixotism and the Novel: Character and Plausibility, Honesty and Fidelity." *Eighteenth Century: Theory and Interpretation* 52, no. 3–4 (2011): 249–69.

Ardila, J. A. G. *The Cervantean Heritage: Reception and Influence of Cervantes in Britain.* Oxford: Legenda, 2009.

Armintor, Deborah. "The Sexual Politics of Microscopy in Brobdingnag." *SEL* 47, no. 3 (2007): 619–40.

Armstrong, Nancy, and Leonard Tennenhouse. "The Problem of Population and the Form of the American Novel." *American Literary History* 20, no. 4 (2008): 667–85.

Auerbach, Erich. *Mimesis: The Representation of Reality in Western Literature.* Princeton: Princeton University Press, 2003.

Bannet, Eve Tavor. "Quixotes, Imitations, and Transatlantic Genres." *Eighteenth-Century Studies* 40, no. 4 (2007): 553–69.

Battestin, Martin. *The Moral Basis of Fielding's Art.* Middletown, CT: Wesleyan University Press, 1959.

Benfey, Christopher. "The Mysterious Mythmaker of New York." Review of *Knickerbocker: The Myth behind New York,* by Elizabeth L. Bradley. *New York Review of Books,* April 29, 2010.

Borges, Jorge Luis. *Ficciones.* Edited and translated by Anthony Kerrigan. New York: Grove, 1994.

——. *Professor Borges: A Course on English Literature.* Translated by Katherine Silver. Edited by Martín Arias and Martin Hardis. New York: New Directions, 2013.

Boswell, James. *Life of Samuel Johnson.* Edited by Pat Rogers. New York: Oxford University Press, 2008.

Boucé, Paul-Gabriel. *The Novels of Tobias Smollett.* London: Longman, 1976.

Boyle, Frank. *Swift as Nemesis: Modernity and Its Satirist.* Stanford: Stanford University Press, 2000.

Brackenridge, Hugh Henry. *Modern Chivalry.* Edited by Claude M. Newlin. New York: American Book Co., 1937.

Braudel, Fernand. *Civilization and Capitalism, 15th–18th Century.* Vol. 3. London: Collins, 1984.

Brewer, David. *The Afterlife of Character, 1726–1825.* Philadelphia: University of Pennsylvania Press, 2005.

Brown, Gillian. "The Quixotic Fallacy." *Novel: A Forum on Fiction* 32, no. 2 (1999): 250–73.

Burgett, Bruce. "Every Document of Civilization Is a Document of Barbary? Nationalism, Cosmopolitanism, and Spaces Between: A Response to Nancy Armstrong and Leonard Tennenhouse." *American Literary History* 20, no. 4 (2008): 686–94.

Bywaters, David. "*Gulliver's Travels* and the Mode of Political Parallel during Walpole's Administration." *ELH* 54, no. 3 (1987): 717–40.

Cervantes, Miguel de. *Don Quixote.* Translated by John Rutherford. London: Penguin, 2003.

———. *The History and Adventures of the Renowned Don Quixote.* Translated by Tobias Smollett. London, 1755.

———. *The History of Don Quixote.* Edited by J. W. Clark. Illustrated by Gustave Doré. London: Cassell, Petter and Galpin, 1867. Based on the Jarvis and Motteaux translations.

———. *The History of the Most Renowned Don Quixote of La Mancha.* Translated by John Phillips. London, 1687.

———. *The History of the Renowned Don Quixote de la Mancha.* Translated by Peter Motteaux. London, 1700.

———. *The History of the Valorous and Wittie Knight-Errant, Don Quixote of La Mancha.* Translated by Thomas Shelton. London, 1612.

———. *The History of the Valorous and Wittie Knight-Errant, Don Quixote of La Mancha.* Translated by Thomas Shelton. London, 1620.

———. *The Life and Exploits of the Ingenious Gentleman Don Quixote de la Mancha.* Translated by Charles Jarvis [Jervas]. London, 1742.

———. *The Life and Notable Adventures of That Renown'd Knight, Don Quixote de la Mancha, Merrily Translated into Hudibrastick Verse.* Translated by Edward Ward. London, 1711–12.

———. *Pleasant Notes upon Don Quixot.* Translated by Edmund Gayton. London, 1654.

Chace, James. "Quixotic America." *World Policy Journal* 20, no. 3 (2003): 7–15.

Chudgar, Neil. "Swift's Gentleness." *ELH* 78, no. 1 (2011): 137–61.

Close, Anthony. *The Romantic Approach to "Don Quixote": A Critical History of the Romantic Approach in Quixote Criticism.* Cambridge: Cambridge University Press, 1978.

Davidson, Cathy. *Revolution and the Word: The Rise of the Novel in America.* New York: Oxford University Press, 2004.

Defoe, Daniel. *The Behaviour of Servants in England Inquired Into.* London, n.d.

Den Hartog, Jonathan. "Transatlantic Anti-Jacobinism: Reaction and Religion." *Early American Studies* 11, no. 1 (2013): 133–45.

Dennis, Larry. "Legitimizing the Novel: Royall Tyler's *The Algerine Captive.*" *Early American Literature* 9, no. 1 (1974): 71–80.

Douglas, Aileen. *Uneasy Sensations: Smollett and the Body.* Chicago: University of Chicago Press, 1995.

Downie, J. A. "The Political Significance of *Gulliver's Travels.*" In *Swift and His Contexts,* edited by John Irwin Fischer, Hermann Josef Real, and James D. Woolley, 1–18. New York: AMS, 1989.

Durant, David. "Aeolism in Knickerbocker's *A History of New York.*" *American Literature* 41, no. 4 (1970): 493–506.

Easson, Angus. "Don Pickwick: Dickens and the Transformations of Cervantes." In *Re-Reading Victorian Fiction,* edited by Alice Jenkins and Juliet John, 173–88. London: Palgrave, 2002.

Elias, A. C. "Swift's *Don Quixote,* Dunkin's *Virgil Travesty,* and Other New Intelligence: John Lyon's 'Materials for a Life of Dr. Swift,' 1765." *Swift Studies* 13 (1998): 27–104.

Elster, Jon. *Alexis de Tocqueville: The First Social Scientist.* Cambridge: Cambridge University Press, 2009.

Engell, John. "Narrative Irony and National Character in Royall Tyler's *The Algerine Captive.*" *Studies in American Fiction* 17, no. 1 (1989): 19–32.

Fergus, Jan. *Provincial Readers in Eighteenth-Century England.* New York: Oxford University Press, 2007.

Ferguson, Robert. "'Hunting down the Nation': Irving's *A History of New York.*" *Nineteenth- Century Fiction* 36, no. 1 (1981): 22–46.

Fielding, Henry. *The Covent-Garden Journal.* Edited by Gerard Edward Jensen. New Haven: Yale University Press, 1915.

———. *Don Quixote in England.* London, 1734.

———. *"Joseph Andrews" and "Shamela."* Edited by Douglas Brooks-Davies and Thomas Keymer. Oxford: Oxford University Press, 1999.

Fiorenza, Elisabeth Schüssler. "Introduction: Exploring the Intersections of Race, Gender, Status, and Ethnicity in Early Christian Studies." In *Prejudice and Christian Beginnings: Investigating Race, Gender, and Ethnicity in Early Christian Studies,* edited by Laura Nasrallah and Fiorenza, 1–23. Minneapolis: University of Minnesota Press, 2009.

Fishelov, David. "Parody, Satire and Sympathy in *Don Quixote* and *Gulliver's Travels.*" *Connotations* 12, no. 2–3 (2002–3): 126–38.

Folkenflik, Robert. Introduction to *Launcelot Greaves,* by Tobias Smollett, edited by Folkenflik and Barbara Laning-Fitzpatrick, i–liv. 1760. Athens: University of Georgia Press, 2002.

Foucault, Michel. *Madness and Civilization: A History of Sanity in the Age of Reason.* Translated by Richard Howard. London: Routledge, 1989.

Frank, Judith. *Common Ground: Eighteenth-Century English Satiric Fiction and the Poor.* Stanford: Stanford University Press, 1997.

Fuchs, Barbara. *The Poetics of Piracy: Emulating Spain in English Literature.* Philadelphia: University of Pennsylvania Press, 2013.

Gallagher, Catherine. "The Rise of Fictionality." In *The Novel,* vol. 1: *History, Geography, and Culture,* edited by Franco Moretti, 336–63. Princeton: Princeton University Press, 2006.

Garcés, María Antonia. *Cervantes in Algiers: A Captive's Tale*. Nashville: Vanderbilt University Press, 2005.

Gerrard, Christine. *The Patriot Opposition to Walpole: Politics, Poetry, and National Myth, 1725-1742*. Oxford: Clarendon, 1994.

Gilmore, Michael. "Eighteenth-Century Oppositional Ideology and Hugh Henry Brackenridge's *Modern Chivalry*." *Early American Literature* 13, no. 2 (1978): 181–92.

Godwin, William. *Considerations on Lord Grenville's and Mr. Pitt's Bills Concerning Treasonable and Seditious Practices and Unlawful Assemblies*. London, 1795.

———. *Political Justice*. Edited by Isaac Kramnick. London: Penguin, 2015.

González Echevarría, Roberto. *Cervantes' "Don Quixote."* New Haven: Yale University Press, 2015.

———. *Cervantes' "Don Quixote:" A Casebook*. New York: Oxford University Press, 2005.

Gordon, Scott Paul. *The Practice of Quixotism: Postmodern Theory and Eighteenth-Century Women's Writing*. New York: Palgrave, 2006.

Graham, John T. *The Social Thought of Ortega y Gasset*. Columbia: University of Missouri Press, 2001.

Greene, Jack P. *The Intellectual Construction of America: Exceptionalism and Identity from 1492 to 1800*. Chapel Hill: University of North Carolina Press, 1993.

Grogan, Claire. "The Politics of Seduction in British Fictions of the 1790s: The Female Reader and *Julie, ou la Novelle Heloise*." *Eighteenth-Century Fiction* 11, no. 4 (1999): 459–76.

Haring, Clarence. *The Spanish Empire in America*. Oxford: Oxford University Press, 1947.

Harkey, Joseph. "The *Don Quixote* of the Frontier: Brackenridge's *Modern Chivalry*. *Early American Literature* 8, no. 2 (1973): 193–203.

Harth, Phillip. "The Problem of Political Allegory in *Gulliver's Travels*." *Modern Philology* 73, no. 4 (1976): 40–47.

Hayes, Julie Candler. "Eighteenth-Century English Translations of *Don Quixote*." In *The Cervantean Heritage: Reception and Influence of Cervantes in Britain,* edited by J. A. G. Ardila. Oxford: Legenda, 2009.

Hazlitt, William. *Spirit of the Age*. London: Everyman, 1964.

Hedges, William. Introduction to *The Old and New World Romanticism of Washington Irving,* edited by Stanley Brodwin, 1–9. New York: Greenwood, 1986.

———. "The Knickerbocker History as Knickerbocker's 'History.'" In *The Old and New World Romanticism of Washington Irving,* edited by Stanley Brodwin, 153–66. New York: Greenwood, 1986

Insko, Jeffrey. "Diedrich Knickerbocker: Regular-Bred Historian." *Early American Literature* 43, no. 3 (2008): 605–41.

Irving, Washington. *A History of New York*. In *History, Tales, and Sketches,* edited by James Tuttleton, 363–730. New York: Library of America, 1983.

Kahn, Paul. *Political Theology: Four New Chapters on the Concept of Sovereignty*. New York: Columbia University Press, 2011.

Kareem, Sarah. *Eighteenth-Century Fiction and the Reinvention of Wonder*. New York: Oxford University Press, 2014.

Laird, Charlton. "Tragedy and Irony in Knickerbocker's *History*." *American Literature* 12, no. 2 (1940): 157–72.

Larkin, Edward. "Nation and Empire in the Early US." *American Literary History* 22, no. 3 (2010): 501–26.

Lennox, Charlotte. *The Female Quixote*. 1752. Edited by Margaret Dalziel. New York: Oxford University Press, 1998.

Lock, F. P. "Swift and English Politics, 1701–14." In *The Character of Swift's Satire*, edited by Claude Rawson, 127–34. Newark: University of Delaware Press, 1983.

Lucas, Charles. *The Infernal Quixote*. London, 1801.

Lynch, Deidre. *The Economy of Character: Novels, Market Culture, and the Business of Inner Meaning*. Chicago: University of Chicago Press, 1998.

Mack, Ruth. "Quixotic Ethnography: Charlotte Lennox and the Dilemma of Cultural Observation." *Novel: A Forum on Fiction* 38, no. 2 (2005): 192–213.

Mackenthun, Gesa. "The Transoceanic Emergence of American 'Postcolonial' Identities." In *A Companion to the Literatures of Early America*, edited by Susan Castillo and Ivy Schweitzer, 336–50. Malden, MA: Blackwell, 2005.

Mandel, Oscar. "The Function of the Norm in *Don Quixote*." *Modern Philology* 55, no. 3 (1958): 154–63.

Manning, Susan. *Poetics of Character*. Cambridge: Cambridge University Press, 2013.

Martin, Wendy. "On the Road with the Philosopher and the Profiteer: A Study of Hugh Henry Brackenridge's *Modern Chivalry*." *Eighteenth Century Studies* 4, no. 3 (1971): 241–56.

McKeon, Michael. "Parables of the Younger Son: Swift and the Containment of Desire." In *Jonathan Swift: A Collection of Critical Essays*, edited by Claude Rawson, 197–215. Upper Saddle River, NJ: Prentice-Hall, 1995.

———. *The Secret History of Domesticity*. Baltimore: Johns Hopkins University Press, 2005.

McMurran, Mary Helen. *The Spread of Novels: Translation and Prose Fiction in the Eighteenth Century*. Princeton: Princeton University Press, 2009.

Mee, John. "Anti-Jacobin Novels: Representation and Revolution." *Huntington Library Quarterly* 69, no. 4 (2006): 649–53.

Mingay, G. E. *English Landed Society in the Eighteenth Century*. London: Routledge, 1963.

Moretti, Franco. *Atlas of the European Novel: 1800–1900*. London: Verso, 1999.

Motooka, Wendy. *The Age of Reasons: Quixotism, Sentimentalism, and Political Economy in Eighteenth-Century Britain*. London: Routledge, 1998.

Nabokov, Vladimir. *Lectures on "Don Quixote."* Edited by Fredson Bowers. New York: Harcourt, 1983.

Newcomb, Lori. *Reading Popular Romance in Early Modern England*. New York: Columbia University Press, 2001.

Nye, Joseph. *Soft Power: The Means to Success in World Politics*. New York: Public Affairs, 2004.

Parker, Alexander. *Literature and the Delinquent: The Picaresque Novel in Spain and Europe 1599–1753*. Edinburgh: Edinburgh University Press, 1967.

Parker, Alice. "Tobias Smollett and the Law," *Studies in Philology* 39, no. 3 (1942): 545–558.

Parkes, Christopher. "*Joseph Andrews* and the Control of the Poor." *Studies in the Novel* 39, no. 1 (2007): 17–30.

Paulson, Ronald. *Don Quixote in England: The Aesthetics of Laughter.* Baltimore: Johns Hopkins University Press, 1998.

Paz, Octavio. *Convergences: Essays on Art and Literature.* Translated by Helen Lane. San Diego: Harcourt Brace Jovanovich, 1987.

Pease, Donald. "Re-thinking 'American Studies after US Exceptionalism.'" *American Literary History* 21, no. 1 (2009): 19–27.

Rasula, Jed. "When the Exception Is the Rule: *Don Quixote* as Incitement to Literature." *Comparative Literature* 51, no. 2 (1999): 123–51.

Reed, Walter. *An Exemplary History of the Novel: The Quixotic versus the Picaresque.* Chicago: University of Chicago Press, 1981.

Rees, Christine. *Utopian Imagination and Eighteenth-Century Fiction.* New York: Longman, 1996.

Robbins, Bruce. *The Servant's Hand: English Fiction from Below.* New York: Columbia University Press, 1986.

Scanlan, Thomas. Review of *Quixotic Fictions of the USA, 1792–1815,* by Sarah F. Wood. *Early American Literature* 43, no. 1 (2008): 233–37.

Schmid, Thomas. "'My Authority': Hyper-Mimesis and the Discourse of Hysteria in *The Female Quixote.*" *Rocky Mountain Review of Language and Literature* 51, no. 1 (1997): 21–35.

Schmitt, Carl. *Political Theology.* Chicago: University of Chicago Press, 1985.

Schopp, Joseph. "Liberty's Sons and Daughters: Susanna Haswell Rowson's and Royall Tyler's *Algerine Captives.*" In *Early American Re-Explored: New Readings in Colonial, Early National, and Antebellum Culture,* edited by Klaus H. Schmidt and Fritz Fleischmann, 291–307. New York: Peter Lang, 2002.

Schultz, Ronald. "A Class Society? The Nature of Inequality in Early America." In *Inequality in Early America,* edited by Carla Gardina Pestana and Sharon V. Salinger. 203–21. Hanover, NH: University Press of New England, 1999.

Scraba, Jeffrey. "Quixotic History and Cultural Memory: Knickerbocker's *History of New York.*" *Early American Studies* 7, no. 2 (2009): 389–425.

Shapiro, Stephen. *The Culture and Commerce of the Early American Novel: Reading the Atlantic World-System.* State College: Pennsylvania State University Press, 2008.

Skinner, John. "*Don Quixote* in 18th-Century England: A Study in Reader Response." *Cervantes: Bulletin of the Cervantes Society of America* 7, no. 1 (1987): 45–57.

Smollett, Tobias. *The Life and Adventures of Sir Launcelot Greaves.* 1760–62. Edited by Robert Folkenflik and Barbara Laning-Fitzpatrick. Athens: University of Georgia Press, 2002.

Spacks, Patricia Meyer. "The Subtle Sophistry of Desire: Dr. Johnson and *The Female Quixote.*" *Modern Philology* 85, no. 4 (1988): 532–42.

Staves, Susan. "Don Quixote in Eighteenth-Century England," *Comparative Literature* 24, no. 3 (1972): 193–215.

Straub, Kristina. *Domestic Affairs: Intimacy, Eroticism, and Violence between Servants and Masters in Eighteenth-Century Britain.* Baltimore: Johns Hopkins University Press, 2009.

Swift, Jonathan. *Gulliver's Travels.* Edited by Claude Rawson and Ian Higgins. Oxford: Oxford University Press, 2005.

Taylor, Michael. "British Conservatism, the Illuminati, and the Conspiracy Theory of the French Revolution, 1797–1802." *Eighteenth-Century Studies* 47, no. 3 (2014): 293–312.

Tenney, Tabitha Gilman. *Female Quixotism.* 1801. Edited by Jean Nienkamp and Andrea Collins. Oxford: Oxford University Press, 1992.

Thomas, Brinley. *The Industrial Revolution and the Atlantic Economy.* London: Routledge, 1993.

Tomlins, Christopher L. *Law, Labor, and Ideology in the Early American Republic.* Cambridge: Cambridge University Press, 1993.

Tyler, Royall. *The Algerine Captive.* Edited by Caleb Crain. 1797. New York: Modern Library, 2002.

Ulrich, Laurel Thatcher. "Martha Ballard and Her Girls: Women's Work in Eighteenth-Century Maine." In *Work and Labor in Early America,* edited by Stephen Innes, 70–105. Chapel Hill: University of North Carolina Press, 1988.

Unamuno, Miguel de. "The Life of Don Quixote and Sancho." In *Selected Works of Miguel de Unamuno,* translated by Anthony Kerrigan, vol. 3, 3–326. Princeton: Princeton University Press, 1967.

Warner, Michael. *Letters of the Republic: Publication and the Public Sphere in Eighteenth-Century America.* Cambridge: Harvard University Press, 1990.

Watts, Edward. *Writing and Postcolonialism in the Early Republic.* Charlottesville: Virginia University Press, 1998.

Welcher, Jeanne K. *Gulliveriana VIII: An Annotated List of Gulliveriana, 1721–1800.* Delmar: Scholars Facsimiles and Reprints, 1988.

Welcher, Jeanne K., and George E. Bush Jr. *Gulliveriana.* Vol. 1. Gainesville: Scholars Facsimiles and Reprints, 1970.

Williams, Daniel. "Authoring the Author: Heroes and Greeks." *Early American Literature* 30, no. 3 (1995): 264–74.

Williams, Stanley T., and Tremaine McDowell. Introduction to *A History of New York,* edited by Williams and McDowell, ix–lxxv. New York: Harcourt, 1927.

Wilson, Diana de Armas. *Cervantes, the Novel, and the New World.* Oxford: Oxford University Press, 2000.

Womersley, David. "Dean Swift Hears a Sermon: Robert Howard's Ash Wednesday Sermon of 1725 and *Gulliver's Travels.*" *Review of English Studies* 60, no. 247 (2009): 744–62.

Wood, Sarah. *Quixotic Fictions of the USA, 1792–1815.* Oxford: Oxford University Press, 2005

INDEX